The Metaphor of God Incarnate

The Metaphor
of God Incarnate
Second Edition

Christology in a Pluralistic Age

John Hick

Westminster John Knox Press
LOUISVILLE • LONDON

First edition published in 1993 by SCM Press, 9-17 St Alban's Place, London N1 0NX. This second edition revised by SCM Press in 2005.

Published in the United States in 2006 by
Westminster John Knox Press
Louisville, Kentucky

Cover design by Mark Abrams

PRINTED IN THE UNITED STATES OF AMERICA

06 07 08 09 10 11 12 13 14 15 — 10 9 8 7 6 5 4 3 2 1

United States Library of Congress Cataloging-in-Publication Data is on file at the Library of Congress, Washington, D.C.

ISBN-13: 978-0-664-23037-1
ISBN-10: 0-664-23037-7

Dedicated to our grandchildren
Jonathan, Emily, Rhiannon and Alexander

Contents

Preface to First Edition

The traditional Christian understanding of Jesus of Nazareth is that he was God incarnate, who became a man to die for the sins of the world and who founded the church to proclaim this. If he was indeed God incarnate, Christianity is the only religion founded by God in person, and must as such be uniquely superior to all other religions.

In this book I criticize this set of ideas and point to an alternative. I argue (1) that Jesus himself did not teach what was to become the orthodox Christian understanding of him; (2) that the dogma of Jesus' two natures, one human and the other divine, has proved to be incapable of being explicated in any satisfactory way; (3) that historically the traditional dogma has been used to justify great human evils; (4) that the idea of divine incarnation is better understood as metaphorical than as literal – Jesus embodied, or incarnated, the ideal of human life lived in faithful response to God, so that God was able to act through him, and he accordingly embodied a love which is a human reflection of the divine love; (5) that we can rightly take Jesus, so understood, as our Lord, the one who has made God real to us and whose life and teachings challenge us to live in God's presence; and (6) that a non-traditional Christianity based upon this understanding of Jesus can see itself as one among a number of different human responses to the ultimate transcendent Reality that we call God, and can better serve the development of world community and world peace than a Christianity which continues to see itself as the locus of final revelation and purveyor of the only salvation possible for all human beings.

All this is inevitably controversial, as indeed everything of serious interest today in theology is controversial. I have, however, tried hard to present issues fairly and to represent the positions of others accurately. Indeed some of those, on both sides of the Atlantic, with whom I disagree most have long been personal friends with whom I have been engaged in a many-year dialogue. The aim of this book is not to polarize positions but to stir public discussion and, hopefully, to move it forward.

I am grateful to my wife Hazel, and to several Birmingham colleagues, who do not necessarily agree with my conclusions, who have made helpful comments on different chapters: Lewis Ayres, Michael Goulder, Gareth Jones, Paul Joyce, Werner Ustorf, and to Tim Musgrove in California, who has also read the proofs. I also want to thank the Editor of *Faith and Philosophy* for permission to draw in chapters 13 and 14 from my article 'Religious Pluralism and Salvation', which appeared in the October 1988 number.

Preface to Second Edition

This book was first published twelve years ago. Since then the focus of much theological discussion has moved from christology to the doctrine of the Trinity. This is partly because theology always does go the rounds of the traditional topics – creation, sin, incarnation, atonement, Trinity, church, heaven and hell – and after a while it feels like time to move on to something else. Why then write more about incarnation instead of engaging with the currently more fashionable idea of the Trinity? Because this doctrine presupposes and depends upon the prior doctrine of the deity (as well as humanity) of Jesus. If Jesus was God incarnate on earth, and at the same time God reigned in heaven, this already creates a binity of Father and Son. When we add the inner experience of God's presence as Spirit, we have a trinity – the Holy Trinity of Father, Son and Holy Spirit who, to preserve monotheism, are three in one and one in three. But there would have been no occasion for this expansion from the unitary God of Judaism to the Trinity of Christianity without the more basic belief in the deity (as well as humanity) of Jesus. For this reason the idea of Jesus as God incarnate remains basic and foundational, and without it the concept of the Trinity evaporates. If a coherent and believable theology cannot establish its earthly base in a literal, ontological incarnation, it cannot take off into the theological stratosphere of the Trinity.

But if, as I argue in this book, divine incarnation is a metaphorical concept, it neither needs nor supports a trinitarian superstructure. And when we look at recent explorative work in christology we find it tending towards a recognition of metaphor and symbol as the characteristic currency of religious thought and language. I have therefore added two new chapters, one about a recent Protestant attempt, and the other a recent Catholic attempt, to find new ways of making the continuing profound spiritual impact of Jesus of Nazareth understandable to the contemporary mind.

John Hick
March, 2005

1

Today's Starting Point

The theological world is today experiencing an intense flurry of activity in the central area of christology, the discussion of the religious significance of Jesus Christ. This is because we are (I believe) on the moving hinge between the structure of Christian belief that dominated Western civilization for many centuries and the still forming new structure of a Christianity that is aware of itself as one valid response among others to the infinite transcendent reality that we call God.

The quest for a new Christian self-understanding in response to multiple changes in human awareness has been going on in various ways for approximately the last two hundred years. Within this period various events and movements of thought have functioned as catalysts, focussing an issue or precipitating a new alignment. In recent years an event of this kind occurred when the British church scene, traditionally dominated by a strong Anglican emphasis on the doctrine of the incarnation, exploded at the publication in 1977 of a volume of essays entitled *The Myth of God Incarnate*. The writers included leading Anglican and other theologians and New Testament scholars whose words, under such a provocative title, could not be ignored. There was uproar in the General Synod of the Church of England, articles for several weeks in the British newspapers, thundering sermons and clerical pronouncements, calls for the Anglicans among the writers to resign their orders, and presently conservative replies, *The Truth of God Incarnate* (Green 1977), *God Incarnate* (Carey 1977), and *The Myth/Truth of God Incarnate* (McDonald 1979), followed later by discussion in *Incarnation and Myth: The Debate Continued* (Goulder 1979), and then *God Incarnate: Story and Belief* (Harvey 1981), *The Logic of God Incarnate* (Morris 1986a) and *The Saga of God Incarnate* (Crawford 1988), as well as numerous articles in journals, including of course further contributions from the original authors. *The Myth* was also published in the United States but made a smaller (though still noticeable) splash in this much larger pond. The main historical thesis of the book – that Jesus himself did not teach that he was God incarnate and that this momentous idea is a creation of the church – was of course in no way new. It had long been familiar and accepted in scholarly Christian circles on both sides of the Atlantic. What was new, in Britain, was that members of the theological establishment were now saying it publicly and concluding that the incarnation doctrine, instead of continuing to be regarded as sacrosanct, should be openly reconsidered.

As I look back at the debate which followed the publication of *The Myth*, what strikes me most now, as one who was involved in it, is how strongly and even frenetically polemical it was. There was emotive rhetoric – for example, at the Anglican Synod the authors of the book were likened to the 'German Christians' who supported Hitler; the *Church Times'* headline was 'Seven Against Christ'; a Greek Orthodox archbishop declared that the writers of *The Myth* had 'fallen prey to an opposition of a demonic character'; and so on. Scholars who took part in the debate often used contemptuous and sarcastic language. It was obvious – but not of course surprising – that deep offence had been caused to cherished ways of thinking, evoking an indignant rallying of the ecclesiastical and theological establishment against a perceived threat.

There was, however, at the same time a hearty welcome to the book from many others, both inside and outside the churches, who were delighted to find theologians writing openly about the historical study of the scriptures and of Christian origins. They, too, were indignant – indignant that the churches had so long encouraged them to go on innocently assuming, for example, that the historical Jesus had said 'I and the Father are one' (John 10.30), 'He who has seen me has seen the Father' (John 14.9), rather than revealing the scholarly consensus that a writer some sixty or more years later, expressing the theology that had developed in his part of the church, put these famous words into Jesus' mouth. Indeed these Christians were indignant that the churches so generally failed to treat them as intelligent adults who could be trusted with the results of biblical and theological scholarship. The shock to the ecclesiastical system was a repetition on a smaller scale of that caused in Britain fourteen years earlier by John Robinson's *Honest to God*.

The generally polemical nature of the debates – and we authors of *The Myth* were as polemical as our critics – meant that a good deal of heat was generated along with the light. Nevertheless it seems clear in retrospect that this rather agitated phase of public discussion had to take place before a more calm and productive conversation could begin. *The Myth* performed the necessary service of pulling down much of the curtain between what the scholars knew and what preachers have been accustomed to tell their congregations. But now, sixteen years later, and after the publication of a flood of further books, many by a new generation of younger scholars, some from the same general point of view as *The Myth* (Race 1983; Newman 1987; Bowden 1988; Coakley 1988; Fredricksen 1988; Casey 1991; Ward 1991; Houlden 1992), and others opposing it (Morris 1986a; Hebblethwaite 1987; Thatcher 1990; White 1991; Sturch 1991), but without the bitterness of the immediate post-*Myth* furore, it seems possible to continue the discussion in a more temperate mood. It is true that whilst much Christian scholarship has gone in the direction represented by *The Myth* the churches as a whole have generally moved in the opposite direction, promoting an unquestioning reaffirmation of traditional dogma and shunning potentially disturbing questions. This has been equally true on both sides of the Atlantic. However, in my view this has not resulted so much from a well-considered weighing of the historical evidence and the theological pros and cons as, in Britain, an alarmed reaction to the realization that Christianity is now a minority faith and, in the United States, an aspect of the broad political-religious swing to the right.

One contribution that I can make to the ongoing conversation is to pose the central question afresh in a less stark and more nuanced way. In the earlier phase of discussion I wrote that 'to say, without explanation, that the historical Jesus of Nazareth was also God is as devoid of meaning as to say that this circle drawn with a pencil on paper is also a square' (Hick 1977, 178). Ignoring the 'without explanation' clause, some took me to be saying (following Spinoza) that the idea of a God-man is a self-contradiction, like a square-circle (Anderson 1978, 94; Brown 1985, 221; Morris 1986a, 21). My intended meaning was that if the doctrine of the incarnation is to be shown to have a believable meaning this must be intelligibly spelled out – adding that 'every content thus far suggested has had to be repudiated' (Hick 1977, 178). I was not, however, suggesting that the idea of divine incarnation can be dismissed *a priori*, without looking at the attempts to explicate it. The question was whether any of these attempts have succeeded. In reply critics made the point that we do not know enough about either divine or human nature to be entitled to say that the two cannot coalesce in the same individual (e.g. Hebblethwaite 1987, 3). There is an important sense in which they were right – though this turns out not to be quite the sense that they had in mind. For our concepts of God are human constructs, and theologians are free to offer their own definitions of the essential attributes in virtue of which God is God. To a lesser extent this also applies to the concept of humanity. Thus it is, within certain limits, up to us to decide what is to count as Jesus being God (did he, for example, have to be omniscient and omnipotent, or are not these after all essential divine attributes?),[1] and what is to count as his being a man (did he, for example, have to be limited in knowledge and power, or could he be an omniscient and omnipotent man?).[2] Given the relatively open character of our concept of humanity, and still more our concepts of deity, it will always be possible to adjust them in relation to each other so as to make a literal understanding of divine incarnation feasible. But the question is whether such manoeuvres are religiously acceptable. Do they enable the thought of Jesus as God incarnate to do the work that traditional Christian theology has required of it? In the history of the church a large number of theories have been offered to explain in what sense Jesus was both divine and human; but in the past they have each had to be rejected as violating the accepted understanding either of deity or of humanity. The question, then, is not whether it is possible to give any coherent literal meaning to the idea of divine incarnation, but whether it is possible to do so in a way that satisfies the religious concerns which give point to the doctrine.

Let us return now to the historical figure who is at the centre of the discussion. I shall usually refer to him as Jesus; for as soon as we add the term Christ we become involved in its ambiguities. The Greek *christos* translated the Hebrew *messiah*, meaning 'anointed', used particularly of kings and carrying no connotation of divinity. Within early Christianity Jesus was identified as God's new anointed one of the royal house of David, who would in his second coming usher in the great Day of the Lord. However, as the second coming failed to occur, Jesus was gradually elevated within the

[1]Thus James Moulder defends the incarnation doctrine by denying 'that omnipotence, or omniscience, or omnipresence are God the Father's essential properties' (Moulder 1986, 299).

[2]Thus Thomas Morris claims that: 'It is not true that an individual must be a contingent being, non-eternal, and non-omnipotent in order to exemplify human nature' (Feenstra 1989, 116–17), and Richard Swinburne declines to set any limits to the degree of power or the extent of knowledge that a human being could have without transcending human limitations (Swinburne 1989a, 57-8).

Gentile church to a divine status, and 'Christ' came to be equivalent in meaning to the pre-trinitarian 'Son of God' and eventually to the trinitarian 'God the Son'. This has now long been its established meaning. However, the present book is concerned with the question whether this is still an appropriate way of thinking about Jesus. And since I conclude that it is not, I shall try to avoid confusion by referring to the individual who has had so momentous an influence in human history simply as Jesus or as Jesus of Nazareth.

It is not always realized that Jesus himself can have had no conception of these issues. He lived in so intense and empowering an experience of the divine presence that his words and his life continue to make God real to those who are inspired by him. But the way in which Jesus understood his role was provided by contemporary Jewish restoration eschatology. 'He thought,' says E.P. Sanders in his authoritative study of *Jesus and Judaism*, 'that the kingdom would come in the near future and that God was at work in a special way in his own ministry' (Sanders 1985, 156). For the historical facts 'show that he fits into the general framework of Jewish restoration eschatology, and they identify him as the founder of a group which adhered to the expectations of that theology' (Sanders 1985, 321). Within this thought-world, 'Jesus saw himself as God's last messenger before the establishment of the kingdom' (Sanders 1985, 319). He was fulfilling the unique role of the final prophet, come to proclaim a New Age, the divine kingdom that God was shortly to inaugurate on earth. However, a movement based upon this expectation could only last for a relatively short time. For the apocalyptic thought-world of first century Judaism has long since vanished. Indeed Jesus' version of it, centred on his own role, lasted for only a few decades among his followers, being replaced by something more able to endure in the pluralistic world of the Roman empire and eventually to become its dominant structure of meaning: Jesus the eschatological prophet was transformed within Christian thought into God the Son come down from heaven to live a human life and save us by his atoning death.

The developed Christian dogma is not of course, strictly speaking, that Jesus of Nazareth was God, in the sense of the God of the Hebrew scriptures, incarnate, but that he was the second person of a divine Trinity incarnate. And so when in these pages I speak of the idea that Jesus was God incarnate I am following a general usage according to which 'God incarnate' is an abbreviation of 'God the Son, second person of the holy Trinity, incarnate'.

Around this central theme a comprehensive body of beliefs developed concerning the original sinfulness and guilt of the human race; a long story of miraculous divine interventions in the course of Jewish history; Jesus' virgin birth, his miracles, atoning death, bodily resurrection and ascension; the church as the body of the redeemed; heaven, hell and purgatory hereafter; as well as a wealth of other matters.

This collection of ideas, constituting the picture in terms of which Christians long understood the universe and their place in it, only began to come under serious strain in the seventeenth century as the modern scientific world-view began to form. This produced a cognitive dissonance which by the end of the nineteenth century had created a rift between those who had gradually come to accept the new knowledge – biological evolution and the historical study of the scriptures being the most contentious issues – and those who, on the contrary, reacted in intensified adherence to their threatened world-view.

Such a deep divergence of viewpoint among Christians has been possible because theology is a human creation. It is the product of devout and faithful men and women (but in fact nearly always, in the past, men), some of them extremely intelligent and thoughtful and others less so, who were, like everyone else, enabled and yet also limited by the presuppositions and cognitive resources of a particular time and place. One can usually tell from their way of thinking to what period and sub-tradition they belonged. And because theology is a human artefact, it has changed almost out of recognition as the circumstances of human life have changed. Ideas which at one time seemed self-evident or divinely authorized have sometimes come in a different age to seem implausible or even offensive. To give just one major example which is relevant to the argument of this book, it was for more than a thousand years a firm Christian dogma that *Extra ecclesiam nulla salus*, 'Outside the church there is no salvation'. Thus for example the Council of Florence (1438-45) declared that 'no one remaining outside the Catholic Church, not just pagans, but also Jews or heretics or schematics, can become partakers of eternal life; but they will go to the "everlasting fire which was prepared for the devil and his angels", unless before the end of life they are joined to the Church' (Clarkson 1961, 78: Denzinger, 714). But very few Catholics would dream of affirming this today, and most who are asked about it only find it embarrassing. Here then is a rather fundamental belief, with vast implications, that held sway throughout most of Christian history up to the present time, but which has now simply been discarded. It cannot, therefore, reasonably be supposed that theological doctrines are unchangeable. The body of doctrine has in fact been developing, sometimes more slowly and sometimes more rapidly, throughout Christian history. Proposals for continued change today should accordingly be considered on their merits. It would be inconsistent, after what has happened to the *extra ecclesiam* dogma, to reject them simply because they involve change, even radical change.

Returning to the nineteenth-century crisis of belief, the scientific challenge to Christian theology which then came to a head has been largely met. The mainstream churches, first Protestant and then Catholic, have allowed their theologies to develop in line with the new knowledge. The effective belief-system of a typical Catholic, Anglican, Presbyterian, Lutheran, Congregationalist, or Methodist in the West today is very different from that of even a hundred years ago. This willingness of the mainline churches to rethink their beliefs, even though at first very reluctantly, in the light of a massive influx of new information, has saved them from becoming marginalized in a cultural ghetto. At the same time Christianity has been sadly weakened by the split between this majority and the continuing powerful minority of fundamentalist believers. As a result there are now in some significant respects two Christianities existing side by side in tension with one another.

But now that orthodoxy has changed in response to the inescapable challenge of modern science, another equally great and equally inescapable challenge has arisen. Whereas the first came largely from new knowledge of the natural world and of our human continuity with it, the second comes from new knowledge of the human religious world and of our continuity with that. This raises questions about the theological core of the Christianity that emerged out of the ecclesiastical debates and council decisions of the first five centuries: namely, that Jesus of Nazareth was God the Son living a human life. For from this there follows the world-centrality of Christianity as the only religion founded by God in person. It is here that the strain is now being felt. For Christianity's implicit or explicit claim to an unique superiority, as the central focus of God's saving activity on earth, has come to seem increasingly implausible within the new global consciousness of our time.

This new global consciousness has prompted a more sensitive awareness of the variety of cultures and faiths within the human family. As a result of the twentieth-century explosion of information about the religions of the world, and an expanding movement of world travel since the Second World War, as well as large-scale immigration into the West from Muslim, Hindu, Sikh, Buddhist, and Taoist and Confucian areas, it has become evident to a growing proportion of educated Westerners that what the Christian faith is to the devout Christian, the Islamic faith is to the devout Muslim, the Buddhist faith to practising Buddhists, the Hindu faith to dedicated Hindus, and so on. Further, it is evident that the religion (if any) to which one adheres, and in terms of which one discerns the meaning of our human existence, normally depends upon the accident of birth. Someone born to Muslim parents in Iran or Indonesia is likely to be a Muslim; one born to Hindu parents in India to be a Hindu; one born to Buddhist parents in Thailand or Sri Lanka to be a Buddhist; just as one born to Christian parents in Poland or Mexico is likely to be a Catholic Christian . . .

Further, it is now a fairly widespread experience that when one comes to know seriously practising adherents of these other faiths one does not find them to be any less sincerely intent on living in obedience to God or to the *Dharma*, any less loving and compassionate towards their fellow humans, or any less honest, truthful, generous or thoughtful, than seriously practising Christians. Again, when one looks at the great saints of these traditions one does not find them to be less impressive than our great Christian saints. Nor again, when one studies their holy scriptures and their theological, philosophical and mystical literature, does one find that our Christian writings are of a different and superior order. Finally, when one examines the long histories of the great traditions and the civilizations built upon them, including the chequered story of our Christian West, one finds that each has been a bewildering mixture of great blessings and appalling evils, and that it is impossible to establish that one has proceeded on a manifestly higher moral level than the others. How do we weigh, for example, the economic backwardness of many Buddhist, Hindu and Muslim societies against the ruthless exploitation of the Third World by the Christian nations of the First World? Or such customs as suttee within Hinduism, or the subordination of women in traditional Islamic societies, against the endemic antisemitism that pervades so much of Christian history? When we try to take all these and innumerable other factors into account we find that we are dealing with unique and, for practical purposes, incommensurable totalities which cannot realistically be set in an agreed order of value.[3]

It is this new public awareness that has undermined the plausibility of the traditional Christian sense of superiority and has thereby set a question mark against its theological core in the dogma that Jesus of Nazareth was God incarnate.

It is not, however, the word 'incarnation', nor even several of its possible meanings, that is now under criticism, but the particular meaning – but not exclusively the particular conceptuality and language – that the church adopted at the Councils of Nicaea (325 CE) and Chalcedon (451 CE). Sarah Coakley (Coakley 1988) has carefully distinguished six senses in which a Christian theology can be said to be incarnational:

(1) In the first sense, an incarnational theology is one that affirms God's involvement in human life. Thus in acting within human history (as depicted throughout the Hebrew scriptures) God is present with us in the flow of time. The basic thought here is that human life and history are important to God, who is at all times 'Immanuel', God with us. In this first sense all versions of Christianity are incarnational; and so also are Judaism, Islam and Sikhism and, in very different ways, extending beyond theism, Hinduism, Buddhism, Taoism, Confucianism, Shintoism and forms of primal religion. This first and most general sense of incarnational thought is not in question here.

(2) A Christian theology can be incarnational in the sense of declaring not only that God is always involved in human life, but also that in the life of Jesus God was involved in a particular and specially powerful and effective way. In other words, Jesus was not just an ordinary man, but one whose relationship to God has a universal significance. However, as Coakley says, 'A definition like this tells us nothing, we note, about more controversial issues such as the personal pre-existence of Jesus, or the fullness, finality or exclusiveness of the revelation claimed to be found in him. None the less this is a common, if vague, understanding of "incarnation"' (104-5). This sense of divine incarnation is likewise not in question here.

(3) Another sense, which takes a major step beyond the previous

---

[3]See further in Chapter 8 and in my 'The Non-Absoluteness of Christianity' (Hick 1993).

two, 'focuses explicitly on the issue of *pre-existence*. "Incarnation" on this view means Christ's coming into flesh, and thus the defining characteristic of "incarnational Christology" is seen as the belief in Jesus personally pre-existing his earthly birth in some divine, or quasi-divine, form (usually the Logos)' (105). It is at this point that I begin in this book to depart from the established tradition.

(4) Another sense again, which makes a still more important claim than the last, is that which 'locates the crucial distinguishing feature of an "incarnational Christology" in the belief in a *total interaction of the divine and the human in Christ*. On this view the incarnation is that complete self-gift of God in Jesus; it is divine revelation *quantitatively* superior to others because here God gives himself fully: he gives nothing less than himself, such that one can talk of Jesus as being "fully God" as well as "fully man"' (105). This is also a sense of divine incarnation which I recommend in this book that we should cease to use.

(5) A theology can be incarnational in the yet further sense of stipulating that Jesus has been and will be the *only* divine incarnation in the previous sense: 'no other person could ever be like this again, or convey God in this way. The "incarnation" on this fifth view means that Christ is in a category distinct from all other forms of revelation; the divine manifestation in him is thus both exclusive and final: it is qualitatively superior to all others, and it can never be surpassed' (105-6). This also is a sense of divine incarnation that I want to discard.

(6) Finally, there is the ecclesiastically defined sense that equates incarnational christology with that of the Council of Chalcedon. 'The assent to belief in the "incarnation" becomes at the same time assent to the substance language of *physis*, *hypostasis*, and *ousia*. This [says Coakley] is a relatively rare, but none the less distinctive and influential, standpoint, of which we also have to take account' (106).[4] This also, of course, is a sense that I want to discard.

As Sarah Coakley points out, these ideas are not mutually exclusive. On the contrary, each later one includes the previous ones. They thus form an ascending scale. And the difference between christologies is a difference in the point at which theologians believe that the progression has gone as far as it should. Thus my own christology stops at sense 2, whereas a traditionally

---

[4]See for example Eric Mascall (Mascall 1977).

orthodox version goes to sense 5, and in a decreasing number of cases to sense 6.

In this book the focus of attention is upon sense number 5, in which it is affirmed that Jesus of Nazareth was the pre-existent divine Son or Logos living a human life. As such he was both fully God and fully a man, so that 'in him the whole fulness of deity dwells bodily' (Colossians 2.9); and he was the only human being who has ever been or will be God incarnate.

This can be described as the standard orthodoxy. My own respected teacher, H.H. Farmer, expressed it as the dogma that 'in Jesus Christ God came into history, took flesh and dwelt among us, in a revelation of Himself, which is unique, final, completely adequate, wholly indispensable for man's salvation' (Farmer 1941, 18). This would be affirmed by the Pope, and is embodied in the World Council of Churches' Basis, in its most recent (1966) formulation, 'the Lord Jesus Christ as God and Saviour'; and it would be difficult for any official church pronouncement explicitly to question it. On the other hand it is in fact questioned today by a large number of highly regarded Christian theologians. The questioning occurs on a continuum from more 'conservative' to more 'liberal' starting points. At the more conservative end, many wish to leave the Chalcedonian formulation behind, regarding it (in Karl Rahner's words) as 'not end but beginning' (Rahner 1965, 149); and the pre-existence of the incarnate one is also often treated as a moot point. Further along the continuum there has been discussion about whether Jesus' uniqueness is one of kind or degree. And further again, amongst those who think of 'incarnation' in terms of degrees of human openness to God, there is a question as to whether Jesus should or should not be thought of as the *only* human being who has been so responsive to God that his life has been significantly revelatory.

This book, then, focuses upon the standardly orthodox doctrine that Jesus was fully God and fully a man and was as such the uniquely complete and final self-revelation of God to humankind. We shall be concerned with this doctrine, with the problems that beset it, and with alternative positive understandings of Jesus that have developed in the modern period. I shall not attempt an encyclopaedic discussion of the long and fascinating story of christological debates. A number of such works are available, the most recent being John Macquarrie's lucid and comprehensive *Jesus Christ in Modern Thought* (Macquarrie 1990). Instead I shall follow a logical thread which begins with the historical question whether Jesus regarded himself as God incarnate; if he did not, whether it is satisfactory to move the basis of Christian belief, as is now rather generally done, from Jesus' own teachings to those of the church, and particularly to the decisions of the great ecumenical councils of the fourth and fifth centuries. I shall then raise the philosophical question whether the idea of Jesus' simultaneous deity and humanity can be coherently spelled out; next turning to the ways in which the idea of the absolute and universal lordship of Jesus has been used to justify great evils in the course of Western history; then to the related ideas of atonement and salvation; and finally to the alternative understandings of Jesus and his message that are available today.

The main conclusion of the book, embodied in its title, is that the idea of divine incarnation in its standard Christian form, in which both genuine humanity and genuine deity are insisted upon, has never been given a satisfactory literal sense; but that on the other hand it makes excellent metaphorical sense. When, for example, Gandhi, asked what his message was, said that his life itself was his message (Judith Brown 1989, 80) he was saying that his message was embodied, incarnated, made visible, in his life. For a human life can 'incarnate', or live out, truths and values. Here incarnation is a metaphorical idea. But more about the nature of metaphor in general, and the metaphor of incarnation in particular, in Chapter 10.

What I shall recommend is acceptance of the idea of divine incarnation as a metaphorical idea. We see in Jesus a human being extraordinarily open to God's influence and thus living to an extraordinary extent as God's agent on earth, 'incarnating' the divine purpose for human life. He thus embodied within the circumstances of his time and place the ideal of humanity living in openness and response to God, and in doing so he 'incarnated' a love that reflects the divine love. This epoch-making life became the inspiration of a vast tradition which has for many centuries provided intellectual and moral guidance to Western civilization. Today many aspects of that tradition have lost their *gravitas* and plausibility, and Western civilization has itself entered a post-Christian phase. But the original inspiration of one who fully trusted in God, though within a human setting very different from our own, is no less powerful than in earlier centuries. If it can be liberated from the network of theories – about Incarnation, Trinity and Atonement –

which served once to focus but now serve only to obscure its significance, that lived teaching can continue to be a major source of inspiration for human life.

This book is accordingly addressed particularly to two groups of readers, a smaller group within the churches and a larger one outside.

The first consists of Christians who are not satisfied to go on living in the intellectual cocoon that we have allowed to form around us, made up of uncriticized traditional ideas which no longer make sense to most of the people among whom we live. And so this book seeks to speak to those who are looking for a Christian faith that is believable not only within the special liturgical world of hymns and prayers and sermons on Sunday, but in the everyday world throughout the week.

The other group is much larger and consists of those, both young and old, who have either left the churches or were never attracted to them, but who are nevertheless genuinely concerned with religious issues. They opt for religious studies courses in colleges and universities; or they read about and seek to encounter Buddhism, Hinduism, Taoism, Islam, Judaism, Bahai, and so on; or they are interested in radio, TV and newspaper treatments of religious questions; or they experiment with forms of meditation; or they are sometimes acutely conscious of the sheer mystery of the universe and of human life – any or some or all of these. In some cases their spiritual hunger has taken them into the New Age movement or into one or other of the new sects. And yet very often they move through these rather than settle in them for life. There is thus a large body of religiously questioning people for whom, in our Western countries, the churches have not offered meaningful or believable answers.

My hope is that some in these two groups may welcome a renewed attempt to focus a central religious issue and to think it through in a straightforward and honest way. For although our age is increasingly post-traditionally Christian, it may well be receptive to a non-traditional Christianity centred upon the universally relevant religious experience and ethical insights of Jesus when these are freed from the mass of ecclesiastical dogmas and practices that have developed over the centuries, reflecting cultures as widely different from ours as the Roman empire and medieval Christendom. Unlike the traditional version, such a non-traditional Christianity must of course see itself, not as the one and only 'true religion', but as one authentic spiritual path among others, open to

influences from the wider religious experience of humankind –
about which more in Chapter 14.

Every topic of real interest in theology today is controversial.
This 'comes with the territory'. And the most controversial area of
all is christology. It is a feature of the present situation that, in
addition to the theological and scriptural debates, powerful
philosophical defences have been offered of the traditional christology. In this book I take these seriously – as indeed they deserve and
require to be taken – and argue with them on their own ground.
Some readers may find these discussions (for example, of the
contributions of Thomas Morris, Richard Swinburne, Stephen
Davis and others) too philosophical for their taste. But it has
nevertheless been essential for me to respond directly to these
contemporary attempts to preserve an endangered dogma. Only
then can I be entitled to come to the conclusion to which I come in
this book.

2

Jesus' Life, Death and Resurrection

The New Testament takes us as far back as we can go towards Jesus of Nazareth. It is for this reason that no other ancient documents have been so intensively studied by the methods of critical research. The process has been going on now for some two centuries, during which time it has produced a bewildering succession and variety of conclusions, many of them mutually at variance. Almost every interpretation offered by one group of scholars has been seriously criticized by another group (cf. Page 1991, ch. 4). Methods and approaches have tended to come and go in waves of fashion, swinging back and forth, or going round in circles, in a way that makes it difficult to know which writers to rely on. However, fortunately, even within this shifting scene there is a modest but significant area of consensus. Whilst the experts range widely along the conservative-liberal spectrum, they have nevertheless produced a sufficient overlap of conclusions for those of us who are not primarily New Testament scholars to have something reasonably solid to start from. Those who support this approximate and always provisional consensus do not, however, agree about its significance; they absorb it into very different over-all interpretations of the New Testament and its central figure. But this is to be expected. For when we come to religiously significant conclusions there are no experts but only, at best, sincere and honest inquirers presenting their own responsibly developed points of view.

The identifiable consensus begins with a distinction between the historical Jesus of Nazareth and the post-Easter development of the church's mingled memories and interpretations of him. And it is a basic premise of modern New Testament scholarship that we have access to the former only through the latter.

We begin, then, with the post-Easter Christian communities and their memories, and developing and diversifying memories of memories, of Jesus. Among these small but growing groups something new and vital and deeply stirring had come about, a contagion of the spirit of Jesus, whom they believed to have been exalted beyond death. The present reality at the time when the New Testament documents were being written was this communal life, inspired by the spirit of the glorified Lord. His influence was felt both through his variously and changingly remembered story and teachings, and also through new revelations proclaimed here and there within local groups by resident and peripatetic Christian prophets reporting their own visions and interpreting the ecstatic 'speaking with tongues'. This was a time of excited and sometimes (from a typical twentieth-century standpoint) fantastic beliefs and practices to whose atmosphere we have a clue in the uninhibited enthusiasms of contemporary Pentecostalism and the unshakeable certainties of marginal sects expecting the imminent end of the world. In that early apocalyptic phase of the Christian movement the canons of plausibility were very different from those operating within today's mainline churches. And it is through writings produced within those vital but volatile communities that we have to try to work our way back in imagination along the trajectories of tradition to the earthly figure of Jesus.

It is widely agreed that the earliest New Testament documents – some of the letters of St Paul – were written about twenty years after Jesus' death (i.e. around 50 CE), with the earliest of the Gospels, that of Mark, some twenty years later and the remainder during the next thirty or so years, moving towards the end of the century. None of the writers was an eye-witness of the life that they depict. The Gospels are secondary and tertiary portraits dependent on oral and written traditions which had developed over a number of decades, the original first-hand memories of Jesus being variously preserved, winnowed, developed, distorted, magnified and overlaid through the interplay of many factors including the universal tendency increasingly to exalt one's leader-figure, the delight of the ancient world in the marvellous, opposition to the mainstream of Judaism from which the church had now been separated, an intensification of faith under persecution, factional polemics within different streams of the Christian community itself, and a policy of presenting events in Jesus' life as fulfilments of ancient prophecy or as exemplifying accepted religious themes. As Howard Kee reminds us, 'historians in this period were not interested simply in reporting events of the past, but saw their role as providing the meaning of those past events for readers in the present' (Kee 1990, 90).

We can have some sort of conception of the literary aetiology of the Gospels if we think by analogy of a medieval European saint, let us say a St Judith, who makes a profound impression upon many of her contemporaries. And then two generations later someone living elsewhere who did not know the saint in person, but who has heard impressive stories of her supernatural sanctity, memorable sayings and miracles of healing, writes a religious tract about her to inspire others. As stories about the saint have circulated through the countryside during the intervening decades they have been simplified, become more pointed and easily remembered, and tailored towards a striking pronouncement, whilst the miraculous elements have tended, in a pre-critical age, to become ever more marvellous. In due course several such Lives appear, presenting partly different portraits of the saint; and it is through the collection of such writings that we today have to form our own impression of her. To some extent our knowledge of St Judith's period can help us gauge the influences that must have affected the developing traditions. Nevertheless it is obviously extremely difficult for historians a thousand years later to arrive at a clear and accurate picture of the historical St Judith. Nor do the activities of a flourishing St Judith Society, embodying a dogmatic belief in the outstanding importance of their saint and circulating material promoting her cult, necessarily help the historian.

There are somewhat analogous difficulties in the case of Jesus. In interpreting the four Gospels, we have to take account of the ongoing life of the Christian communities whose faith, ideas, assumptions, prejudices and disputes are reflected both in the Gospels themselves and in the remaining New Testament documents. For the societies which produced these writings constituted the living medium within which the traditions about Jesus grew and by which they were moulded into their present forms. And as we seek, so far as we can, to penetrate behind these documents to Jesus of Nazareth, we must also, as scholars have been stressing in recent years, take into account a wealth of knowledge about the Judaism of Jesus' time. Indeed in the light of information, much of it fairly recently available, about early rabbinic Judaism, 'Few . . . will contest that [Jesus'] message was essentially Jewish' (Vermes 1991, 113). We also have to remind ourselves that the Gospels were written, in a period between forty and seventy years after the time of Jesus, in a quite different cultural milieu from that of the original events. Paula Fredricksen summarizes the contrast as follows:

'from oral to written; from Aramaic to Greek; from the End of time to the middle of time; from Jewish to Gentile; from the Galilee and Judea to the Empire' (Fredricksen 1988, 8). Clearly, the attempt to form a picture of the life that lay forty to sixty or seventy years behind the written Gospels cannot yield a great deal in the way of fully assured results.

Is there, however, anything that can be said today with any degree of assurance about the earthly Jesus whose short career has made so profound a long-term impact as to be the most influential life ever lived?

Scholars have listed such generally agreed points as that Jesus was a Galilean Jew, son of a woman called Mary; that he was baptized by John the Baptist; that he preached and healed and exorcized; that he called disciples and spoke of there being twelve; that he largely confined his activity to Israel; that he was crucified outside Jerusalem by the Roman authorities; and that after his death his followers continued as an identifiable movement. Beyond this an unavoidable element of conjectural interpretation goes into our mental pictures of Jesus. My own picture falls within the tradition of 'liberal' interpretation established by Schleiermacher, Strauss, Harnack and others. As I see it, religiously the most important fact about Jesus must have been his strong and continuous awareness of God as *abba*, 'father'. From the point of view of the psychology of religion we can say that only an extremely intense God-consciousness could have sustained Jesus' firm prophetic assurance and charismatic power. It is evident that in his own consciousness God was the great over-arching reality in relation to whom he lived. The heavenly Father was utterly real to him – as real as the men and women with whom he interacted every day or the Galilean hills among which they lived. When Jesus declared God's gracious and yet demanding love, and God's judgment upon hypocrisy, and pronounced God's forgiveness for sinners, he was speaking out of a direct sense of a supernatural loving, judging, forgiving presence, so that his words had the powerful ring of authenticity. God was evidently so real to Jesus that in his presence the heavenly Father became a living reality to many of his hearers. As Günther Bornkamm says, 'To make the reality of God present: this is the essential mystery of Jesus' (Bornkamm 1960, 62). Jesus' words, spoken out of this powerful God-consciousness, were often profoundly challenging and yet at the same time utterly convincing, so that the lives of many were revolutionized in their encounter with him. As we read in Matthew's Gospel, 'the crowds were astonished at his teaching, for he taught them as one who had authority, and not as their scribes' (Matt. 7.28).

Jesus' intense God-consciousness was of course inevitably structured in terms of the religious ideas of his own culture. The basic concept with which to understand his own existence in relation to God was that of prophet. But it seems that Jesus was conscious, not just of being a prophet, but probably of being the last prophet. 'Jesus,' says E. P. Sanders, 'saw himself as God's last messenger before the establishment of the kingdom' (Sanders 1985, 319). He came as the eschatological prophet, urgently proclaiming the imminent approach of the Day of the Lord. He and those who responded to him were living consciously in the last months or years before the great Day when the present world order would be swept away and God's kingdom established on earth. Widely circulated apocalyptic writings looked forward to this coming new age when 'the God of heaven will set up a kingdom which shall never be destroyed, nor shall its sovereignty be left to another people' (Daniel 2.44). The Dead Sea Scrolls also show, as Howard Kee says, 'how vital the expectation was within first-century Judaism that the present age was coming to an end, to be replaced by the new age in which God would vindicate the faithful and establish his rule over the world!' (Kee 1990, 17). According to one popular expectation, in the coming age Israel would be restored, Jerusalem would be the centre of the world, and peace and justice would reign universally. But beyond this there was a bewildering variety of differing strands of thought expressing the themes of God's long-awaited new age and the expectation of 'one who is to come' to inaugurate it.

However, the expected End, which was also to be God's new Beginning, was delayed from year to year and from generation to generation. As one of the Qumran documents says: 'The final End is taking more time than the prophets predicted, for marvellous are God's mysteries . . . The last days will come according to God's appointed time' (I QpHab 7.7-14; Schillebeeckx 1979, 121). But Jesus seems to have been vividly conscious that the End was at last close at hand and that he was called urgently to summon Israel to repentance so that it might be ready for the great day: 'Jesus came into Galilee, preaching the gospel of God, and saying "The time is fulfilled, and the kingdom of God is at hand; repent, and believe in the gospel"' (Mark 1.14). As Mircea Eliade says, 'Following the prophets, following John the Baptist, Jesus predicted the imminent transformation of the world: this is the essence of his preaching' (Eliade 1982, 332).

Although scholars have raised questions about Jesus' own use of the idea, one apocalyptic strand expected a saviour figure to appear from the sky. In the Danielic vision of the future,

> behold, with the clouds of heaven
> there came one like a son of man,
> and he came to the Ancient of Days
> and was presented before him.
> And to him was given dominion
> and glory and kingdom,
> that all peoples, nations, and languages
> should serve him;
> his dominion is an everlasting dominion
> which shall not pass away, and his kingdom one
> that shall not be destroyed (Daniel 7.13-14).

Either Jesus himself or the developing mind of the church believed that when Jesus returned on the great Day he would be this Son of Man appearing in the clouds.

The other familiar image which Judaism offered to identify the eschatological prophet was that of Messiah. It is far from certain that Jesus applied this to himself. Leslie Houlden reminds us that in the time of Jesus 'it is not the case that Judaism was full to the brim with expectations of the Messiah' (Houlden 1992, 18). More probably it was the church that subsequently made this identification. But by the time the Gospels began to be written, the two images of the Son of Man and the Messiah had become more or less fused in the Christian mind, so that when in the Markan passion story Jesus, before the Sanhedrin, is asked if he is the Messiah, he replies, 'I am; and you will see the Son of man seated at the right hand of Power, and coming with the clouds of heaven' (Mark 14.62). It is a widespread critical opinion that these words are not in fact historical. They are, says Schillebeeckx, 'what the post-Easter church put into Jesus' mouth later on' (Schillebeeckx 1979, 315). But the general apocalyptic expectation of a decisive divine intervention in human history is reflected at many points in the New Testament and must surely go back to Jesus himself. He is reported in the earliest Gospel to have said, 'Truly, I say to you, there are some standing here who will not taste death before they see that the kingdom of God has come with power' (Mark 9.1). And at many other points the Synoptic Jesus speaks of the imminent end of the age. As E. P. Sanders concludes, 'the facts about Jesus, his predecessors and the Christian movement indicate that he himself expected the kingdom to come in the near future' (Sanders 1985, 118). This expectation seems, as he says, 'to have been shared by the entirety of the early Christian movement, and Paul characterized as "the word of the Lord" the promise that those who are still alive when the Lord returns will not precede those who have already died (1 Thess. 4.15)' (Sanders 1985, 93). The expectation had important practical consequences. It meant that Jesus' moral teaching did not involve a critique of the social, political and economic structures of his time in the manner of some of the earlier Hebrew prophets and of contemporary liberation theology; for the present social order was soon to disappear and be replaced by God's manifest rule on earth. But although Jesus was thus not a social reformer, nevertheless to preach the imminent end of the present world order did at that time have inevitable political implications: it meant the early end of Roman rule. And in a period when Jewish rebellion against that rule was very much in the air – *Acts* (ch. 5) refers to revolts led by Theudas and by Judas the Galilean, and there were to be the Jewish war of 66-70 CE and the rebellion led by Bar Kochba in 135 CE – to imply the impending end of Roman rule could be dangerous talk. It was indeed apparently the main reason for Jesus' crucifixion, this being 'a Roman form of punishment reserved particularly for political troublemakers' (Fredricksen 1988, 104). To quote a leading historian of the period, 'The context of Jesus' execution was clearly the suppression of Jewish revolt against the rule of Romans and their collaborators in Judea. Any proclamation of the coming reign of God immediately suggested to the Jerusalem authorities that the restoration of a Jewish kingdom was involved' (Grant 1971, 59).[1]

Jesus' central message, then, was a call to repent, to believe that the kingdom was about to come, and to begin to live the life of the new age. This was the life of love. Here Jesus stood within a strand of Jewish thought that became prominent in the first century CE. David Flusser refers to it as 'the new sensitivity in Judaism' and 'the

---

[1]Howard Kee points out: 'The inscription placed above Jesus' head as he was lifted on the cross confirms that he is dying on a political, anti-Roman charge, rather than as a violator of Jewish law' (Kee 1990, 85-6).

new Jewish ethics' (Flusser 1991, 167-8). It had indeed already been expressed during the first century BCE in *Ecclesiasticus*; and the double commandment to love God and neighbour 'clearly was coined before the time of Jesus' (Flusser 1991, 170). Schillebeeckx tells us that this theme of outgoing love was part of the Galilean ethos of that time, setting many Galileans at odds with the more legalistic attitude prevailing in Jerusalem. He says, 'For these Greek-speaking Jews, much inclined as they were to *philanthropia*, a universal "love of humanity", a good deal of what the others were accustomed to call "the Law", was actually incompatible with the Law proper, that is, God's decalogue, the Ten Commandments. In Galilee, as opposed to Jerusalem, this Graeco-Jewish outlook was in fact the "general thing" (which is why Judea could not expect "any good" to come out of Galilee, out of Nazareth)"' (Schillebeeckx 1979, 118-19).

But Jesus' own conception of love of neighbour seems to have been more profound and total, or at least to have made a more powerful impact, than that of others who were teaching along much the same lines. He taught a complete trust in God in which one forgets one's private interests and so becomes free to serve others in their needs. He called his hearers to give and forgive without limit; to treat all people, including the despised Samaritans and the overbearing Romans, as their neighbours; and to live without anxiety for tomorrow, trusting in God's providential care. They would thus be true children of their heavenly Father and heirs of the kingdom: 'Love your enemies and pray for those who persecute you, so that you may be sons of your Father who is in heaven; for he makes his sun rise on the evil and on the good, and sends rain on the just and the unjust' (Matt. 5.44-45).

Jesus' teaching and healing ministry was brief but intense, probably lasting no more than two years. The impact of his personality and of his words and actions during this short period must have been tremendous. But the greater the impact, the more likely that he would come to the attention of the Roman authorities as one who was proclaiming the end of the established order. And the Jewish authorities in Jerusalem, to whom he was a Galilean critic of the Law as they understood it and one who had even spoken of the destruction of the Temple, as well as being a threat to their concordat with Rome, had no inclination to protect him, but on the contrary collaborated in his arrest. Indeed it seems that in a sense Jesus himself may also be said to have collaborated in his fate in that

he saw martyrdom as virtually inevitable when he went up to
Jerusalem to confront the Jewish-Roman establishment at its
centre. When he was told that Herod wanted to kill him he is
reported to have said, 'I must go on my way today and tomorrow
and the day following; for it cannot be that a prophet should perish
away from Jerusalem' (Luke 13.33). Later Christian thought has
created doctrines according to which Jesus' death was a divinely
planned sacrifice for the salvation of the world: he was bearing on
our behalf God's just punishment for sin or in some other way by his
death winning forgiveness for the human race. I shall be discussing
these atonement theories in Chapter 11. But in the minds of the
Jews of Jesus' time, including presumably his own mind, there was
the idea that the sufferings of a faithful servant of God work
vicariously for the good of Israel. A number of traditional themes
contributed to this idea. One was the 'suffering righteous one' of the
Psalms (22; 34 and 37) and another was the 'suffering servant' of
Isaiah 53. It was also an established conviction that 'without the
shedding of blood there is no forgiveness of sins' (Hebrews 9.22).
The widespread assumption of the salvific benefit won by a martyr's
death may well lie behind the Markan saying attributed to Jesus that
his coming death would be 'a ransom for many' (Mark 10.45). But it
was also integral to this set of ideas that the righteous sufferer will be
vindicated in the end. And as the belief in bodily resurrection
became fairly general during the century before Jesus, the vindication of the righteous was assumed to mean their resurrection. All
this clearly sets the scene for the New Testament accounts of Jesus'
death, understood as being salvific, and of his resurrection interpreted as God's decisive vindication.

The term 'resurrection' has been used throughout Christian
history to refer to the transitional event or events in virtue of which
the Jesus movement survived the death of its founder, withstood
persecution, flourished and went on to become the religion of the
Roman empire and so of the Western world and its colonial
extensions. Precisely what this transitional event was we cannot
now discern with confidence. By the time the Gospels were being
written, two generations later, it was believed to have been a
revivifying of Jesus' corpse in a mysteriously transformed state,
followed by his bodily presence on earth for a period of several
weeks and then his bodily ascension up into a cloud. However, it has
often been pointed out that the earliest strata of the New Testament
do not include any reference either to the empty tomb or to a visible

or tangible body of the risen Jesus. The conviction that he had risen, or ascended, or is in glory, evidently arose prior to and independently of the later physical resurrection stories with which we are familiar from the Gospels.

What, then, caused the first disciples to believe, after Jesus' crucifixion, that he was now alive as their exalted and glorified Lord? Any answers are inevitably under-determined by the historical evidence. My own preferred conjecture starts from the earliest account that we have of an 'appearance' of the risen Lord, that of Paul on the Damascus road some two or three years after the crucifixion. Paul, as later reported in Acts 9.3-8 (repeated in 22.6-11 and, in a developed form, in 26.12-18), experienced a blinding light and heard (inwardly, according to one of the accounts) a voice but did not see any bodily presence; if he had, this would also have been seen by the others present. Paul himself equated this experience with the paradigm 'appearances' to Peter and the twelve (I Cor. 15.8); and Barnabas likewise described the Damascus road experience as Paul's 'seeing of Jesus' (Acts 9.27).[2]

It seems a reasonable conjecture that the original resurrection event consisted in Peter at least, but perhaps others also of the twelve, and perhaps some of the women, having an experience essentially similar to that of Paul, an experience of a supernatural light around them within which they were conscious of the glorified presence of Jesus. The near-death experiences which have been reported so abundantly in recent years, since improved methods were developed for resuscitating 'clinically dead' patients, often include something rather like this in the form of a bright light, or a brightly shining figure, from which there emanates a profound accepting love and peace. Christians who have had this experience generally identify the 'being of light' with Christ; and the original resurrection 'appearances' may quite possibly have been waking versions of this same type of experience.

On this hypothesis the stories of the empty tomb (Mark 16.5; Matthew 28.6; Luke 24.3; John 20.2); the three hours of darkness 'over all the land (*or* all the earth)' (Matt. 27.45); the rending of the temple curtain 'from top to bottom' (27.51); the earthquake

---

[2]Howard Kee, commentating on Paul's reference in I Corinthians 15.8 to his Damascus road experience, says: 'There he [Paul] makes no distinction between his having seen Jesus and the appearances of Jesus to the disciples. Equally important is that apparently they also saw no difference between Paul's experience and theirs, since they accepted him as having been called to apostleship by the risen Christ, just as they had been' (Kee 1990, 1).

(27.51); the raising from their tombs of 'many bodies of the saints who had fallen asleep [i.e. died]' and their entering into Jerusalem and being seen by many (27.52-53); the second earthquake two days later (28.2); the angel who 'descended from heaven and came and rolled back the stone, and sat upon it', his appearance being 'like lightning (28.2-3)'; the guards fainting (28.4); the appearances of Jesus at the tomb, and on a mountain in Galilee (28.9-10, 16-20); and, in Luke, Jesus' appearance on the Emmaus road (Luke 24.13-35); and to the eleven in Jerusalem (24.36-49); and in Acts (and also in Luke 24.50-52) his bodily ascension, disappearing upwards into a cloud (Acts 1.9-11); not to mention the appearances and long discourses described in John's Gospel – are all later elaborations as the story developed through the decades. For as we try to trace the stream of tradition back through successive layers we find less and less of the physically miraculous and more of the spiritually transforming. In John, towards the end of the first Christian century, there is an elaborate narrative expressing the virtual deification of Jesus in the mind of his part of the church; in Luke and Matthew, one to three decades earlier, we have a wealth of prodigious miracles, some of which (above all, the bodily appearances of Jesus) have played a central role in Christian faith whilst others (such as the concurrent bodily resurrection of many saints of old, seen publicly in the streets of Jerusalem) have generally been quietly forgotten. In Mark, between one and two decades nearer to the events themselves, there are no appearances but only the announcement at the empty tomb that Jesus is risen. (It is part of the scholarly consensus that the last section of Mark's Gospel, recounting resurrection appearances, is a later addition.) And coming from nearly a generation earlier still there is the story of Paul's blinding light and (perhaps inner) voice. There is thus reason to think that – as indeed we should expect on general psychological grounds – the tradition developed from the remembrance of a numinous and transforming experience into a story of miraculous physical events. This pattern suggests that the original happening is more likely to have been in the realm of inner spiritual experience than in that of outer sense experience. But we have to add that any unqualified assertions about what occurred in the days and weeks after Jesus' death, whether in terms of spiritual encounters or of physical miracles, can never be fully substantiated from an historical point of view.

As a general argument against 'spiritualizing' conceptions of

Jesus' resurrection such as I have just been recommending it has often been urged that only a manifest physical miracle could have saved his movement from collapse after the crucifixion, when the disciples fled in despair. However, Schillebeeckx opposes this familiar argument. He says that if those who reason in this way 'want to convince me in this regard, they must first show me why, when John the Baptist had been beheaded, his movement was able simply to continue on Jewish ground – as if that death entailed no break at all. Did the Jewish mentality change within a year or two (that is, with the death of Jesus) so fundamentally that people suddenly began to think that Jesus' death set a big question-mark against his entire ministry here on earth?' (Schillebeeckx 1979, 393). And it is indeed important to remember that in Jewish thinking the deaths of martyrs were not taken as discrediting them but on the contrary as giving them an even more exalted place in popular esteem and in the divine plan.

So what I myself see when I try to peer back through the New Testament documents to the person who lies at a distance of some two generations behind them is a man, Jesus, whose immensely powerful God-consciousness made God, and God's demanding but liberating claim upon men and women, intensely and startlingly real. He did not intend to found a continuing church or a new religion, and he was mistaken in his expectation of an early end to ordinary human history. Nevertheless he was so transparently open to the divine presence that his life and teaching have a universal significance which can still help to guide our lives today.

3

From Jesus to Christ

A further point of broad agreement among New Testament scholars is even more important for understanding the development of christology. This is that the historical Jesus did not make the claim to deity that later Christian thought was to make for him: he did not understand himself to be God, or God the Son, incarnate. Divine incarnation, in the sense in which Christian theology has used the idea, requires that an eternally pre-existent element of the Godhead, God the Son or the divine Logos, became incarnate as a human being. But it is *extremely* unlikely that the historical Jesus thought of himself in any such way. Indeed he would probably have rejected the idea as blasphemous; one of the sayings attributed to him is, 'Why do you call me good? No one is good but God alone' (Mark 10.18).

Of course no statements about what Jesus did or did not say or think can be made with certainty. But such evidence as there is has led the historians of the period to conclude, with an impressive degree of unanimity, that Jesus did not claim to be God incarnate. This is so generally agreed today that a few representative quotations, drawn from writers who themselves affirm an orthodox christology, will suffice for our present purpose. Thus the late Archbishop Michael Ramsey, who was himself a New Testament scholar, wrote that 'Jesus did not claim deity for himself' (Ramsey 1980, 39). His contemporary, the New Testament scholar C.F.D. Moule, said that 'Any case for a "high" Christology that depended on the authenticity of the alleged claims of Jesus about himself, especially in the Fourth Gospel, would indeed be precarious' (Moule 1977, 136). In a major study of the origins of the doctrine of the incarnation James Dunn concludes that 'there was no real evidence in the earliest Jesus tradition of what could fairly be called a consciousness of divinity' (Dunn 1980, 60). Again, Brian Hebblethwaite, a staunch upholder of the traditional Nicene-Chalcedonian christology, acknowledges that 'it is no longer possible to defend the divinity of Jesus by reference to the claims of Jesus' (Hebblethwaite 1987, 74). Yet again, David Brown, another staunch upholder of Chalcedon, says that 'there is good evidence to suggest that [Jesus] never saw himself as a suitable object of worship' and that it is 'impossible to base any claim for Christ's divinity on his consciousness once we abandon the traditional portrait as reflected in a literal understanding of St. John's Gospel' (David Brown 1985, 108).

These quotations (which could be multiplied) reflect a remarkable transformation resulting from the modern historico-critical study of the New Testament. Until about a hundred years ago (as still very widely today in unlearned circles) belief in Jesus as God incarnate was assumed to rest securely upon his own explicit teaching: 'I and the Father are one', 'He that hath seen me hath seen the Father', and so on. Now, however, to quote one of the most recent defenders of a Chalcedonian christology, Adrian Thatcher, 'there is scarcely a single competent New Testament scholar who is prepared to defend the view that the four instances of the absolute use of "I am" in John, or indeed most of the other uses, can be historically attributed to Jesus' (Thatcher 1990, 77).[1]

This recognition is sometimes, though not always, associated with the idea that Jesus became the Christ in being resurrected by God. This in turn connects with a very early adoptionist strand of New Testament thought. As James Dunn says, 'primitive Christian preaching seems to have regarded Jesus' resurrection as the day of his appointment to divine sonship, as the event by which he became God's son' (Dunn 1980, 36). Thus Luke's version of Peter's speech at Pentecost refers to Jesus as 'a man attested to you by God with mighty works and wonders and signs which God did through him in your midst' (Acts 2.22), and says: 'This Jesus God raised up, and of that we are all witnesses . . . Let all the house of Israel therefore know assuredly that God has made him Lord and Christ, this Jesus whom you crucified' (2.32,36). Again, Paul speaks of Jesus as a human being ('descended from David according to the flesh') who was 'designated [*horisthentos*] Son of God in power, according to the Spirit of holiness by his resurrection from the dead' (Romans 1.3-4). In this, one of the earliest christologies, the human Jesus was

---

[1]Despite this, some theologians continue to use 'I and the Father are one' as establishing, for example, that 'Jesus is humanly conscious of being one with God his Father' and that 'The word of God becomes humanly aware of itself in the human consciousness of Jesus' (Dupuis 1991, 61).

raised to an unique and highly exalted role (though not to deity) shortly after his death.

All this rules out the once popular form of apologetic which argues that someone claiming to be God must be either mad, or bad, or God; and since Jesus was evidently not mad or bad he must have been God (e.g. Lewis 1955, 51-2). With the recognition that Jesus did not think of himself in this way christological discussion has moved from the once supposedly firm rock of Jesus' own claim to the much less certain ground of the church's subsequent attempts to formulate the meaning of his life.

It is worth pausing to reflect on the magnitude of this change. From at least the fifth to the late nineteenth century Christians generally believed that Jesus had proclaimed himself to be God the Son, second person of a divine Trinity, living a human life; and their discipleship accordingly included this as a central article of faith. But that supposed dominical authority has dissolved under historical scrutiny. This result of New Testament scholarship would until comparatively recently have been inexpressibly shocking in church circles; and as late as the sixteenth century in Protestant and the seventeenth in Catholic countries those propounding it would have been in grave danger of being executed for heresy. Indeed many of the results of nineteenth- and twentieth-century scholarly research would probably have been regarded as demonic by the church leaders at Nicea and Chalcedon,[2] or by Thomas Aquinas and the other medieval theologians, or Luther and Calvin and the other Reformers, or indeed by Christians generally down to only a few generations ago – as indeed they often still are among the large majority of Christians who continue to be unacquainted with the modern study of the Bible. This ignorance on the part of church members, usually undisturbed by their pastors, still makes it difficult for basic theological issues to be discussed in the church in an open and genuinely enquiring way.

Many Christian theologians today – but no longer, as in former generations, almost all – continue to adhere to the Nicene-Chalcedonian dogma. But now that its centuries-old foundation has collapsed they have had to find a new basis for it. They have accordingly decided that the doctrine of the incarnation does not require the knowledge or consent of the historical Jesus himself.

---

[2]The Chalcedonian Definition supports its two-natures dogma by affirming that it is 'as the Lord Jesus Christ taught us'.

Indeed David Brown argues that 'it is incoherent to suppose that a human mind could be conscious of its own divinity' (Brown 1985, 109 and ch. 6). And responding to the 'new paradox of God incarnate who does not know that he is God incarnate', Brian Hebblethwaite protests that 'to refer dismissively to the notion that Jesus was God but was unaware of it is to fail to grasp the point of kenotic christology' (Hebblethwaite 1979, 90). In other words, in the incarnation God the Son became so self-emptied of the attributes of deity that he was unaware that he was God. We must presently (in Chapters 6 and 7) look carefully at the viability or otherwise of this idea.

But assuming for the moment, and for the sake of argument, that the idea of an incarnate God who is ignorant of his own deity can be made intelligible and its implications made acceptable, the next question will be: how is it possible for the church to know something so important about Jesus that he did not know himself?

This question has elicited four lines of response, sometimes appearing separately but more often in various combinations.

The first involves a qualification of the admission that Jesus was unaware of and did not teach his own deity. This response holds that he was *implicitly* aware of it in his uniquely intimate filial relationship with the heavenly Father, and that he *implicitly* taught it by his actions, particularly in abrogating the law of Moses and in forgiving sins. Thus in constructing its incarnational doctrine the church was only making explicit what had been implicitly there from the beginning.[3] An implicit awareness is not in the nature of the case susceptible of proof or disproof, and its affirmation or denial must be prompted by a wider theological position. Thus the Roman Catholic scholar Gerald O'Collins acknowledges 'the difficulties inherent in exploring the knowledge and inner experience of any human being – particularly, one who lived nearly two thousand years ago', and asks 'which of us is wise enough or holy enough to speak with great assurance about the knowledge and mind of Jesus?' (O'Collins 1983, 184-5). Which indeed? And yet despite this, and indeed in defiance of it, O'Collins feels able confidently to affirm 'a self-consciousness and self-presence in which [Jesus] was intuitively aware of his divine identity' (185)!

---

[3]Thus C.F.D. Moule argued that 'Jesus was, *from the beginning,* such a one as appropriately to be described in the ways in which, sooner or later, he did come to be described in the New Testament period – for instance as "Lord" and even, in some sense, as "God"' (Moule 1977, 4).

James Dunn likewise implies such an implicit awareness when he says, 'We cannot claim that Jesus believed himself to be the incarnate Son of God; but we can claim that the teaching to that effect as it came to expression in later first-century Christian thought was, in the light of the whole Christ-event, an appropriate reflection on and elaboration of Jesus' own sense of sonship and eschatological mission' (Dunn 1980, 60). This carefully constructed sentence by a leading New Testament scholar who is a firm Chalcedonian believer deserves attention. One notes first that it does not aspire beyond the pre-trinitarian notion of 'Son of God' to the properly trinitarian idea of 'God the Son'. One also notes that it makes use of the highly elastic notion of the 'Christ-event', at which we must look presently. But passing over these points, what was 'Jesus' own sense of sonship'? It was that expressed by his use of *abba*, 'dear father'. Although there is dispute as to precisely what *abba* meant at that time – and James Barr has recently argued forcefully that it did not have the specially intimate sense that has so often been attributed to it, but simply meant 'father', whether used by children or by adults (Barr 1988a & b) – and also as to how widely it was in use by other Jewish charismatics (Dunn 1980, 26-7), I do not want to resist the widely received view that Jesus' use of the word did constitute a genuinely new contribution to Western spirituality. To think of God as our heavenly Father was by no means new, but Jesus seems to have made the idea distinctively central and powerful and thus to have initiated a new development through its use within what was to become Christianity. For in the Lord's Prayer he taught his disciples to address God in this same familiar way. Paul later interpreted the practice as involving a mystical or metaphysical incorporation into the life of the risen Christ. But here, as generally, Paul fits Jesus into his own theology with little regard to the historical figure. It is, however, surely wholly credible that Jesus' awareness of the heavenly Father was much more powerful and intense than that of any of his contemporaries. But we have to add, and indeed emphasize, that to experience God as one's heavenly Father is not the same as experiencing oneself as uniquely God the Son, second person of a divine Trinity.

Again, what was Jesus' 'eschatological mission', referred to by Dunn? Was it not his calling to be the final prophet, a human being speaking at a crucial moment as God's messenger? The role of the final prophet was unique, in that it could never recur, so that 'Jesus sensed an *eschatological uniqueness* in his relationship with God'

(Dunn 1980, 28). But this also is a long way from Jesus thinking that he was himself God (i.e. God the Son).

And so to take these two items – Jesus' use of *abba* and his eschatological message – as sufficient to give an implicit dominical authority to the church's belief in Jesus' deity is to tread upon very shaky ground.

What, however, of the suggestion that in 'abrogating the law of Moses' and in 'forgiving sins' Jesus was implicitly claiming a divine authority?

Did Jesus in fact abrogate the Torah, and did he in fact do what only God can do in forgiving sinners? As the literature shows, there is much scope here for scholarly disagreement. E. P. Sanders, after a careful examination of texts, says, 'We have found one instance in which Jesus, in effect, demanded transgression of the law; the demand to the man whose father had died ['Follow me, and leave the dead to bury the dead', Matt. 8.22]. Otherwise the material in the Gospels reveals no transgression by Jesus. And, with one exception, following him did not entail transgression on the part of his followers. On the other hand, there is clear evidence that he did not consider the Mosaic dispensation to be final and absolutely binding'; and Sanders suggests as the reason for this that 'It was Jesus' sense of living at the turn of the ages which allowed him to think that the Mosaic law was not final and absolute' (Sanders 1985, 267). And he concludes concerning the forgiveness of sins: 'The oft-repeated claim that Jesus "put himself in the place of God" is overdone. He is often said to have done so in forgiving sins; but we must note that he only pronounced forgiveness, which is not the prerogative of God, but of the priesthood.'[4]

These are points of the kind that will long continue to be argued back and forth by New Testament scholars. There are also several other relevant debated passages, particularly the parable of the vineyard, in which the son is killed (Mark 12.1-11; Matthew 21.33-41; Luke 20.9-18); and the Markan saying, 'But of that day or that hour no one knows, not even the angels in heaven, nor the Son, but only the Father' (Mark 13.32); and again the saying in Matthew, 'All things have been delivered to me by my Father; and no one knows the Son except the Father, and no one knows the Father except the Son and anyone to whom the Son chooses to reveal him'

---

[4]Sanders 1985, 240. The 'oft repeated claim' is made, for example, by E. Schweizer (1971, 14), and Walter Kasper (1976, 102).

(Matthew 11.27). The authenticity of each of these passages, as sayings of Jesus, has been seriously questioned, and their significance much debated. But rather than attempting a detailed examination of each it will be sufficient to quote here the conclusion to which James Dunn comes at the end of his detailed discussion of all the synoptic material bearing upon Jesus' self-understanding: 'Just when our questioning reaches the "crunch" issue (Was Jesus conscious of being the divine Son of God?) we find that it is unable to give a clear historical answer' (Dunn 1980, 29). The evidence does not permit proof or even an objective degree of probability. There has to be historical judgment in the balancing of diverging considerations; and the conclusions drawn from such balancing exercises inevitably reflect the wider standpoint and commitment of the writer. I agree at this point with David Brown's remark about 'the state of play among the experts' concerning Jesus' self-awareness that 'the philosophical theologian cannot help but suspect that apologetic reasons lie behind much of the energy devoted to the question' (David Brown, 1985, 107). There is indeed often a circularity in the use of scripture to establish debated theological conclusions. Generally a broad theological stance comes first and guides a selection from the wide range of New Testament materials to cohere with that position. It would therefore be hazardous to rest a faith in the deity of Jesus on the historical judgment that he himself implicitly claimed this. If one has already accepted a form of orthodox christology one can reasonably interpret some of Jesus' words and actions, as presented by the Gospel writers, as implicitly supporting that belief. But it seems clear that one cannot justifiably arrive at the belief simply from the New Testament evidence as this has thus far been analysed and interpreted by the scholarly community.

A second response to the realization that Jesus himself did not claim to be God incarnate has been the use of the concept of the 'Christ-event'. This helpfully elastic idea is now widely used to take the weight off the pillar of dominical authority, now found to be hollow, by shifting it to the historically solid fact of the church's teaching. For the 'Christ-event' is supposed to consist not only in the life of Jesus but also in the formation of the church and the growth of its faith in Jesus' deity. It is this larger complex, rather than Jesus' own words and actions, that are now said to authorize the belief that he was God incarnate.

The notion of the Christ-event seems to have appeared first in

Rudolf Bultmann's existentialist interpretation of the New Testament, according to which Christian faith is a response, not to the largely unknown Jesus of Nazareth, but to the present notion of Jesus as the Christ; so that whenever 'the Christ' is preached this is a 'continuation of the Christ-event' (Bultmann 1955, 286). In Bultmann's work the use of the Christ-event idea reflected a strong historical scepticism and a consequent move from an ontological to an existentialist understanding of Christ. However, in the work of another New Testament scholar, John Knox, the Christ-event has an ecclesiastical (and thus social) rather than an existential (and more individual) meaning. The Christian faith is not centred in the person of Jesus of Nazareth alone but in the church's developing memory – not, however, ordinary literal memory but a metaphorical 'memory' – of him as its divine Lord (Knox 1967, 2f.). For Knox, 'The phrase "Jesus Christ our Lord" designates, not primarily an historical individual in the past, but a present reality actually experienced within the common life' (Knox 1967, 2). Indeed, 'The Church is the *distinctive* Christian reality . . . And it is because the Church *is* [Christ's] body and, in history, his only body, that we often use the words "Christ" and "Church" interchangeably, saying "in Christ" when we are wanting to refer to what it really means to be – and really to be – in the Church. It is this embodiment or incarnation (that is, the Church) which is most immediately – indeed alone is immediately – *known* . . . And so I say again, the Incarnation originally took place, not within the limits of an individual's individual existence, but in the new communal reality, in principle co-extensive with mankind, of which he was the creative centre' (Knox 1967, 66-7).

At this point I will only make a comment and ask a question. The comment is that this kind of thinking, in which Christianity is no longer centred upon the person of Jesus but now upon the church, has moved a long way from the traditional belief that Jesus, the historical individual, was himself God the Son incarnate. And the inevitable question becomes: has the Christian church, as a reality within human history, been so gloriously different from all other human societies as to justify a claim to divinity? To think of Jesus as divine makes some kind of intuitive sense; but does it make the same sense to think of the Christian church as divine?

Other major contemporary theologians use the Christ-event concept as a way of repairing the fabric of orthodox doctrine after the effects of New Testament criticism. Thus John Macquarrie says that

> the use of this conception does to some extent relieve the problems that arise from our lack of information about the historical Jesus. The coming into being of the church or the Christian movement is, shall we say, more visible and clearly attested in history than the personal career of the rabbi of Nazareth. And if we think of Jesus and the community as together embraced in the Christ-event, this is not only being true to the inescapably social character of all human existence, it also dissolves some questions that used to be debated with some heat among churchmen, who disagreed about what comes from Jesus and what comes from the community. Whether, for instance, the so-called "dominical" sacraments were instituted by Jesus or by his followers or perhaps partly by both is a question of little consequence once it is acknowledged that there is no sharp dividing line between Jesus and the community. Even more importance was attached in some of the older books on christology to the question of how Jesus understood himself. Did he think of himself as Messiah, or did he call himself Son of Man in some special eschatological sense of that term? Did he first apply to himself the imagery of the suffering servant of deutero-Isaiah? Did he think of himself as standing in a unique relationship to the Father? Or did some or all of these ways of thinking originate among his disciples? There can, I think, be no certain answer to these questions. But I also think that the importance of such questions has been exaggerated. We do not need to know the inner thoughts of Jesus, and in any case we cannot. When one places him in his context and acknowledges that he cannot be abstracted from his community and the responses of that community, to be gathered from the appellations it applied to him, then many of our questions, although they continue to have a certain historical interest, are of no great moment for christology (Macquarrie 1990, 21-2).

One sees here how useful the idea of the 'Christ-event' can be in defusing potentially explosive questions. It no longer matters how Jesus understood himself. It no longer matters, for example, whether he thought of himself as standing in an unique relationship to the heavenly Father. For the incarnation consists, for Macquarrie, in the existence of the Christian community, including the beliefs that it developed about Jesus. To affirm the incarnation is thus to affirm the church and the Christian story by which it lives; and this does not require a prior or independent judgment that the story is literally true. A somewhat similar position is presented by Schubert Ogden when he says that 'the real subject of the christological assertion is not the historical Jesus, or, as we may now say more precisely, the *empirical*-historical Jesus, for which the earliest stratum of Christian witness must be used as historical source. Rather, the subject of the christological assertion is the *existential*-historical Jesus, for which this same earliest stratum of Christian witness plays the very different role of theological norm' (Ogden 1982, 56).

The concept of the 'Christ-event' does, however, have the merit of drawing attention to something important. The meaning, for others, of anyone's life consists not only in the concrete actuality of that life itself but also in the way(s) in which he or she is perceived, revered or denigrated, remembered and responded to by others. This is true of all historical figures, both good and evil, whether St Francis or Attila, George Washington or Hitler. They have become part of public history in terms of the memories and stories, loyalties and hatreds of others, and are known by the values which they are seen as incarnating. This is also true of Jesus. We know of him only because others responded to him, with yet others responding to their responses, so that a movement developed which almost inevitably came to regard him as divine in the highly elastic sense in which outstanding religious and political figures were often so regarded in the ancient world. This 'soft' divinity, expressed in the 'son of God' metaphor, eventually developed into the 'hard' metaphysical claim that Jesus was God the Son, second person of a divine Trinity, incarnate. But to use the 'Christ-event' concept to validate this development involves arbitrarily stretching that highly flexible 'event' at least as far as the Council of Nicaea (325 C E), and preferably to include the Council of Chalcedon (451 C E).

The third response to Jesus' lack of divine self-consciousness, or at any rate to the lack of any indication of such, is closely akin to this. But instead of using the concept of the 'Christ-event', and extending it to include the development of trinitarian orthodoxy, it speaks of the Holy Spirit as having guided the church in its theological development. This is mainly a Roman Catholic position. Thus M. Schmaus says that 'What the Holy Spirit gave to the disciples was a true understanding of Jesus Christ and his work' (Schmaus 1972, 42), and Hugo Meynell says of the growth of the church's christology, 'From an orthodox Christian viewpoint the development is to be ascribed ultimately to Divine providence' (Meynell 1986, 107). Vatican II declared that 'This tradition which comes from the apostles develops in the Church with the help of the Holy Spirit' (Abbott 1966, 116 – Dogmatic Constitution on Divine Revelation, ch.2, para. 8). And Cardinal Ratzinger even says of the history of the church: 'This history is in its entirety a manifestation of the Holy Spirit' (Ratzinger 1987, 131). Richard Swinburne, as an Anglican, argues that divine revelation requires either an infallible interpreting authority, which may be either a pope or councils (or both), or 'a general direction by God, allowing for errors here and there but guaranteeing the basic structure of belief' (Swinburne 1989, 82-3). And Stephen Davis, as a Protestant Evangelical, says of the Chalcedonian christology, 'I confess to a strong belief that the church was led to the classical doctrine by the Holy Spirit' (Davis 1988, 43). The claim to divine guidance of the church's developing theology is prompted by the immense differences between that theology and the message of Jesus himself. But it should be evident that an appeal to the Holy Spirit cannot add anything to the case for the truth of the Chalcedonian or any other dogma. In propounding the further dogma that those who created the original dogma were divinely guided, one is simply shifting the point of debate from a first-order belief to the second-order belief that the first-order belief is divinely guaranteed. But we have no way of determining whether the councils were in fact divinely inspired other than by evaluating their pronouncements. If we can accept these as true we might accept that the authors were inspired in making them; if not, not. There is an obvious circularity here: one believes the dogma to be true because the ecumenical councils were divinely guided in declaring it, and one believes that they were divinely guided because one believes the dogma to be true. There is no escape here from the question of the first-order grounds for the dogma. This third response is thus deceptively redundant.

The fourth strand of response to the recognition that the historical Jesus did not think of himself as God incarnate has been a move from the earthly Jesus to (in the Catholic tradition) the heavenly or cosmic Christ, or (in evangelical Protestantism) to the presently experienced risen Jesus, as the object of Christian faith.

The Catholic focus is expressed by Eric Mascall: 'That the Christ whom we know today is the historical Christ is basic to our faith, but we do not depend for our acquaintance with him on the research of historians and archaeologists. He is also the heavenly Christ, and as such is the object of our present experience, mediated through the sacramental life of the Church' (Mascall 1985, 38-9).

The evangelical language of 'Jesus being with me', 'guiding my decisions', and so on, reflects a world-wide type of religious experience in which a guru or a god is felt to be spiritually present with the believer. One thinks, for example, of the Christian hymn 'In The Garden', with its refrain 'He walks with me and he talks with me and he tells me I am his own'; or of the 'spiritual', 'I Have a Little Talk with Jesus, and I Tell Him About My Troubles', ending 'Just a little talk with Jesus makes it right, all right'. Perhaps continuous with this from the point of view of psychological description is the vivid sense, widely reported, that a loved person who has died (usually recently) is invisibly present, comforting or guiding or challenging one in some present situation.

I would not by any means wish to rule out the possibility that those who have died may sometimes be present to the living in this way, and that this may also have been true of Jesus during the days and weeks after his death. But the evangelical experience of conversing today with an invisible Jesus – or, sometimes, for Catholics, with an invisible Virgin Mary or a glorified saint – must be understood, along with the awareness of the cosmic Christ, in a way that also applies to comparable phenomena within other religious traditions. Numerous examples of vivid experiences of what is taken to be a personal divine presence can be found in William James' *Varieties of Religious Experience* (Lecture III) and in the contemporary collection, *Seeing the Invisible: Modern Religious and Other Transcendent Experiences*, drawn from the reports collected by the Alister Hardy Research Centre at Oxford. These record many cases of an experience of encounter with Jesus, pictured on the basis of the Gospel stories (Maxwell 1990, 78-9, 83, 104-5, 142, 150, 166). There are similar accounts from Hindu sources of experiences of encounter with the Lord Krishna (Klostermeier, 1969, 15), or with Mother Kali (Isherwood 1965, 65f.). Sometimes a voice is heard, and sometimes the experiencer is surrounded by a bright light (James 1960, 251f.; Maxwell 1990, 165), as in the instance of Paul on the Damascus road. As in the case of all forms of religious experience, a religious and a naturalistic interpretation are both possible. From a naturalistic point of view all such experiences are to be dismissed as hallucinatory. But from a religious point of view they are to be tested by their fruits, and if

these promote the salvific human transformation from self-centredness to a new centring in the divine Reality they are to be accepted
as ways in which the Transcendent has come to consciousness in the
experience of people formed by these different traditions. They are
thus jointly products of the universal presence of the ultimately
Real, of the special circumstances that cause individuals at particular moments to be open to that reality, and of the concepts and
images in terms of which their conscious experience is constructed.[5]

We have now taken note of the various ways in which theologians
have responded to the fact that Jesus did not claim to be God
incarnate. And we have seen that none of these ways can relieve
upholders of Jesus' deification of the task of justifying that
momentous move. Such justification involves showing both that the
process by which the deification came about is one that we can
regard as valid, and that the resulting doctrine is in itself coherent
and credible.

But before examining the coherence of the traditional doctrine
let us look, in the next chapter, at the way in which as a matter of
history it seems to have come about.

[5]For a justification of this position, see Hick 1989.

4

The Church's Affirmation of Jesus' Deity

Our next task, then, is to look at the historical development which led from the earthly Jesus of Nazareth to the divine Christ of orthodox Christian faith, theology, preaching and sacraments. How did this immensely significant transition come about? In posing this question we have to appreciate how different was the intellectual milieu of the first century of the common era from that of our own industrialized, science-dominated, secularized modern West. Here are some words of caution from James Dunn: 'What would it have meant to their hearers when the first Christians called Jesus "son of God"? . . . we must endeavour to attune our listening to hear with the ears of the first Christians' contemporaries. We must attempt the exceedingly difficult task of shutting out the voices of early Fathers, Councils and dogmaticians down the centuries, in case they drown the earlier voices, in case the earlier voices were saying something different, in case they intended their words to speak with different force to their hearers' (Dunn 1980, 13-14). From our point of view today it would require earth-shaking miracles, overturning the whole established secular world-view, to cause an historical individual to be regarded as being also God. For we have come under the influence of centuries of Christian thought to mean by God the eternal, omnipotent, omniscient creator of the universe. But in the ancient world the concept of divinity was much less clearly defined and the conditions for its use much less demanding. This was a world in which there were, in St Paul's phrase, 'many gods and many lords' (I Corinthians 8.5). Thus to quote Archbishop Michael Ramsey again, 'The title "Son of God" need not of itself be of high significance, for in Jewish circles it might mean no more than the Messiah or indeed the whole Israelite nation, and in popular Hellenism there were many sons of God, meaning inspired holy men' (Ramsey 1980, 43). Spelling this out more fully Dunn points out that in the Roman world of the New Testament period 'divine' and 'son of God' and even 'God' were used more or less

interchangeably. Heroes 'were frequently called "divine" in
Homer, and from Augustus onwards "divine" became a fixed term
in the imperial cult, "the divine Caesar". At the other end of the
spectrum it could mean simply "pious", "godly" . . . Once again we
find that heroes were sometimes called "god"; and that "god" was a
regular title of emperors and kings from Hellenistic times onwards
– we may think, for example, of Antiochus Epiphanes (= God
made manifest)' (Dunn 1980, 16-17).

Referring specifically to the 'son of God' concept, Dunn says that

> some of the legendary heroes of Greek myth were called sons of
> God – in particular Dionysus and Heracles were sons of Zeus by
> mortal mothers. Oriental rulers, especially Egyptian, were called
> sons of God. In particular, the Ptolemies in Egypt laid claim to the
> title 'son of Helios' from the fourth century B C onwards, and at
> the time of Jesus 'son of God' (*huios theou*) was widely used in
> reference to Augustus. Famous philosophers also, like Pythagoras
> and Plato, were sometimes spoken of as having been begotten by a
> god (Apollo). And in Stoic philosophy Zeus, the supreme being,
> was thought of as father of all men . . . (Dunn 1980, 17).

Dunn concludes, 'The language of divine sonship and divinity was
in widespread and varied use in the ancient world and would have
been familiar to the contemporaries of Jesus, Paul and John in a
wide range of application' (Dunn 1980, 17). It is further evidence of
this that the Dead Sea Scrolls refer to one who 'shall be called the
son of the Great God. He shall be hailed as the Son of God, and they
shall call him the Son of the Most High.'[1] This flexible and
permissive usage continued well into the common era. For
example, Clement of Alexandria writing around 200 said, 'Some,
too, of the Indians obey the precepts of Buddha; whom, on account
of his extraordinary sanctity, they have raised to divine honours'
(Clement 1956, 316; Book I, ch.15). Having divine honours, being
divine, being a god, or a son of God, all belonged to the same broad
spectrum of the divine.

In view of this elasticity of the idea of divinity in the ancient
world, including first-century Judaism, it is in no way surprising or
remarkable that Jesus should have come to be regarded as

---

[1] Cited by Martin Hengel, 1975, 44. This fragment, 4Q246, is translated by Geza
Vermes as follows: 'The son of God he will be proclaimed and the son of the Most
High they will call him' (*The Independent*, 1 September 1992).

belonging to the class of divine persons. Even during his lifetime his special quality as a holy prophet and an impressive preacher and healer may well have been recognized in this way. As the New Testament scholar Maurice Casey says, 'Jesus could have been called a son of God by anyone who thought that he was a particularly righteous person: given his ability as an exorcist, people who believed themselves possessed by evil might well use the term of so obviously holy and effective a figure' (Casey 1991, 46). And after his death, and the resurrection events, when he came to be identified by his followers as the Messiah, of the royal line of David, the title 'son of God' would again be natural and appropriate. Indeed we can even say that it would have been surprising if Jesus had not shared in the widespread honorific divinizing of outstanding religious figures and if the Hebraic 'son of God' metaphor had not been applied to him.

I say 'metaphor', although our modern distinction between the literal use of language and its various metaphorical and other non-literal uses was not sharply drawn in the ancient world. In the Hebrew tradition the significance of a personally or communally remembered event or encountered person was readily expressed in metaphorical and mythic terms. This was 'a culture accustomed to midrashic expansion' (Casey 1991, 52). Indeed the entire biblical language about God and God's manifestations in the world is very largely metaphorical. God is described in the Hebrew scriptures as king, shepherd, father, rock. In the New Testament the key image is father, so that this and its correlative image of a son have become central to Christian discourse. In their original scriptural use these are – in terms of our modern distinction – manifestly metaphors. Literally, a father is a male parent. God, however, is Spirit, beyond the biological distinction between male and female, and does not literally beget children – although the idea of Jesus' 'virgin birth' (or, more precisely, virginal conception) comes perilously close to that. But when we speak of God as our heavenly Father we are using a powerful metaphor which pictures the divine attitude to human-kind as importantly like that of an ideal parent.

In the case of 'son of God' language, then, we have what was in the ancient world a widely used and readily understood metaphor, though subsequent Christian theology was to treat it as having a literal meaning. I shall cite here the Jewish scholar Geza Vermes: '"son of God" was always understood metaphorically in Jewish circles. In Jewish sources, its use never implies participation by the person so-named in the divine nature. It may in consequence safely be assumed that if the medium in which Christian theology developed had been Hebrew and not Greek, it would not have produced an incarnation doctrine as this is traditionally understood' (Vermes 1983, 72).

It has, however, seemed to some, and it may be the case, that St Paul constitutes an exception or a partial exception, as one whose way of thinking was distinctively Jewish but who nevertheless arrived at the idea of Jesus as the unique Son of God incarnate. Paul can be, and has been, understood in various ways; for he is (in his letters) generally hortatory and rhetorical rather than conceptually precise. He is preaching to particular Christian groups rather than writing systematic theology. He speaks of Jesus as the Lord Jesus Christ, and as the Son of God, and in his last letter, to the Colossians – if this is indeed by Paul (many scholars doubt it) – his language moves in the direction of deification. But the question is, of course: what did this language mean to the writer and his readers in the first century? The central imagery that Paul uses, that of father and son, inevitably suggests (and suggested even more strongly in the ancient world) the subordination of the son to the father. And in Paul's writings God and God's Son cannot be said to be co-equal, as the Persons of the Holy Trinity were later declared to be. The notion of Jesus as God's Son is indeed pre-trinitarian. Paul's carefully stated theological view, in the Epistle to the Romans, seems – in line with Luke's Petrine sermon at Pentecost in Acts – to be that Jesus was a man who was raised by God in his resurrection to a special and uniquely important status. He says of Jesus that he was 'descended from David according to the flesh and designated Son of God in power according to the Spirit of holiness by his resurrection from the dead' (Romans 1.3-4). The Son's subordinate role is further made unmistakably clear in I Corinthians where, speaking of the future general resurrection, Paul says that Christ will appear first, 'then at his coming those who belong to Christ. Then comes the end, when he delivers the kingdom to God the Father after destroying every rule and every authority and power. For he must reign until he has put all his enemies under his feet . . . When all things are subjected to him, then the Son himself will also be subjected to him who put all things under him, that God may be everything to everyone' (I Corinthians 15.23-28).

It has, however, been argued on the basis of the kenosis theme of the hymn in Philippians 2.5-11 ('he emptied himself, taking the form of a servant, being born in the likeness of men . . .'), and such passages as Galatians 4.4 ('God sent forth his Son, born of woman . . .') that for Paul Jesus was a pre-existent being whom God sent into the world – an idea that might connect with Jewish conceptions of intermediate entities (Wisdom, Word, angels) between God and humanity. If so, Paul is nearer to the developed idea of divine incarnation than the general tenor of his writings suggests. But the question has proved to be highly debatable and is indeed the kind of objectively undecidable issue in New Testament exegesis that is likely to go on nurturing conflicting views. James Dunn concludes, after a thorough examination of all the relevant texts, that 'It is possible that in the two passages when he speaks of God sending his Son (Rom. 8.3 and Gal. 4.4) he means to imply that the Son of God was pre-existent and had become incarnate as Jesus; but it is as likely, indeed probably more likely, that Paul's meaning did not stretch so far, and that at these points he and his readers thought simply of Jesus as the one commissioned by God as one who shared wholly in man's frailty, bondage and sin, and whose death achieved God's liberating and transforming purpose for man' (Dunn 1980, 46). But since it makes little difference at this point whether Paul was nearer to the earlier or to the later Christian understandings of Jesus, I shall not pursue the question further. Provisionally, I see his thought as roughly a third of the way along the historical path leading from the honorific designation of the human Jesus as 'son of God', and then more particularly as 'the son of God' (with the capital S in due course supplanting the lower case), and finally, after several centuries of debates, as God the Son, second person of a divine Trinity.

The growing and developing church had to explain its beliefs to the Greek-speaking culture of the Mediterranean world, and at the same time to itself, in acceptable philosophical terms; and after the emperor Constantine's conversion to Christianity the peace of the empire required a unitary body of Christian belief. Accordingly in 325 Constantine convened the Council of Nicaea 'for the purpose of restoring concord to church and empire' (Pelikan 1985, 52); and it was here that the church first officially adopted from Greek culture the non-biblical concept of *ousia*, declaring that Jesus, as God the Son incarnate, was *homoousios toi patri*, of the same substance as the Father. The original biblical metaphors were henceforth relegated for theological purposes to the level of popular language awaiting interpretation whilst for official purposes a philosophical definition took their place. A metaphorical son of God had become the metaphysical God the Son, second person of the Trinity. The political significance of this was that the Christian emperor now had the status of God's viceroy on earth. Thus the contemporary historian Eusebius, writing about Constantine's victory over his rival Licinius, says that Constantine and his son 'under the protection of God, the universal King, with the Son of God, Saviour of all, as their leader and ally, drew up their forces on all sides against the enemies of the Deity and won an easy victory' (Eusebius 1952, 386; Book X, ch.9, para. 4).

The Nicene formulation was expanded, using the same philosophical conceptuality, at the Council of Chalcedon in 451, affirming that Christ was '*homoousios* with the Father as to his Godhead, and at the same time *homoousios* with us as to his manhood . . . made known in two natures [which exist] without confusion, without change, without division, without separation . . .' And it is this Chalcedonian formulation that has ever since constituted the official Christian language about Christ.

The metaphorical language of the Bible communicates naturally to all who inhabit or can imaginatively enter its universe of discourse. We still have fathers and sons and, less universally, kings and shepherds as part of our conceptual world; and with only a little effort of the imagination we can appreciate the ancient habit of thinking of one who is spiritually close to God, a faithful servant of God, as a son of God. Such metaphors communicate successfully because they were formed within the ordinary discourse of the time. But the Chalcedonian formula is a philosophical artefact having whatever meaning it is defined to have. Such formulae are impressive precisely because their sole meaning is technical and known only to the learned. Critical philosophical scrutiny of such conceptual constructions must, however, always be in order. And in this case the possibility that has to be considered is that the formula, which at first seems so firm and definitive, is incapable of being explicated in any religiously acceptable way. The intention behind it was to exclude any understanding of Jesus that denied either his full and authentic deity or his full and authentic humanity. But perhaps this cannot be done! If the formula is such that any spelling out of its meaning will have implications that conflict with one or other of these desiderata, then the formula is a failure. If every attempt to explicate it proves unacceptable, it can only function as a ritual utterance whose sense must not be examined too closely and which can only serve to inhibit and stultify thought.

That this is indeed the case is, I believe, the lesson of the christological debates from before the time of Nicaea to the present day. It cannot of course be proved that no one will in the future succeed in making the two-natures formula intelligible in a religiously valuable way. But it can, I think, be shown that this has not yet been done, despite the fact that so many of the best Christian minds have either attempted it, or recoiled from the task as hopeless, in generation after generation.

In the next chapter, then, we turn to these attempts.

5

Two Natures – Two Minds?

The Council of Chalcedon (451 C E) defined what was thenceforth the orthodox doctrine of the incarnation as follows:

> Therefore, following the holy fathers, we all with one accord teach men to acknowledge one and the same Son, our Lord Jesus Christ, at once complete in Godhead and complete in manhood, truly God and truly man, consisting also of a reasonable soul and body; of one substance [*homoousios*] with the Father as regards his Godhead, and at the same time of one substance with us as regards his manhood; like us in all respects, apart from sin; as regards his Godhead, begotten of the Father before the ages, but yet as regards his manhood begotten, for us men and for our salvation, of Mary the Virgin, the God-bearer [*Theotokos*] one and the same Christ, Son, Lord, Only-begotten, recognized in two natures, without confusion, without change, without division, without separation; the distinction of natures being in no way annulled by the union, but rather the characteristics of each nature being preserved and coming together to form one person [*prosopon*] and subsistence [*hypostasis*], not as parted or separated into two persons [*prosopa*], but one and the same Son and Only-begotten God the Word, Lord Jesus Christ; even as the prophets from earliest times spoke of him, and as our Lord Jesus Christ himself taught us, and the creed of the Fathers has delivered to us (Bettenson 1956, 72-3).

The particular conceptuality used here, expressed in the terms *ousia* and *hypostasis*, was familiar in educated circles in the fifth century and throughout the medieval period, but has now long ceased to be current. But the task facing one who wishes to reaffirm a Chalcedonian christology is not that of translating into contemporary terms a Hellenistic account of how the one person, Jesus, could have two natures; for no such account is contained in the original formula. As a historian of the period says, 'Chalcedon has proved less a solution than the classic definition of a problem which constantly demands further elucidation' (Young 1983, 72-3). The problem does not lie in an outmoded language and conceptuality but in the fact that the Council in effect merely asserted that Jesus was 'truly God and truly man' without attempting to say how such a paradox is possible. The orthodox task is to spell out in an intelligible way the idea of someone having both a fully divine nature, i.e. having all the essential divine attributes, and at the same time a fully human nature, i.e. having all the essential human attributes. Merely to assert that two different natures coexisted in Jesus 'without confusion, without change, without division, without separation' is to utter a form of words which as yet has no specified meaning. The formula sets before us a 'mystery' rather than a 'clear and distinct idea'. Further, this is not a divine mystery but one that was created by a group of human beings meeting at Chalcedon in present-day Turkey in the mid-fifth century. Many attempts were made in the great period of christological debates, both before and after Chalcedon, to give intelligible meaning to the idea of a God-man. However, they all failed to meet the basic Chalcedonian desiderata, namely to affirm *both* Jesus' deity *and* his humanity, and accordingly they had to be rejected as heresies. I do not propose to describe this series of often highly ingenious attempts here: there are plenty of excellent textbooks which do this.[1] I will, however, mention one sample attempt. The theologian Apollinaris in the fourth century suggested (or seems to have suggested; for there are historical questions about precisely what many of the ancient thinkers, including Apollinaris, actually said) that a human person consists of spirit (*nous*), soul (*psyche* = mind) and body (*sarx*), and that in the case of Jesus his spirit was the eternal divine Logos whilst his mind and body were human. This suggestion offered a clear sense in which Jesus could be said to be both divine and human. But it had to be declared heretical for the convincing reason that without a human spirit Jesus would not have been genuinely human. And all the other attempts in that period to explain the idea of divine incarnation likewise failed to do justice to one or other of the basic dogmatic data. The result is that we inherit the original Chalcedonian formula but with no clearly spelled out meaning attached to it.

The twentieth century has accordingly seen a number of attempts to express the religious essence of Chalcedon without recourse to the

[1]For example, Young 1983 and 1991.

traditional two-natures language. The main constructive suggestion has been that the two 'natures' should be understood as two minds, the divine mind of the Logos/Son and the human mind of Jesus of Nazareth. This appeals to a number of philosophical theologians today. As A.T. Hanson says, 'It seems probable that this account of two consciousnesses will become the accepted method today for those who wish to defend the Chalcedonian christology in such a way as to make it intelligible to modern minds' (Hanson 1984, 471-2). There are several versions of this two-minds proposal,[2] but I do not intend to describe and discuss them each separately. Instead I shall concentrate upon one of the most recent and probably the most philosophically sophisticated, that of Thomas Morris in *The Logic of God Incarnate*, in which he defends the high-orthodox position that 'Jesus of Nazareth was one and the same person as God the Son, the Second Person of the divine Trinity' (13). There is much more in Morris' book than his two-minds theory, and I have discussed the work as a whole elsewhere (Hick 1993). Here I shall confine myself to the two-minds christology. It is, I shall try to show, an excellent example of the way in which the determination to make sense at all costs of the idea of divine incarnation leads into an entangling net of unpalatable consequences. Given suffficient logical dexterity (which Morris possesses in abundance) the task can be accomplished; but only for one who is willing to 'bite the bullet' of accepting its unacceptable implications. For the sense of 'incarnation' that is left to Morris, after a series of unavoidable qualifications, is only a thin shadow of what was affirmed at Chalcedon.

Morris proposes that 'in the case of God Incarnate, we must recognize something like two distinct ranges of consciousness. There is first what we can call the eternal mind of God the Son with its distinctively divine consciousness, whatever that might be like, encompassing the full scope of omniscience. And in addition there is a distinctly earthly consciousness that came into existence and grew and developed as the boy Jesus grew and developed. It drew its visual imagery from what the eyes of Jesus saw, and its concepts from the languages he learned. The earthly range of consciousness, and self-consciousness, was thoroughly human, Jewish, and first-century Palestinian in nature' (102-3). He continues:

---

[2]O'Collins 1983; Brown 1985; Thomas Morris 1986a; Swinburne 1989; Sturch 1991. A somewhat similar idea was earlier expressed by Bernard Lonergan: see Meynell 1986, ch. 8.

We can view the two ranges of consciousness (and, analogously, the two noetic structures encompassing them) as follows: The divine mind of God the Son contained, but was not contained by, his earthly mind, or range of consciousness. That is to say, there was what can be called an asymmetric accessing relation between the two minds. Think, for example, of two computer programs or informational systems, one containing but not contained by the other. The divine mind had full and direct access to the earthly human experience resulting from the Incarnation, but the earthly consciousness did not have such a full and direct access to the content of the overarching omniscience proper to the Logos, but only such access, on occasion, as the divine mind allowed it to have. There thus was a metaphysical and personal depth to the man Jesus lacking in the case of every individual who is merely human (103).

In further explication of the idea of two minds, one enclosed within the other, Morris offers three further analogies. One is that of a dreamer, participating in the stream of dream events and yet aware at some overarching level that it is all a dream. Here the 'overarching' consciousness corresponds to the divine and the dream material to the human mind. A second analogy is that of the 'levels' of consciousness referred to in standard psychological theory: 'The postulated unconscious, or subconscious, mind would stand in an asymmetric accessing relation to the conscious mind somewhat parallel to that postulated between the divine consciousness and the earthly consciousness of God Incarnate' (105). And a third is that of the two consciousnesses in a case of multiple personality: 'in some cases of multiple personality, there exists one personality with apparently full and direct knowledge of the experiences had, information gathered, and actions initiated by one or more other personalities, a sort of knowledge which is not had by any other personality concerning it. In other words, there seem to exist asymmetric accessing relations in such cases, interestingly though of course not perfectly parallel to the sort of relation claimed by the two-minds view to hold between the divine and human minds of Christ' (106).

What all these analogies have in common is that they are concerned with the *cognitive* relationship between the two minds, divine and human. These are seen as repositories of information, as noetic structures or belief-systems; and the theory is concerned with the way and the extent to which each mind is conscious of the contents of the other. But such a view of mental life is one-dimensional. (As such, it is consonant with Morris' general treatment of a religion as consisting essentially in a set of beliefs, a Western post-Enlightenment view which has now long been under serious criticism – see, e.g., Smith 1991). For a living consciousness is not only a noetic structure but a dynamic activity, processing information received through the senses, continuously exercising a power of choice and decision, adopting attitudes, exerting oneself volitionally; and one perceives the world with varying affective tones, and feels emotions which are sometimes powerful and determining. This difference between Morris' one-dimensional conception of the mind and the multi-dimensional reality is important. I shall argue that a purely noetic account of the relation between the divine and human minds cannot amount to a religiously significant sense of 'incarnation', but that on the other hand when we expand it to include volition and emotion, Morris' two-minds christology becomes unacceptable for another reason – to which I shall come presently.

But let us proceed in stages. Consider first the hypothetical case of *complete* asymmetry of access. Here there are two streams of consciousness, A and B, one including the other in the sense that A is aware of everything occurring in the B stream of consciousness whilst B is entirely unaware of the contents of the A consciousness. Thus God the Son could know all that was going on in the conscious, and also in the unconscious, mind of Jesus whilst Jesus was entirely unaware that the Son was thus monitoring him, or even unaware of the Son's existence.

Now this – as Morris himself notes (158-9) – is something that the doctrine of divine omniscience (without having to specify the Son as the omniscient mind) already entails. For an omniscient God must be aware at all times of the contents of every stream of human consciousness. But such asymmetrical cognitive accessing would not constitute divine incarnation in any religiously significant sense. For if this consists in God's full one-way awareness of human consciousnesses, then God is incarnate in everyone. Further, God must be as fully aware of what is going on in the most wicked and depraved as in the most holy of human mentalities and therefore, on the possible view we are considering, equally incarnate in them all. Clearly the traditional notion of a unique divine incarnation in Jesus Christ could not be sustained by such exclusively one-way cognitive accessing alone. Morris is aware of this, and his theory does not in fact postulate such an exclusively *one way* access between the two minds. It is, rather, at least partly and spasmodically two-way. He says (in a passage already quoted), 'The divine mind had full and direct access to the earthly, human experience resulting from the Incarnation, but the earthly consciousness did not have such full and direct access to the content of the overarching omniscience proper to the Logos, but only such access, on occasion, as the divine mind allowed it to have. There was thus a metaphysical and personal depth to the man Jesus lacking in the case of every individual who is merely human' (103).

The nature of the limited access of the human to the divine mind which Morris postulates needs to be specified more fully. I can see two rather different possibilities. One involves a mutual relationship and interaction between the two minds, divine and human. That is to say, at certain times and to a certain degree the human mind of Jesus became conscious of being an object of awareness of the vaster encompassing consciousness of God the Son. He thus became conscious of being in a state of mutual I-Thou awareness with the second person of the Trinity. In these moments he was conscious of being in the presence of God the Son and at the same time aware that God the Son was conscious of him. Such a picture would seem to fit the New Testament indications – except of course that the encompassing divine presence of which Jesus was so vividly aware was not the second person of a trinity but simply God, known as *abba*, father. But, further, Jesus' relationship to God, as reflected in the Synoptic Gospels, had not only a cognitive but also a conative or volitional aspect. Not only was he (at least during the period of his public ministry, and perhaps earlier as well) overwhelmingly conscious of the reality and presence of God, but he was in an active relationship in which he prayed to God, heard God's voice, and responded in his actions to God's will for him. His life was continuously guided by his sense of God's purposes for human life on earth and for himself in particular as God's messenger proclaiming the imminent coming of the Kingdom.

Now this kind of interaction, in which a person is overwhelmingly conscious of God's presence, speaks to God, hears God's voice (whether inwardly or outwardly), is aware of and does God's will, is one in which many men and women have participated in varying degrees. Outstanding examples include Moses, Jeremiah, the Isaiahs, Muhammad, Guru Nanak, St Francis, Kabir,

Ramakrishna, and many others down to our own day. This kind of openness and responsiveness of the human to the divine is the basis for the understanding of Jesus' relationship to God proposed by the grace or inspiration christologies of such recent theologians as Donald Baillie and Geoffrey Lampe (see further in Chapter 10). According to them Jesus was conscious of the environing divine presence, and was responsive to the divine will, to such an extent that he could be said (in a natural metaphor) to have incarnated a love that reflected the divine love. However, this is not the kind of spelling out of the two-minds idea that Morris intends; for he wants it to carry the same weight as the Chalcedonian two-natures christology.

Another possible way of spelling out a limited access of the human to the divine mind is in terms not of occasional consciousness-consciousness interaction but of occasional consciousness-consciousness unity. That is to say, from time to time and perhaps with varying degrees of clarity, the human mind of Jesus became conscious of its identity with the divine mind of God the Son. In these moments Jesus was consciously divine, aware that he was God the Son incarnate. This is consonant with the picture of Jesus offered in the Fourth Gospel – except that there Jesus is depicted as believing that the divine presence with whom he was in unity was God the Father: 'I and the Father are one' (John 10.30), 'he that hath seen me hath seen the Father' (John 14.9).

This option assimilates Jesus' God-consciousness to that reported in unitive mysticism. Normally, in theistic mysticism, a final distinction is preserved between the human mystic and the divine Being. Occasionally, however, such mystics – Jewish, Christian and Muslim – have at least seemed to transcend this distinction. But it is in Hindu advaitic thought that the identity of the purified human consciousness with the divine Reality is most explicitly taught. According to this, when we transcend egoity we discover in a moment of salvific illumination that we are one with the infinite and eternal Brahman: *Tat tvam asi*. Several Hindu philosophers (e.g., Gandhi 1984, 46) have pointed out the analogy between the claim of the Fourth Gospel's Christ to unity with the Father, and the Vedantic idea that only our false individual ego-hood conceals from us our own identity with the absolute reality of Brahman and that in a fully enlightened mind that final identity comes to consciousness.

The limitation of such an interpretation of the two-minds theory is that it fits the divine Christ of the Fourth Gospel but not the more historically believable Jesus of the Synoptics. One can rule, by stipulative definition, that a man who is consciously God is still to be counted as fully human. But such a one would nevertheless not be one of us, sharing our human condition. Even if he was only aware on rare occasions of his identity as God the Son he would at other times presumably remember and live in terms of these all-important moments. Thus even if one were to grant the possibility of God becoming incarnate, on the Fourth Gospel model, as a physically human being who is (always or sometimes) conscious of being divine, and thus eternal, omnipotent and omniscient, this would not be the Jesus whom historical research has glimpsed through the Synoptic traditions.

Let us now return to Morris' response to the point that a one-way cognitive access account of incarnation would amount to no more than the fact of God's omniscient awareness, not only of Jesus' consciousness, but of all human consciousnesses. Morris says:

> Consider a case of telepathy. Person A has telepathic access to the mind of person B. Suppose if you like that A telepathically has complete access to the mind of B. Does it follow that B's thoughts are A's thoughts, that B's mental states are A's mental states? Of course not. From B's believing that it is raining outside and A's having perfect telepathic access to the mind of B, it does not follow that A believes it is raining outside, for A can have independent reason to think that B is wrong. The accessing relation itself does not alone constitute ownership. So from God's standing in a perfect accessing relation to all our minds it does not follow that all our minds *are* his mind or that all our thoughts are his thoughts. And so of course it does not follow that each of us is God Incarnate (159).

It seems from this passage that the divine mind's access to the human mind is only to count as incarnation if there is also identity of ownership of the thoughts within the two minds. However, Morris goes on to point out that, in view of our historical picture of Jesus, identity of ownership would not in fact be an asset. For 'most theologians who take seriously the real humanity of Jesus, however orthodox they might be, will want to allow . . . the possibility of the earthly mind of Jesus containing some false beliefs, beliefs, for example, concerning the shape of the earth, or the nature of the relative movement of the sun and the earth, among other things' (159-60). Have we then now, with this correction, arrived at last at an adequate concept of incarnation, namely as God the Son's complete accessing of the contents of Jesus' earthly mind, whilst being aware in so doing that some of Jesus' beliefs are mistaken?

No; for this model will apply equally to all other human minds. And so Morris at this stage accepts that his original account of incarnation as consisting in 'an asymmetric accessing relation between the two minds' (103) is not sufficient. Some additional factor is required. The additional factor, he says, is a unity of 'causal and cognitive powers'. In the case of two human beings, A and B, A having telepathic access to B's mind, the state of B's mind at a given moment is a result (at least in part) of B's exercise of her own causal powers, whilst A's accessing of her mind is an exercise of his own causal powers. Two numerically distinct sets of causal powers are thus involved. But the case of Jesus was different and unique: 'He was not a being endowed with a set of personal cognitive and causal powers distinct from the cognitive and causal powers of God the Son. For Jesus was the same person as God the Son. Thus, the personal cognitive and causal powers operative in the case of Jesus' earthly mind were just none other than the cognitive and causal powers of God the Son' (161-2).

These 'cognitive and causal powers' are clearly now crucial to Morris' final theory. What are they? Presumably our cognitive power is our capacity to cognize, whilst our causal power is our capacity to initiate change, in other words our will. That causal power, in the case of a mind, is volitional, is evident in Morris' text from the fact that he speaks of a person attaining to a given mental state 'as the result of the exercise of her own cognitive and causal powers' (161). For clearly it is by the exercise of her will, thereby making choices, that she comes at that particular moment to be in this particular mental state rather than some other.

Let us then consider the implications of the idea that the volitional activity in virtue of which the human mind of Jesus was at each moment in the state in which it was, was the volitional activity of God the Son. Morris, with his exclusive attention to the cognitive relation between the two minds, only applies this principle to their belief-systems or noetic structures. He says that the results of the operation of the cognitive and causal powers of God the Son 'through the human body, under the constraints proper to the conditions of a fully human existence, were just such as to give rise to a human mind, an earthly noetic structure distinct from the properly divine noetic structure involved with the unconstrained exercise of divine powers' (162). But to take account only of noetic structures is to operate with the inadequately one-dimensional, purely intellectual, view of mental life that we noted earlier. In reality the will operates not only in forming beliefs but also, importantly, in the person's activity in the world in relation to other people. And here a unitary will, which is the will of God the Son, would mean that when Jesus decided to say or do anything, God the Son was so deciding; and likewise when Jesus resisted temptation, the will that resisted was that of God the Son. Morris is, in other words, at this point embracing the view that Jesus had no separate human will and that the will operative in his life was the divine will of the second person of the Trinity.

However, throughout his book Morris is very good at recognizing difficulties and trying to meet them. And he is aware that the idea that the will whereby Jesus made his choices from moment to moment was the will of God the Son was condemned as the monothelite heresy by the Sixth Ecumenical Council, meeting at Constantinople in 680-81. This council was concerned to preserve Jesus' full humanity, including his human will, and appealed to such texts as 'I seek not mine own will, but the will of the Father which hath sent me' (John 5.30) and 'Father, all things are possible unto thee; take away this cup from me; nevertheless, not what I will but what thou wilt' (Mark 14.36). And so in another passage Morris affirms a free human will of Jesus in addition to the divine will of the second person of the Trinity. The relationship between the two wills, he suggests, was that Jesus was humanly free, including being free to sin, but that if he had in fact tried to sin, the divine will would have intervened to stop him. For he insists that Jesus possessed 'the divine property of being necessarily good' (152). And so Morris asks, 'Was [Jesus'] choosing rightly a free act of his? Well, it must be admitted from the outset that he could not have chosen otherwise. His divine nature would have prevented it' (150). He was thus free, and yet necessarily good. Morris helps us to understand this by the imaginary case of someone, Jones, who is placed in a room and told not to leave it for two hours. But, 'Unknown to him, electrodes have been implanted in his brain which upon activation will prevent his deciding, or attempting, to leave the room before the two-hour mark' (151). In fact, however, the electrodes never need to be activated. In one sense, then, Jones freely remained in the room, in another sense he was not free to do otherwise. And analogously, 'As Jones was unaware of the electrodes . . . Jesus was unaware in his earthly consciousness that he was necessarily good, unable to sin' (153).

This is certainly a very strange kind of freedom, depending as it does upon ignorance. It seems that in Morris' sense I am free to do anything that I cannot do but think that I *can* do! However, I do not want to press this peculiarity; for even if we allow this conception of Jesus' freedom, it will still not save the two-minds theory of incarnation.

We have seen that Morris has to grant that a complete cognitive access of the divine mind to the human mind is not enough, since this applies to all human minds. He is accordingly compelled to add the all-important clause that 'the personal cognitive and causal powers operative in the case of Jesus' earthly mind were just none other than the cognitive and causal powers of God the Son' (161-2). For it is this that distinguished Jesus from all other human beings. And yet, as we have seen, this distinguishing circumstance just amounts to there being a single will, which is the will of God the Son. Morris is aware, however, that he must on pain of heresy avoid this conclusion. And so, as we have seen, he asserts that there were two wills, human and divine; and adds that if the human will ever tried to make a decision that deviated from those of the divine will, the divine will would overrule it. But in Morris' illustrative story it is stipulated that the person in the room did not in fact try to leave, and so did not need to be prevented by the implanted electrodes. The analogy in the case of Jesus would be that he never began to initiate a wrong action, and so did not need to be prevented by the encompassing divine mind from proceeding from such a beginning. But of course we are not entitled to stipulate this. Granting, for the sake of argument, that Jesus never in fact performed any action that was in the slightest degree wrong, how do we know that he never, as a man, intended to do something wrong but was internally prevented from translating the intention into action by the over-ruling will of the Logos? His outwardly perfect life might, for all that we can know, conceal many wrong inner impulses that were nipped in the bud before developing into overt actions. But even such unfulfilled beginnings of evil must themselves count as imperfec-tions; for in order for the divine mind to overrule them there must have been something there that required to be overruled.

What we have, then, is a human Jesus who never did a sinful action but concerning whose inner moral life we can, on Morris' theory, say nothing; for any inner defects would have been systematically prevented from expressing themselves in outward actions. I suggest that the resulting picture does not amount to divine incarnation in the Chalcedonian sense that Morris is trying to make intelligible and believable. We are left with the human Jesus, to whose mind God the Son has full cognitive access; and if, or whenever, the human mind began to make a wrong decision, God the Son prevented him from proceeding with it. That is to say, Jesus is God incarnate in the sense that God singled the human Jesus out for a special role – namely by not allowing him to go wrong.

It follows that if God, in addition to being omnisciently aware of the full contents of someone else's mind, were to prevent her from making any wrong choices, that person would be another instance of God incarnate. But has not the heart of the Chalcedonian conception now been missed out – namely the unique personal presence of God in a human life, so that those who talked with the human Jesus were talking with God the Son? The nearest that Morris' theory comes to this is that those who talked with Jesus were talking to a man whom God the Son was invisibly monitoring and preventing from going astray.[3]

In a more recent article (Thomas Morris 1989) Morris has suggested that support for a two-minds christology can be derived from the multimind or society of mind conception of mental life. This is the view advanced by some contemporary psychologists and artificial intelligence theorists that the mind is a society of small minds or mental modules. Is not the idea that the mind is thus composite compatible with, and indeed hospitable to, Morris' two-minds theory? Morris refers to Robert Ornstein's *Multimind* (Ornstein 1986); but a more sophisticated pluralistic conception of the mind, offering the possibility of a more detailed support to a basically orthodox christology, can be found in Marvin Minsky's *Society of Mind*.[4] According to this, minds are hierarchically ordered societies of mental elements, with higher layers monitoring and influencing lower layers. On each level there is both co-operation and competition between different modules – ideas, memories, volitions, emotions, – with influences from the next higher level sometimes intervening in the process. Thus our consciousness is all the time receiving both material supplied from

[3]For a different criticism of Morris' theory, concluding that 'Morris's Jesus is in the end scarcely a human figure at all', see Thatcher 1990, 46-8, 94-5.

[4]Marvin Minsky 1987. This theory of mind, and its possible applications to christology, were brought to my attention by Tim Musgrove in a paper at present unpublished.

lower levels and also influences from higher levels of the complex society which is our total mental life.

The application of this picture to christology could be in adding a further level, the mind of the Logos, to oversee and direct the activity of the society which is Jesus' human mind. The divine mind would thus work through a mental structure which would be wholly human, constituting the human mind of God the Son. Or, as an alternative application, one could think of the society of mind not as hierarchically but as heterarchically structured, conscious activity being the outcome of the push and pull of variously competing and cooperating sub-minds. The divine mind would then function as one of these sub-minds, thus allowing both for Jesus' temptations, ignorance and mistaken beliefs in the non-divine modules of his mind and yet also for a successful overall divine direction of his life.

It seems to me entirely plausible that the human mind can be regarded as a complex system of systems, as was first argued by William James (James 1890, ch. 10), rather than a single unitary system. But I do not think that this can get us any nearer to a viable conception of divine incarnation than the point at which Apollinaris arrived in the fourth century. For a composite mind whose determining element is divine (but which we nevertheless rule to be as a totality human) would not have the freedom to act wrongly. The human part might intend to sin, but the divine part, being unable to sin, would necessarily over-rule or circumvent the intention. Such a person could not be tempted as we are tempted, or become good by overcoming temptation, and accordingly could not embody our human moral ideal. Nor – in relation to the doctrine of atonement – could his death constitute the sacrifice of a life of perfect human obedience to God. The two-minds christology has thus not advanced, through the introduction of the society of mind concept, beyond the impasse in which we left it earlier.

Richard Sturch (Sturch 1991), has attempted to improve upon Morris' version of the two-minds christology by his own 'central self' theory. The central self is the I, ego, *moi*, and Sturch claims that 'What a "central self" theory gives us, and Morris's, similar though it is, does not, is an awareness on the part of the Logos . . . that the human life "accessed" is *His own*' (133). As in Morris' theory, there are two consciousnesses: 'besides the human awareness "I experience X and Y", which Jesus has like the rest of us, there is also a divine awareness "I experience X and Y and also P and Q", where P and Q stand for experiences of God the Son' (132).

But whereas – I have argued above – on the question of Jesus' moral freedom Morris' conception falls apart into a human mind which may or may not always intend rightly and a divine mind which overrules any wrong tendencies in that human mind, Sturch says, 'So far as I can tell, the points raised by Hick do not affect the position taken in the present work' (133 n.24). But this, I think, is only because he does not directly tackle the specific problem that proved fatal for Morris' theory: was Jesus free to commit sin? Sturch says, 'The will and consciousness of God the Son were those of the same person (*prosopon* and *hypostasis*) as those of the first-century Jewish carpenter, but they were not, so to speak, present in His human brain' (140). So God the Son's volitions were the volitions of Jesus, but were not 'present in His human brain'. Was Jesus' brain, directing the rest of his body, then by-passed in the moral decision-making of the divine self of God the Son? Might the human brain of Jesus intend to do something wrong, but the divine self nevertheless cause his body to act rightly instead? The more the picture is spelled out, the less plausible it becomes. Sturch only adds to the confusion when he says that 'the human [will and consciousness] were guided and enlightened by the Holy Spirit, and the divine knows all that passes in the human life as its own' (140). For the question recurs: was Jesus free to reject the Holy Spirit's guidance and enlightenment? If not, he was not genuinely human; and if he was free, in his human brain, to will wrongly, how do we know that he never did and that the divine central self, which was 'not, *so to speak*, present in His human brain' [my italics], caused him to act differently? The only refuge left for this endangered theory would seem to lie within the helpful vagueness of the 'so to speak'!

I conclude that the two-minds christology fails to give an intelligible meaning to the idea of divine incarnation and is in the end no better than the two-substances christology which it seeks to replace. Indeed the old Chalcedonian formula, which in effect simply asserted Jesus' deity and humanity without attempting to explain how this might be so, had the advantage of mystery, an advantage which Morris and Sturch have forfeited by attempting to spell the mystery out in an intelligible way!

6

Divine Self-emptying?

Although the idea of a divine kenosis or self-emptying goes back to Philippians 2.5-11, its use to solve the puzzles created by the two-natures dogma is fairly modern. The theme of divine condescension, the eternal Son of God coming down from heaven to earth for our salvation, was stressed in the early church, for example by Hilary of Poitiers, Cyril of Alexandria and Pope Leo. But these had no thought of God the Son divesting himself of any of his divine attributes in order to become a man. It was the nineteenth-century Lutheran theologian Gottfried Thomasius who first proposed that we could properly acknowledge Jesus' genuine humanity – which was at that time being emphasized afresh – by supposing that in taking human nature the pre-existent Son laid aside some of his divine qualities. Thomasius suggested that we 'posit the incarnation itself precisely in the fact that he, the eternal Son of God, the second person of the deity, gave himself over into the form of human limitation, and thereby to the limits of a spatio-temporal existence, under the conditions of a human development, in the bounds of an historical concrete being, in order to live in and through our nature the life of our race in the fullest sense of the word, without on that account ceasing to be God' (Welch 1965, 48).

Since then a range of kenotic theories have been developed, mainly in Germany and Britain. Their aim has been both to do justice to Jesus' nature as an authentically human and historical figure whilst also (particularly in the minds of some of the more recent kenoticists) avoiding the seemingly intractable problems which had become increasingly evident in the Chalcedonian two-natures formula. Their course is laid out by the basic logic of the situation. Starting from the evidence of the Synoptic Gospels we have to say that the historical Jesus lacked at least some of the attributes of God. For example, he was neither omniscient nor omnipotent. The first question, then, is whether he lacked these (and also other) attributes in the absolute sense that he simply did not possess them; or only in the sense that he possessed them but systematically refrained from exercising them.

Although advocated by some Lutheran theologians, the latter possibility (sometimes called *krypsis*, or concealment) has not generally commended itself. For an omnipotent Jesus who consciously refrained from using his limitless power, and who was omniscient but pretended to human ignorance, would scarcely count as a fellow human being. He might be declared by stipulative definition to be so; but from an ordinary point of view he would be a superhuman being. The fears and anxieties to which we are subject, the temptations that afflict us, and the mystery of death that faces us, would all be unreal to him, so that he would live in a different world of meaning from we ordinary mortals. It would be impossible to see in him the perfection of our common human nature, towards which we should strive as his disciples.

And so the major kenotic theories speak not merely of a concealment of divine attributes but of an actual divine self-emptying, self-retraction, divestment of powers, a shedding of absolute qualities in order to take on humanity – and yet without the one who does this ceasing to be fully and unequivocally God the Son. Clearly there is at least a seeming contradiction here; and as in the case of the two-natures christologies the question is whether sense can nevertheless be made of it. This is what the kenotic theorists try to do. In my opinion they do not succeed. They set forth the general idea of a radical divine self-giving, the Saviour coming to us in the humility of weakness, poverty and vulnerability; and they show the religious value of such a picture as a supreme manifestation of divine love. But when they come to the apparent contradiction of a being who is God and yet lacks the attributes of God, all that they can do is to offer analogies which fail to reach the key issue, and then appeal to mystery.

At this point we should look more closely, as a representative sample, at one of the major presentations from the heyday of kenotic christology. I shall select one that is being commended by advocates of the kenotic idea today, that of Bishop Frank Weston in *The One Christ*, first published in 1907. Brian Hebblethwaite refers to Weston as one in whose writings kenotic christology has been 'refined and expounded with great care and penetration', and says that 'it is possible to regard his treatment of the self-restraint of the divine Logos in living and acting through manhood at each stage of Jesus' life as one of the best and most morally convincing statements

of the kenotic view' (Hebblethwaite 1987, 30, 57). And Stephen
Davis says that 'Weston's unjustly forgotten book is in my opinion
one of the best ever written on Christology' (Davis 1988, 198). These
are strong commendations.

Frank Weston (1871-1924) was, as his biography shows (Maynard
Smith 1926), a missionary bishop in the heroic mould - utterly
dedicated to the work of Christ as he understood it, and one who
came to identify himself with the African Christians of his diocese in
what is today Tanzania, seeking to promote their welfare and to
protect them from what he saw as the two evils of 'Mohammedanism'
and European commercialism. He was an Anglo-Catholic in the
honourable tradition of those who were also Christian socialists. The
first edition of his book, *The One Christ*, was published in 1907 when
Weston, at the age of thirty-six, was Canon and Chancellor of the
Anglican cathedral in Zanzibar, a second and revised edition
appearing in 1914 (Weston 1914). Weston was passionately opposed
to the Anglican modernists of his time who were questioning the
traditional Chalcedonian christology, and with it the historicity of the
virgin birth and the bodily resurrection of Jesus. He attacked the
authors of *Foundations: A Statement of Christian Belief in Terms of
Modern Thought* (1912), edited by the New Testament scholar B. H.
Streeter; and when the Bishop of Hereford appointed Professor
Streeter a canon of his cathedral, Weston, now Bishop of Zanzibar,
solemly declared his own diocese to be out of communion with the
diocese of Hereford! He was thus a celebrated public defender of
orthodoxy as he understood it.

The style of Weston's book is that of much theological writing in his
generation, on a more rhetorical and less rigorously precise level
than would be expected in an Oxford B D thesis (which the book
originally was) today. From a vantage point more than eighty years
later the book is also pre-critical in its use of the scriptures. For
Weston regarded the New Testament criticism of his day as
dangerous error and was accordingly able, for example, to quote the
Fourth Gospel discourses as *ipsissima verba* of the historical Jesus.
Nevertheless he thought hard, with a sincere dedication to seek the
truth, he had a partially new approach to the subject, and he had the
honesty and clarity of mind to see and to face, even if he could not in
the end rebut, the very considerable objections which his theory
provokes.

We should begin, as Weston does, with his psychology. This does
not by any means coincide with standard modern psychology.

According to Weston we consist, first, of what he variously calls a self, ego, subject, person, or 'I', and second, a human nature through which this operates. A human nature consists of body and soul, the soul (i.e. the mind) including both the intellectual powers of reason, will and feeling and the 'animal' powers of sense, appetite and emotion. What is unusual about Weston's scheme is the presence of the self/ego/person/'I' as something distinct from the mind (or soul). However, this distinction is essential for his christology. 'Christology,' he says, 'assumes in a man a certain underlying reality called "I", inseparable from soul [=mind] and body in existence, yet in fact distinct from and the ground of both . . . The essential functions of this "I" require the soul, through which "I" wills, thinks, and chooses; and for its true and complete life it requires the body, the material expression of which the soul is the essential form. But the "I" is not the soul, nor the body, nor the composition of the two, but the ground in which both subsist' (Weston 1914, 16). The reason why Weston's christology requires this dichotomy between the "I" on the one hand and the mind-and-body on the other is that 'The Catholic Church bears witness that in Jesus of Nazareth the "I" is the Eternal Word of God, and none other' (16). However, this distinction between the 'I' and the mind-and-body is not only required by Weston's theory but at the same time the source of its problems. For if the 'I' or self or ego is to be anything at all it must at least include consciousness, indeed self-consciousness. And the dilemma to which the distinction leads concerns the relation between the two simultaneous states of the divine consciousness which Weston postulates, one discarnate and the other incarnate. But in order to see how the problem arises we must turn to his argument.

His basic suggestion is that the 'human nature of the Incarnate was constituted, in its first moment of existence, not in a human person, or subject, or actor; but in the Incarnate Word, who has been its subject, possessor, actor, ego, person, since it came into existence in Mary's womb' (17). Weston accordingly sees the divine self of God the Son as living in two sets of relationships – his eternal relationships within the Trinity and the historical relationships of his incarnate existence. But whereas the divine 'I' is distinct from the human nature which he assumes, he is not similarly distinct from the divine nature; for each of the triune divine 'I's is identical with the one divine nature. Accordingly 'it is useless to enquire whether the Incarnate Word uses divine Mind or Will, as it is wrong to postulate an abandonment of them by Him. He *is* the divine Mind and Will; and in every moment of the Incarnate's life we are bound to acknowledge that where He is there is the divine Nature, with all the powers and activities that are to be ascribed to it; there it is, a unity, the divine Essence, which is the Word Himself' (13).

Thus when Weston speaks, in the Nicene-Chalcedonian tradition, of 'the union of the divine and human natures in the one person, Christ' (63), he is speaking of God the Son, with the fullness of divine attributes, as the ego, self or 'I' that manifested itself in and through the body/mind that we know historically as Jesus of Nazareth. The human nature which the divine Logos (= Son) assumed was thus 'impersonal', i.e. without a human 'I', ego, self – the 'I' which used this nature being the eternal divine Logos or Son. Of these three terms which Weston uses synonymously I shall henceforth generally use only one, namely 'self'.

Weston is sometimes treated as an exponent, and indeed a leading exponent, of the kenotic type of christology. However, he distinguishes his own theory from kenoticism, concerning which he writes a chapter of sometimes strong criticism. He insists that the Logos did not, in becoming incarnate, cease to possess any of his divine attributes. He did, however, in that state voluntarily limit his exercise of them to the extent that he was not conscious of possessing them. And yet at the same time – and it is here that the problems arise – it remained true of the eternal Logos that 'Whatever of self-limitation is required, He always remains in possession of His powers, recognizing a law of restraint where restraint is necessary' (150). The result – human nature indwelt by a divine self – shows 'the beauty and excellencies of manhood when framed without sin, developed without flaw, and continuously maintained in personal union with the eternal Son of God' (150).

As we have seen, Weston follows the orthodox tradition that the humanity assumed by the Logos was 'impersonal' (*anhypostatic*) humanity, i.e. not a particular human person complete with self-directing ego, but the mental and physical machinery through which such an ego operates. In this case the ego or self that operated the human psycho-physical machinery was the eternal divine Logos. But – and this is the aspect of Weston's thought that many have labelled kenotic – in order to operate within the limitations of human nature, even ideal human nature, the Logos had to practise self-restraint: 'the Incarnate must not think or say or do what is beyond the capacity of the co-operative powers of manhood, sinless, perfect, and constituted in Himself' (153). As Weston's analogies (to which we shall come presently) make clear, he is thinking of God the Son in his incarnate state as voluntarily restricting his own mental activity within the limits proper to a human being.

At the same time, however, Weston affirms of Jesus 'an inerrancy in His human mind, due to the fact that it is the assumed and proper expression of Him who is, personally and essentially, Creator and Truth' (156). Jesus did not of course have beliefs about everything; but on everything concerning which he did have beliefs, he believed correctly – 'we cannot for a moment believe that the Incarnate ever spoke a single word, of which in His universal life as Logos he could say: "That is not exactly and finally true"' (226).

The incarnate Son's communion with God the Father was mediated through his human mind. And so Jesus prayed to God and was conscious of doing his heavenly Father's will. And as Jesus grew from babyhood to youth to manhood, so his consciousness of God developed from that appropriate to a perfect baby to that appropriate to a perfect man. 'For in considering the self-emptying of the eternal Son we have not to discuss how much of His power he retained, but how far at any stage of His life the manhood that He had assumed was able to mediate His power' (162).

The problem that confronts Weston, and with which he was honest and clear-sighted enough to struggle, is how the self of Jesus could be the eternal, omniscient, omnipotent self of the second person of the Trinity and simultaneously the self of a time-bound, normally ignorant and weak human being. This is the problem on which critical discussion of Weston's theory has to concentrate. He speaks of the Logos discarnate and incarnate in terms of two different sets of relationships of the one divine self. On the one hand there are the relations in which the Logos is involved within the internal life of the Trinity and in an unlimited relationship to the entire created universe as its Lord. And on the other hand there are the finite relationships of the incarnate Son to his fellow humans and to the world which they and he inhabit. The issue that we are trying to clarify concerns the relationship between these two – between the eternal heavenly Logos with the full attributes of deity and the same Logos incarnate in a finite human nature. For Weston insists that there is only one Christ (hence the title of his book), only one divine self, in both the discarnate and incarnate states. So he says that 'the action by which the eternal Son restrains Himself, while allowing divine aid to reach the manhood, belongs not to the relations of the Incarnate, but to those of His universal [i.e. discarnate] activities . . . He lives under a law of self-restraint that He imposed upon Himself as unlimited Logos . . . The eternal Son gives the motive-force to the relationships of the Incarnate at every moment' (160-1). A significant ambiguity must be noted here. The second sentence in this quotation suggests a prior discarnate resolution which the divine Son later carries out in his incarnate life. On the other hand the third sentence suggests a continuous willing by the Son of the limitations of his own incarnate existence. However, it does not in the end make any significant difference which interpretation we adopt. For Weston is insistent that there is only one divine self both making the resolution and carrying it out.

The resulting picture, then, is of the infinite and eternal self of the second person of the holy Trinity willing the limitations of his own consciousness in his incarnate state. Since the second person of the Trinity, being eternal, continued his heavenly existence throughout the thirty or so years of his earthly life, the Logos was during that period operating simultaneously in heaven and on earth. Thus, speaking of the time when Jesus lay unconscious in Mary's womb, Weston says that 'the acceptance of practical unconsciousness is seen to be the momentary expression of the will of the living, unlimited Logos' (177). The same divine self – for there is, once again, for Weston only one self in both the incarnate and discarnate states – is simultaneously both infinite and yet finite, omniscient and yet humanly ignorant, omnipotent and yet humanly weak. The question is whether this set of ideas can be developed into a coherent hypothesis.

Weston attempts to make sense of his suggestion by means of a series of analogies. One is that of St Francis de Sales, who acted as a confessor to his own father and mother, whom as a son he loved and revered. 'But the moment he entered the tribunal of penance with one of them he found himself unable to exercise filial love or make use of his knowledge of their lives. He was merely a priest; shriving their souls; related to them only in and through his priesthood. He was the subject of two relationships with them; of both he as their son was the first term; but in respect of the particular, limited relationship of priesthood he was seen to be restrained in the exercise of his sonship' (166-7). Thus the one self, Francis, had simultaneously two ranges of consciousness, a wider one as son, and a narrower one formed by the voluntary self-limitation of his awareness to that of a priest – this latter being analogous to the eternal Logos' limited human consciousness. Another (I omit an intermediate story about an African king reduced to slavery, 171-2), is that of

> a man, the favourite son of a commanding officer, enlisting in the army, and being transferred to his father's regiment. His self-consciousness as son of his father belongs to the sphere of his full, proper life; but within the particular, narrow relationships set up by his enlistment he is the subject of a limited consciousness; knowing himself only a son in conditions of military service. And it is only in the measure that the limited consciousness is allowed to prevail over the wider that his military life is really effective and tolerable. He is one single person; he has no dual consciousness; but the content of his self-consciousness as a soldier is less than the content of his consciousness as son, free in his father's house (172).

In such cases there is a 'single person in a dual relationship to his environment' (172). However, Weston is conscious that 'These analogies fail us just in the point where we need most help' (173). For there is in these stories – as there must be in all analogies drawn from human life – a straightforward continuity of personal consciousness in the two states of, as we may call them, glory and humiliation. But in the case of a divine incarnation the situation must be more complicated. For the self-consciousness of the incarnate one is limited and clouded by his human nature. He is not conscious, as in the analogies, of who he really is; that is to say, the earthly Jesus was not conscious of being the eternal Logos, the second person of the holy Trinity. Nor was the earthly Jesus aware of himself in glory willing his own state of humiliation. How then can the self of the earthly Jesus be identical with the heavenly self which is simultaneously willing his (Jesus') own limitations of consciousness? This does not seem to be a coherent possibility. And yet the unity of the divine self in both discarnate and incarnate states is Weston's central thesis. 'The importance of arriving at a conception of a single consciousness of the Christ cannot,' he says, 'be overestimated' (174). And so, 'as Incarnate He is at every moment observant of and obedient to a law of self-restraint which He as unlimited Logos wills should be imposed upon Himself' (175).

The problem which Weston has created is how to think of a single divine self which is simultaneously in an unlimited discarnate and a limited incarnate state, and in the first state willing the limitations of the second. How can the one undivided divine self be at once unlimited (in heaven) and limited (on earth)? Weston is acutely aware of the problem and does not shrink from facing it. He asks, 'How can the Logos as self-limited be the subject of the passion, the agony, the desolation and death upon the cross, and yet at the same moment be the living and life-giving Son of God?' (181). His answer is splendidly honest: 'No one has answered the question, no one can answer it' (181). He then, however, less admirably, joins those who take refuge in the idea of a divine mystery: 'They only plead the infinite power of the divine love. They wisely refuse to limit the divine power by the measure of what is possible to man. And with them we may well pause; fortifying our faith by the contemplation of the Father's love and omnipotence, in the face of the supreme mystery of redemption' (182).

Weston does, however, attempt yet another analogy to lighten the mystery:

It is as if a king's son were to will, for purposes of his father's policy, to leave his palace and to dwell a workman among workmen; to pass through all the troubles and vicissitudes of the life of a manual labourer, and to refuse to receive anything from others that he could not naturally receive and use as a working man. Those who recognize him and in their hearts bow before him are forbidden to acknowledge him or to help him in any way. Imagine a time of distress, and the king's son numbered among the unemployed and chosen to be one of their leaders. He goes with them into the king's presence; he is as they are in the king's sight; and the answer that he receives is that nothing can be done for any one of them. Outside the palace he shares the grief, the distress, and the hunger of the unemployed; and none may help him apart from the whole body of weary sufferers. He is, by a primary act of will, one of the unemployed. As the days pass the distress deepens; and finally a riot ensues. In the riot he is severely handled; he lies at death's door in the prison infirmary. He is recognized, but must be treated only as an unemployed workman, now a prisoner awaiting his trial. Yet all the while he is a king's son. However, he is resolved only to know himself as a king's son in conditions of manual labour. The law of self-restraint that he imposed upon himself when in his father's palace must hold. He will not, must not break it (182-3).

But once again Weston sees clearly that 'The main point in which the analogy fails us in this connection is that, of course, the son could not be at one and the same moment in his father's house as royal son and in the streets as unemployed' (183). He then appeals to yet another analogy, that of a priest who must not, as a witness in a murder trial, divulge information received in the sacred confidentiality of confession (184-5). Here again, the same self operates in a larger and a narrower consciousness. 'But,' he has at the end to acknowledge, 'when all is said these analogies have not taken us very far towards seeing the possibility of the co-existence of the two states of the Logos' (185).

Thus Weston's attempt ends in what he has to accept as mystery. And this is true generally for the kenotic theologians. They regularly say that we cannot hope to understand the process or manner of the divine self-emptying. Thus P.T. Forsyth, a leading member of this school, said, 'We cannot form any scientific conception of the precise process by which a complete and eternal being could enter on a process of becoming, how Godhead could accept growth, how a divine consciousness could reduce its own consciousness by volition' (Forsyth 1910, 293-5). And another leading kenotic theologian of the same period, H.R. Mackintosh, said, 'Somehow – to describe the method exactly may of course be beyond us – somehow God in Christ has brought His greatness down to the narrow measures of our life, becoming poor for our sake' (Mackintosh 1912, 446). We cannot, he thinks, hope to understand the divine kenosis: 'We can but believe in it as more than we could ask or think' (476). And Charles Gore, holding like Weston that 'in some manner the humiliation and the self-limitation of the incarnate state was compatible with the continued exercise of divine and cosmic functions in another sphere' (Gore 1907, 93), has to admit that this is 'in a way we cannot conceive' (207). Contemporary kenoticists speak in similar ways. Thus Stephen Davis says, 'Of course we cannot use kenosis (or any other theory) to remove the mystery of the classical doctrine' (Davis 1988, 53). And Brian Hebblethwaite, speaking of 'a mysterious and baffling act of the transcendent God in making himself personally present and known in human form', says that 'We do not grasp the essence of the incarnation any more than we grasp the essence of God'

(Goulder 1978, 28). The fallacy, however, within such appeals to mystery as a substitute for conceptual clarity is that the kenotic christology is not a revealed truth but, as Davis correctly terms it, a theory. It is a humanly devised hypothesis; and we cannot save a defective hypothesis by dubbing it a divine mystery.

7

Further Problems of Kenosis

On the face of it the idea of God ceasing to possess any of the essential divine attributes is, as we have seen, highly paradoxical. Thomas Morris brings out the extent of the paradox in his suggestion that divine immutability should be understood 'as a property, or modality, of the exemplifications of those attributes constitutive of deity, kind-essential for divinity. In brief, any individual who has a constitutive attribute of deity can never have begun to have it, and can never cease to have it. He has it, rather, immutably' (Morris 1986a, 96-7). Clearly, immutability in this sense precludes the possibility of God ceasing to have any of the attributes in virtue of which God is God.

Is it possible, however, to escape this conclusion by distinguishing between divine attributes that are not kind-essential for divinity and that can accordingly be left behind in the process of incarnating, and those others that are retained because they are essential and must therefore continue to characterize God even when incarnate? This is the way proposed by Stephen Davis. He is well aware, however, of the problems involved in using this distinction. He says,

> What would have to happen for God to remain divine and to become a man? Naturally, a complete answer to that question is beyond my knowledge. But *one* of the things that would surely have to happen would be that God would have to give up whatever divine properties (accidental ones of course; the essential ones cannot be given up if God is to remain God) are inconsistent with being human. It would also entail God's not assuming whatever accidental human properties are inconsistent with being divine. The whole picture depends upon there not being any essential divine properties that a human being cannot have and on there not being any essential human properties that God cannot have (Davis 1988, 52, cf. Davis 1983).

On the face of it this is a stiff requirement. Nevertheless it can be met quite easily simply by adopting whatever definitions will enable one to meet it. For we are free up to a point to declare of any divine or human quality that it is or is not essential, as one's theory requires. This is just what Davis does. He takes as an absolute datum the dogma that Jesus was God incarnate and infers from this that such qualities as omnipotence, omniscience, incorporeality, which he acknowledges that Jesus did not possess, are therefore not essential divine attributes! Hence, 'If Jesus was God; and if Jesus was non-omnipotent; then being omnipotent is not essential to God' (Davis 1988, 72). And the same has to be said of several other attributes. As I indicated in Chapter 1, it is always possible to save the traditional dogma by stipulating definitions that allow it to be true. But we have to count the cost. The danger here is that in adjusting the concept of God to make divine incarnation possible one may jettison aspects of the concept that are religiously essential.

For the same evidence that leads us to say that the historical Jesus was not omnipotent, omniscient or incorporeal also leads us to say that he was not omnipresent but present only at one place at a time; not eternal, but came into existence in his mother's womb at a certain point of time; hence that he cannot have been the creator of everything that exists other than himself and did not possess aseity or self-existence. Having emptied the divine nature of so much that has usually been included within it Davis asks, 'which properties of God, then, are essential?', and answers, 'I suppose it would be the properties (whichever they are) that are consistent with the incarnation, properties such as *being divine, being self-identical, existing*' (Davis 1988, 72). Existing and being self-identical must indeed be properties of anything that exists, including God. But are there any distinctive properties essential to being God? Davis' only remaining suggestion is 'being divine'. But what is it to be divine? Part of the traditional answer is that being divine consists in being the eternal, omnipotent, omiscient, omnipresent and self-existent creator of everything that exists, other than God. But all these attributes have been set aside by Davis as accidental, since the historical Jesus did not possess them. Thus in making conceptual space for divine incarnation, Davis has had to reject much of the traditional Christian understanding of God. He has had to reject even more of it if we follow Anselm, who claims that it does not make sense to speak of aseity as an accidental property; to have aseity (i.e. to exist eternally, to be uncreated, and not to be dependent for existence upon anything else) is to have that status necessarily. If this is correct it poses an uncomfortable dilemma for Davis. He must either say that aseity is not the basic divine attribute that it has so long been supposed to be, or else that the earthly Jesus possessed aseity – thereby denying his genuine humanity.

However, Davis has a way, as he hopes, of avoiding this dilemma. He grants that there are a number of divine attributes which (whether or not 'essential') are, as he says, 'ungiveupable'. He offers as examples 'being creator of the heavens and the earth' and 'not having been created'. Presumably aseity is another and more comprehensive example. Davis then applies a *qua* clause to these ungiveupable properties: 'Jesus Christ has some properties *as* God and some *as* a human being . . . Thus we can sensibly say such things as "Jesus Christ is, as God, unable to die" and "Jesus Christ is, as a human being, able to die"' without nonsense' (Davis 1988, 56). He supports this proposal, in the manner of the earlier kenoticists, with an analogy:

> Suppose a certain person named Malan is both mayor of the town and athletic director of the local college. Malan does have certain rights and responsibilities as mayor (e.g. signing into law resolutions passed by the city council) and certain rights and responsibilities as athletic director (e.g. signing checks paid out of the athletic department's budget). Someone might then ask: 'Well then, is this one person Malan able to sign bills into law or not?' In one sense the answer is yes – the one person Malan does have that ability. But in another sense, the question is ill-formed. It ought to ask, 'Does Malan, as mayor, have that ability?' Then of course the answer is yes (just as the answer to 'Does Malan, as athletic director, have that ability?' is no). Similarly, the objection raised ['is the one person Jesus Christ able to die or not?' (56)] is ill-formed. In one sense (a sense that will lead to paradox), the one person Jesus Christ was able and was not able to die. Better, however, to say: he was, as human, able to die; he was not, as divine, able to die (Davis 1988, 57).

Davis grants that his analogy is not exact, in that whereas we can see how a human being can be both a mayor and an athletic director, we cannot see how Jesus could be both God and a man. In other words the analogy does nothing to solve the logical problem of incarnation. However, it is not intended to do this, but rather, presupposing incarnation, to show how it could be true that Jesus Christ was both able to die and yet not able to die – namely, as God he was immortal whereas as man he was mortal.[1] But even with this restricted aim the analogy fails (as in the case of the other kenotic analogies) at a crucial point. For in the Malan story we have two roles performed at different times by the same unity of consciousness, memory and will: Malan functioning as athletic director in the afternoon can remember what he did as mayor in the morning. But we do not have analogous serial roles in the case of Jesus; he was not sometimes divine and sometimes human; nor do we have a situation in which Jesus, as human, can remember what he previously did as God. He has to be both human and divine at the same time – the problem that proved fatal (as I pointed out in the last chapter) to Weston's kenotic theory.

Thomas Morris suggests a possible way, which however he does not recommend, of saving the kenotic theory. This would be to say that omniscience, for example, is indeed a necessary attribute of the immutable God, but only in the modified form of 'the property of being omniscient-unless-freely-and-temporarily-choosing-to-be-otherwise' (Thomas Morris 1986a, 99); and similarly with the other divine attributes. We could then maintain that omniscience, etc. are properties that God immutably has, but that they nevertheless allow for a temporary abeyance during the period of incarnation. Morris thinks that this is 'the strongest and most sophisticated form of the kenotic approach to reconciling the divinity of Christ with the evident limitations evinced in his earthly career' (Thomas Morris 1986a, 100). It is certainly sophisticated. But, as Morris also notes, it clashes with any traditionally orthodox understanding of God: 'A form of divine immutability compatible with a divine person's ceasing to know a vast number of truths is very different from anything traditional theists have wanted to ascribe to God' (Thomas Morris 1986a, 101). Indeed this version of kenoticism, which is as theologically unattractive as it is philosophically ingenious, illustrates again the fact that it is always possible to save a particular element within a larger theological complex by making appropriate adjustments at some other point; but that such manoeuvres are liable to result in more loss than gain. One difficulty has been resolved, but only by creating a new and equally formidable problem elsewhere.

---

[1]The use of reduplicative, or *qua*, propositions is also advocated by Peter Geach (1977, 25-8), and by R.T. Herbert (1979, ch.4), and is criticized by Thomas Morris in 1986b.

But let us try yet another approach, distinguishing now between the metaphysical and the moral qualities of God. The metaphysical attributes will be aseity (including eternal existence without dependence for existence upon anything else), omnipresence, omnipotence, and being the creator of everything that exists, other than God. The moral qualities will be goodness, love, justice, mercy and wisdom. Can we, then, say (with, for example, Thomasius[2]) that the metaphysical attributes of the second person of the Trinity were temporarily laid aside in the incarnation whilst the moral attributes were retained – so that Jesus incarnated the goodness and love, justice, mercy and wisdom of God, but not the divine omnipotence, omniscience, etc.?

At first sight this is an attractive possibility. It is initially much more plausible to suggest that Jesus incarnated the divine love than that he incarnated the divine omnipotence or omniscience. For whilst he was manifestly not all-powerful or all-knowing, he did both teach and live out the commandment of love. His life expressed a self-giving *agape* for the men and women whom he encountered, opening the kingdom of heaven to the poor and humble, and being ready to die in the fulfilment of his mission. In the metaphorical sense of 'incarnation' his life was an incarnation of *agape*, and since all *agape* is a reflection of the divine *agape*, he can indeed be said to have 'incarnated' God's love.

It is when we try to translate this into non-metaphorical terms that the problems multiply. For what is distinctively divine about God's moral attributes is their infinity or unlimitedness. Human beings can be good, loving, wise, just, merciful; but only God is infinitely so. Thus for God's moral qualities to become fully embodied in a human being, that human being would have to possess those qualities to the unlimited divine extent. But this does not seem possible. The characteristics of a finite human person can only be finite. What we therefore have to say is not, with St Paul, that 'in [Jesus Christ] the *whole fulness* of deity dwells bodily' (Colossians 2.9), but that Jesus lived out *as much* of the divine goodness, love, etc. as could be expressed in the thirty or so years of a particular human life in a particular time and place.

That Jesus' earthly goodness and love were a limited reflection of the infinite divine goodness and love is the point at which this

---

[2]Gottfried Thomasius in Welch 1965, 70. Ronald J. Feenstra, in Feenstra 1989, argues for the logical possibility of such a position.

increasingly modified version of traditional christology comes close to the metaphorical conception of incarnation. For this latter holds that the 'incarnation' of divine love occurs in all human lives in so far as they are responsive to God's loving presence and thus reflect the divine love on earth in humanly limited ways. Jesus was clearly such a person to an eminent degree.

The further question whether he 'incarnated' the divine love more than anyone else who has ever lived, or that he was totally motivated by love at every moment of his life, is not capable of being answered on the basis of historical evidence. Christian tradition has, however, in effect answered it in the dogma of Jesus' sinlessness, a dogma which leads back to a 'high' christology. For sinlessness must count as at least a negative criterion of divinity. But that Jesus was at every moment of his life morally perfect has to be an affirmation of faith rather than an historical report. Indeed it is a faith-affirmation that must over-ride several items in the Gospel records. For Jesus is reported not only to have said, 'Why do you call me good? No one is good but God alone' (Mark 10.18), but also to have done various things that would be counted by many as less than perfect if done by anyone else: he treated his family with disdain (Mark 3.31-5) and said 'If any one comes to me and does not hate his own father and mother and wife and children and brothers and sisters . . . he cannot be my disciple' (Luke 14.26); he used violence in the Jerusalem temple (Matt. 21.12); he evinced what would today be regarded as a racist attitude to the Gentile woman who begged him to cure her daughter, saying 'Let the children [i.e. the Israelites] first be fed, for it is not right to take the children's bread and throw it to the dogs' (Mark 7.27); and he cursed a fig tree and made it wither because it had no fruit when he was hungry (Mark 11.13-4, 20). These are small enough blemishes in the life of a great saint; but they do not on the face of it cohere with the dogma of Jesus' absolute moral perfection as uniquely sinless, the only person who has ever lived entirely without ethical flaw of any kind.

It is of course open to one who is committed to the dogma of Jesus' sinlessness to hold that, since Jesus was God incarnate, any apparently less than perfect actions of his must have been impeccable by God's standards, even if not by ours. But this would be to affirm a dogma regardless of contrary evidence and then to use the dogma to negate that evidence; and this is not a procedure that would be regarded as intellectually respectable in other spheres.

Returning, then, to the idea of Jesus incarnating the moral but not the metaphysical attributes of God, I conclude that this has not been spelled out intelligibly as a literal hypothesis, although it makes good sense as a metaphorical truth. That is to say, Jesus was so open to God's presence and so obediently responsive to God's will that he 'incarnated' a love that reflects the divine love (but not the divine omnipotence, omniscience, etc.) in a life of selfless witness and service, even to the point of death.

That the kenotic idea is best understood as metaphor is in effect supported by Bishop Stephen Sykes' treatment of it in his original and perceptive discussion of 'The Strange Persistence of Kenotic Christology' (Sykes 1986). He adopts the theory, originated by Ernst Lohmeyer in 1927 and widely accepted, that Philippians 2.5-11 are the verses of a hymn which Paul was quoting; and he believes that the hymn was probably used in the early church at baptisms. For its form is the universal structure of religious initiations – an abandoning of one's former life and status, a symbolic humiliation or death, and a rising again into a glorious new identity. The humiliation of Christ, even to the point of crucifixion, 'is that with which the believer is identified in the baptismal humiliation' (Sykes 1986, 363). The believer then rises into the new life of mutual self-giving, or kenotic love, within the Christian community.

Sykes suggests that the rooting of the kenosis metaphor in the structure of Christian baptism, with the theme of a self-giving divine love behind it, accounts for its persistence in Christian theology despite 'the corrosive criticism of its successive dogmatic forms' (Sykes 1986, 361). For the metaphor of divine self-emptying, reflected in the symbolic self-emptying of baptism, has a life and validity of its own independently of the nineteenth- and twentieth-century attempts to harness it to solve the metaphysical puzzles created by Chalcedon; and it remains largely unaffected by the failure of these attempts. Kenosis is a vivid metaphor for the self-giving quality of the divine love as revealed in Jesus, and for the self-giving love to which we are called as his disciples. But when the metaphor is used to try to make literal sense of the idea of incarnation, by suggesting that God the Son divested himself of certain of his attributes in order to become a man, it generates too many problems to be acceptable. These kenotic theories are examples – though Sykes would probably not want to put it as strongly as this – of a good metaphor being turned into bad metaphysics. Sykes' own way of putting it is that the true meaning of the kenotic metaphor is to be found in the historical reality of 'an institution performing certain rituals in the belief that they thereby participated in a new redeemed humanity' (Sykes 1986, 366).

That the Philippians hymn was not intended by Paul, or by its original unknown composer, as a solution to the problem of a two-natures christology is supported by the setting of the passage in Paul's text, where it is an exhortation to imitate the selflessness of Jesus: 'Do nothing from selfishness or conceit, but in humility count others better than yourselves. Let each of you look not only to his own interests, but also to the interests of others. Have this mind among you, which you have in Christ Jesus, who . . .' (Philippians 2.3-5). The metaphor of self-emptying thus serves the practical purpose of guiding us rightly in our lives by pointing us away from self-centredness towards a radical recentring in God – a recentring embodied, in Paul's experience and/or in his theology, in the life of the Christian community.

This understanding of kenosis is closely analogous to what I am arguing in this book concerning the doctrine of the incarnation itself. A good metaphor – Jesus as a 'son of God', one in whom the divine Spirit was powerfully present and whose life has revealed to others the reality and love and claim of God – was turned into the metaphysical theory that Jesus had two natures, one human and the other divine. That theory has never been able to be formulated in a coherent and intelligible way that is also religiously acceptable; but the living metaphor in which it is rooted, combined with the aura surrounding dogmatic formulations within the church, has ensured that the attempts to make sense of it continue to this day. The original metaphor of incarnation can express the distinctively Christian response to Jesus as mediating God's saving presence. This response was embodied in a life of common discipleship, thereby creating the Christian community. And the son of God metaphor is part of the private, idiosyncratic family speech of this community. But it should not be turned into a metaphysical dogma which is supposed to have objective and universal truth.

8

Historical Side-effects of the Church's Dogma

The history of every major religious tradition includes great moral evils committed by its adherents. Sometimes these have not only been justified on prudential grounds by those who committed or acquiesced in them but have been validated by appeal to the official teachings of the tradition itself. For example, the Vedic teachings about caste have been used in Hindu India to justify the treatment of millions as worthless outcastes. In some Islamic countries hideously inhumane forms of punishment have been justified by appeal to the Qur'an. This chapter is concerned with parallel Christian phenomena, in which great historical evils have been validated specifically by appeal to the doctrine of the incarnation.[1]

These evils – antisemitism; the colonial exploitation of the Third (or two-thirds) World; Western patriarchalism; and the Christian superiority-complex in relation to the peoples of other faiths – have not been caused by the incarnation dogma. They have been caused by the greed, cruelty and prejudice which Christianity has proved powerless to overcome in its adherents. But this chapter is concerned, not with the fact of these evils as such but with the ways in which they have been defended by appeal to the idea of Jesus' deity. The conclusion is not that the doctrine is thereby shown to be false, but a recognition that it is inherently liable to dangerous misuse by fallen human nature. This is one element in a cumulative case, along with the fact that it was not taught by Jesus himself, and the fact that it has never been formulated in a viable way, for a re-understanding of God's activity in the life of Jesus that is compatible with the new perception of Christianity as one salvific path among others.

---

[1]For a broader discussion of the relationship between Christian doctrine and the exercise of power by Christians, see Driver 1981 and Bowden 1988, ch.8.

Antisemitism did not begin with Christianity; but when Christianity became the religion of the Roman empire the persecution of the Jews, instead of ending, soon escalated. As Rosemary Ruether says, 'we must recognize Christian anti-Semitism as a uniquely new factor in the picture of antique anti-Semitism. Its source lies in the theological dispute between Christianity and Judaism over the messiahship of Jesus, and so it strikes at the heart of the Christian gospel. It was this theological root and its growth into a distinctively Christian type of anti-Semitism that were responsible for reversing the tradition of tolerance for Jews in Roman Law' (Ruether 1974, 28). This Christian antisemitism rose to appalling heights in the medieval period, then waned somewhat, but rose again in the nineteenth and twentieth centuries to reach a new extreme of truly demonic intensity in the Nazi attempt to exterminate the Jewish population of Europe. Throughout this long history antisemitism has justified itself as a morally appropriate treatment of those who had committed deicide by crucifying God incarnate. The fact that it was not Jews but their Roman overlords who saw him as a potential political threat, who executed Jesus, is discounted; for the Gospels, written in a period of acute tension between church and synagogue, and probably within a Gentile Christian community (Casey 1991, 27f.), are concerned to place the blame firmly upon the Jews.

This motif is at its strongest in the Gospel of John, which brands the Jews as enemies of God in a way that has poisoned the Christian imagination for many centuries. Thus the Johannine Jesus, amongst other attacks on 'the Jews', says 'you seek to kill me, because my word finds no place in you' (8.37); 'You are of your father the devil, and your will is to do your father's desires' (8.44); and, concerning his own teaching, 'He who is of God hears the words of God; the reason why you do not hear them is that you are not of God' (8.47). To quote Rosemary Ruether again, 'By mythologizing the theological division between "man-in-God" and "man-alienated-from-God" into a division between two postures of faith, John gives the ultimate theological form to that diabolizing of "the Jews" which is the root of anti-Semitism in the Christian tradition' (Ruether 1974, 116). The charge of deicide – which of course presupposes Jesus' deity – continued to justify anti-Jewish attitudes during recurrent phases of violent persecution throughout the mediaeval period and was still exploited by the more secular antisemitism of the nineteenth and twentieth centuries. Indeed the charge of deicide was only formally rescinded by the Roman Catholic Church in 1965 at the Second Vatican Council. But neither at Vatican II nor in any subsequent official pronouncement has there been a full facing by the church of the distinctively Christian character of antisemitism. One could wish for more public utterances like the inscription that was put up in 1955 at the Anglican cathedral at Lincoln in England. This replaced one set there in 1255 to record the supposed ritual murder of a Christian boy by Jews. The new 1955 inscription says, 'Trumped-up stories of "ritual murders" of Christian boys by Jewish communities were common throughout Europe during the Middle Ages and even much later. These fictions cost many innocent Jews their lives. Lincoln had its own legend, and the alleged victim was buried in the Cathedral. A shrine was erected above and the boy was referred to as "little St. Hugh" . . . Such stories do not redound to the credit of Christendom and so we pray – "Remember not Lord our offences, nor the offences of our forefathers"' (Sonn 1989, 438).

The connection between the deification of Jesus and antisemitism is not of course a straight line of logical necessity. It would have been possible for Christians to believe that the Jews had rejected Jesus by failing to see him as God incarnate, and yet not to have felt it right to persecute and slaughter them. The connection lies in the historical fact that Jesus' deity was used to validate and intensify prejudice against a people who, because they adhered to their own distinctive faith and form of life, were forced into ghettoes and into unpopular occupations and then used as scapegoats for society's ills. But the virulent intensity of the worst persecutions, and the religious rhetoric which enabled many otherwise good people to support them or turn a blind eye, depended upon the faith that the Jesus whom Judaism failed to accept was none other than God in person living a human life – with the conscious or unconscious inference that the Jews must be rejected by the Christian world and may properly be ill-treated in whatever way is currently in practice.[2]

If for other reasons – particularly its not having been taught by Jesus himself, and the fact that no one has as yet succeeded in giving it an acceptable literal meaning – the doctrine were to be re-understood as a metaphorical statement of Jesus' significance for Christians, the demon of antisemitism would be deprived of a powerful psychological weapon. As I have already said, this is not in itself a reason to abandon the doctrine of the incarnation; but it is a

[2] For a comprehensive history of Christian antisemitism see Cohn-Sherbok 1992.

reason to look again carefully to see if there are sufficiently good reasons to retain it in its traditional form.

Turning to a second area of history, the fifteenth to nineteenth centuries, Western imperialist exploitation of what is today called the Third World was another major historical evil that has justified itself in the public conscience by its claim to serve the divine lordship of Christ. European colonization in Africa, India, South America and the Far East was initially an outlet for the explorers' adventurousness and their appetite for treasure. But the development of trade required military intervention to protect it, then political annexation to control the native people and keep out the rival traders of other nations, and finally led to the massive and systematic exploitation of the subject populations. Their mineral and other natural resources were exported to enrich Spain, Britain, Portugal, France and Germany, and later to feed the European industrial revolution; their people became a captive market, often buying back their own materials, now processed into finished artefacts in the West; and in the case of Africa many of their people were subjected to the ultimate exploitation of being forcibly abducted as slaves in the United States and elsewhere.

This massive exploitation of the peoples of the Third World by the technologically more powerful nations of the First World was justified as a duty, a shouldering of 'the white man's burden', his vocation to take charge of backward continents so that they might benefit from the saving gospel of Christ and the blessings of Western civilization.

Many illustrations can be given of the way in which the universal claim of Christ to rule human life, and to offer the only escape from perdition, was used to provide a moral and religious validation for the imperial enterprise. A couple of well-known examples will suffice here.

One is the sixteenth-century Spanish conquests in South America, whose motivation was, in the words of the historian Anne Peck, 'to win gold and glory for their king and themselves, and heathen people for the Catholic faith' (Peck 1941, 91). She adds that 'every conquistador of the sixteenth century was still a crusader, carrying the Cross into pagan lands'. Another standard history says:

> The Spanish expeditions to America and the West Indies, as recorded by the Spanish chroniclers, were marked by ferocious cruelty, unlimited bloodshed, unparalleled lust for treasure. A

kindly reception by natives was recompensed by the wholesale enslavement of the people for enforced labour in the search for gold and other wealth. Nor was any vestige of humanity shown in the treatment of the various tribes thrown into bondage. . . . Yet these expeditions were conducted under the pretence of advancing civilization and hallowed by the presence of priests. The hideous barbarities committed were cloaked by the fact that the Holy Cross was planted on Pagan shores and the heathen forced to accept the outward forms of Christianity . . . An almost indiscriminate slaughter was countenanced as a necessary prelude to the foundation of Christianity (Akers 1930, 6-7,9).

Another example is that of the British empire. As its historian, James Morris, says,

The mission stations which, throughout the second half of the nineteenth century, sprang up throughout the tropical possessions, were manned by and large by militants with no doubts – this was a Christian Empire, and it was the imperial duty to spread the Christian word among its heathen subjects . . . The administrators of the Empire too, and very often its conquerors, were generally speaking practising Christians; the new public schools at which so many of them were educated were invariably Church of England foundations, with parson-headmasters . . . Explorers like Speke or Grant saw themselves as God's scouts. Generals like Havelock and Nicholson slaughtered their enemies in the absolute certainty of a biblical mandate . . . and most of the imperial heroes were identified in the public mind with the Christianness of Empire – not simply humanitarianism, not Burke's sense of trusteeship, but a Christian militancy, a ruling faith, whose Defender on earth was the Queen herself, and whose supreme commander needed no identification. Every aspect of Empire was an aspect of Christ (James Morris 1968, 318-19).

Examples of this attitude could be multiplied; but as a final historical vignette, Count Zinzendorf, the Moravian leader, counselled the slaves in the Caribbean island of St Thomas in 1739, 'God punished the first negroes by making them slaves, and your conversion will make you free, not from the control of your masters, but simply from your wicked habits and thoughts, and all that makes you dissatisfied with your lot' (Erskine 1981, 21).

As in the case of Christian antisemitism, belief in the divine status of Christ did not logically require this human aberration. But given a 'fallen' human nature, unredeemed by fifteen to eighteen centuries of the church's influence, the Christian belief-system provided a sanction for the ruthless exploitation of the Third World by Christian Europe and North America. And again, as in the case of antisemitism, whilst the misuse does not show that the belief in the deity of Jesus is mistaken, it does cause us to ask whether an idea which has been so readily available to validate massive human evil is really an essential element of the Christian faith.

A third area in which the dogma that Jesus was God incarnate has been used to justify prejudice and injustice is in the social subordination of women. This has not of course been peculiar to Christian cultures. Patriarchalism, or more precisely male dominance, has reigned more or less throughout the world at least from the time of the rise of monotheism – which has always been male monotheism. The cause must lie in the male version of human nature. There is a vicious circle here: male 'chauvinism' creates God in its own image and then, in Mary Daly's famous phrase, 'When God is male, the male is God' (Daly 1973, 19).

Jesus himself seems to have been exceptionally sympathetic towards women. It is possible to see him as ahead of the culture of his time in the respect that he accorded to his female followers. And in the early church, as from time to time throughout church history, significant women leaders have been rediscovered by recent feminist scholarship. But the church as a whole took a patriarchal path, possibly initially under the leadership of St Paul. His theological justification of male dominance is well known; for example, 'I want you to understand that the head of every man is Christ, the head of a woman is her husband, and the head of Christ is God . . . For a man ought not to cover his head, since he is the image and glory of God; but woman is the glory of man. For man was not made from woman, but woman from man. Neither was man created for woman, but woman for man . . . As in all the churches of the saints, the women should keep silence in the churches. For they are not permitted to speak, but should be subordinate, as even the law says. If there is anything they desire to know, let them ask their husbands at home. For it is shameful for a woman to speak in church' (I Corinthians 11.3, 7-9 and 14.33-35). This attitude validated within Christendom a general degrading of women, thought of as associated with earth and flesh in contrast to heaven and spirit, and as epitomizing temptation and sin in contrast to spirituality and virtue. Thus Thomas Aquinas held that, 'As regards the individual nature, woman is defective and misbegotten . . . For the good of order would have been wanting in the human family if some were not governed by others wiser than themselves. So by such a kind of subjection woman is naturally subject to man, because in man the discernment of reason predominates' (Aquinas 1976, I, Q.92, art.1).

This is a general theological validation of male dominance; but the specific relevance of the doctrine of the incarnation becomes evident in the debates about the ordination of women in the Catholic, Anglican and Orthodox churches. God the Son, being male, became incarnate as a man, not as a woman, and therefore only men can be God's priestly representatives on earth. Thus the Vatican's Declaration on the Question of Admission of Women to the Ministerial Priesthood in 1976 said that there must be a 'physical resemblance' between a priest and Christ. (On the other hand the Catholic theologian Karl Rahner condemned the Declaration as heretical at this point – Ruether 1989, 47.) Thus the dogma of Jesus' deity lends itself to exploitation by male chauvinists in perpetuating the subordination of women within the church. Once again, this does not establish the falsity of the dogma; but it does prompt us to look at it again to see whether it really is an essential Christian belief.

The fourth historical situation to which I want to point has an even more direct connection with the idea of Christ's status as the unique incarnation of the second person of a divine Trinity, namely the attitude of Christians to the people of the other great world religions. This has for centuries consisted, and still today consists to too great an extent, in a religious superiority-complex which readily manifests itself in arrogance, contempt, condemnation and hostility. Such an attitude has affected, and still for many pervasively affects, the relationship between the Christian minority of the human race and the non-Christian majority. The missionary movement that was carried on the back of the imperial expansion of the West generally regarded Hinduism, Buddhism, Islam, Taoism, Sikhism and African primal religion as areas of spiritual darkness from which souls were to be rescued by conversion. As late as 1960 the Chicago Congress of World Mission declared that 'In the years since [World War II], more than one billion souls have passed into eternity and more than half these went to the torment of hell fire without even hearing of Jesus Christ, who He was, of why He died on the cross of Calvary' (Percy 1961, 9). And there continue to be large and powerful fundamentalist constituencies within which such ideas are still alive, still affect human attitudes, still determine the use of resources, and still influence political policies.

The connection between this Christian superiority complex and the traditional doctrine of the incarnation is evident. If Jesus was God incarnate, the Christian religion is unique in having been founded by God in person. The Christian story is that in Jesus God came down to earth and inaugurated a new and redeemed community, the church; and it seems self-evident that God must wish all human creatures to become part of this community; so the church is called to convert the human race to the Christian faith. However, this implication has long since come to seem unrealistic. The independence of previously colonial territories has dismantled the imperial umbrella under which the missionaries worked. And with the continuing population explosion throughout much of the Third World the Christian proportion of the world's population has shrunk and is likely to continue to shrink. It is probable that early in the twenty-first century Islam will have become numerically the largest of the world religions. In this new situation, in which Christianity no longer expects to cover the earth, Christian thought is in a serious state of cognitive dissonance. One response is an intensification of fundamentalist faith within a large wing of the churches. On the more liberal wing, various epicycles of theory have been developed to avoid the absolutist implication of the incarnation dogma. Already in the nineteenth century the ideas of 'implicit faith' and 'baptism by desire' were in use, according to which individuals who have not had a proper opportunity to respond to the gospel, but whose spiritual state is nevertheless such that they *would* respond if it were properly presented to them, are unconsciously included within the sphere of salvation. In the twentieth century Karl Rahner has developed the concept of 'anonymous Christians', which was in effect adopted (though without using Rahner's term) at the Second Vatican Council and reiterated by the present pope in his first encyclical, *Redemptor Hominis*, 1979, in which he declared that 'every man without any exception whatever has been redeemed by Christ, and . . . with man – with every man without any exception whatever – Christ is in a way united, even when man is unaware of it' (para. 14). However, it becomes clear in a more recent encyclical, *Redemptoris Missio*, 1990, that this is not intended to cancel the drive to convert the entire human race to an explicit Christian faith. For here the pope says that 'Dialogue should be conducted and implemented with the conviction that the church is the ordinary means of salvation and that she alone possesses the fullness of the means of salvation' (para. 55), and urges renewed support for the missionary societies, quoting with approval the statement 'This must be our motto: All the churches united for the conversion of the whole world' (para. 84).

An 'inclusivism' according to which non-Christians are included within the sphere of Christian salvation probably represents the nearest approach to a consensus among Christian thinkers today. It is, however, being criticized by a growing minority as a continuation in a milder form of the old theological imperialism. For it still holds that salvation is, exclusively, Christian salvation, won by the atoning death of Christ, although the benefits of that death are now generously extended in principle to all human beings.

The alternative being proposed both to the older exclusivism and the newer inclusivism is a pluralism which recognizes the validity of all the great world faiths as authentic contexts of salvation/liberation, not secretly dependent upon the cross of Christ. Those of us who advocate this pluralist option do so because it seems to us to be more religiously realistic than the older alternatives. For we see taking place within each of the great traditions at their best, and to more or less the same limited extent, the salvific transformation of human life, individually and corporately, from destructive self-centredness to a new orientation centred in the divine Reality. It cannot, alas, be claimed that any of the great traditions has been more than very partially successful in this; for each has also been burdened by immense historical evils which have counteracted the good that they have done. But viewed as complex, long-lived totalities, each is an unique mixture of good and evil, and none stands out as more salvifically effective than another. So far as human discernment can tell, the great traditions seem to be contexts of salvation/liberation to a more or less equal extent. This is of course a large-scale empirical judgment. I have elsewhere indicated grounds for it (Hick 1993); but I recognize that it cannot be proved and that it is open to endless discussion. I would only insist that the onus of proof lies upon anyone who claims that a particular tradition – presumably their own – is demonstrably morally and spiritually superior to all others.

Once again, then, if the dogma of Jesus' deity were to become understood, not as a literal claim with universal implications, but as internal Christian metaphorical discourse, a barrier would be removed from the relationship between the Christian and other sections of humankind.

9

Plural Incarnations?

As the ancient Ptolemaic picture of the universe, with our earth at its centre, was gradually replaced in the Christian consciousness by the enormously expanded universe disclosed by modern astronomy, Western thinkers began to speculate about the possibility of divine incarnations on other planets. The thought has produced opposite reactions.

Some have seen it as a threat to the traditional understanding of redemption as brought about by the death of Jesus on our earth. The sceptical Tom Paine, for example, wrote in *The Age of Reason*:

> From whence then could arise the solitary and strange conceit, that the Almighty, who had millions of worlds dependent on his protection, should quit the care of all the rest, and come to die in our world, because they say one man and one woman had eaten an apple! And, on the other hand, are we to suppose that every world in the boundless creation, had an Eve, an apple, a serpent, and a redeemer? In this case, the person who is irreverently called the Son of God, and sometimes God himself, would have nothing else to do than to travel from world to world, in an endless succession of death, with scarcely a momentary interval of life.[1]

On the other hand some imaginative artists have grasped the thought of many divine incarnations as an expansion of the gospel to that of a truly cosmic Christ. Alice Meynell's poem 'Christ in the Universe' well expresses this:

> Nor, in our little day,
> May His devices with the heavens be guessed;
> His pilgrimage to tread the Milky Way,
> Or His bestowals there, be manifest.

[1] Paine 1890, 47-8. The possibility of plural incarnations, and the problems that this might create, have been discussed more recently by Ninian Smart 1960, 95f.; Roland Puccetti 68, 136ff.; Thomas Morris 1986a, 170ff.; Richard Sturch 1991, 194ff.

> But in the eternities
> Doubtless we shall compare together, hear
> A million alien gospels, in what guise
> He trod the Pleiades, the Lyre, the Bear.
>
> Oh be prepared, my soul,
> To read the inconceivable, to scan,
> The infinite forms of God those stars unroll
> When, in our turn, we show to them a Man.

Or again, Sydney Carter's

> Who can tell what other cradle
> High above the Milky Way
> Still may rock the King of Heaven
> On another Christmas Day?

And many today have had the scope of their theological imaginations enlarged by C. S. Lewis' allegory of Narnia with the numinous figure of Aslan, who is the divine Logos incarnate as a mighty lion.

In recent theological writings Christian thought has continued to move in opposite directions. Thomas Morris, referring to his own two-minds christology (discussed in Chapter 5), with its conception of the divine mind of the Logos enclosing and being in an asymmetric accessing relationship with the human mind of Jesus, says that '[In that case] there seems to be no good reason to think that this accessing relation could not hold severally between any number of finite, created minds, or ranges of consciousness, and the properly divine mind of God the Son. And if this is possible, multiple divine incarnations are possible in any number' (Thomas Morris 1986a, 183). Indeed he sees it as an advantage of his type of christology that it allows for the possibility of multiple incarnations, so that 'if we are to allow in principle the widest range of possibilities concerning multiple divine incarnations, we should endorse the two-minds view' (Morris 1986a, 183). (Whilst Morris holds that multiple divine incarnations are logically possible, he does not argue that in fact 'there have been, or are, or will be multiple incarnations of God in creaturely natures' – Morris 1986a 186.) The connection between a two-minds christology and the possibility of plural incarnations does not, however, hold in any exclusive way. On the contrary, the idea of many incarnations is equally viable given any basically Chalcedonian form of christology. For all such christologies posit two realities, the eternal divine Son and the human nature which the Son assumes. And it would seem that this assuming of human nature could in principle occur any number of times.

Morris presumably has in mind plural incarnations in different worlds, not in the same world; and so he would not necessarily disagree with Brian Hebblethwaite's rejection of the idea of several earthly incarnations. Hebblethwaite says:

> The suggestion that Jesus might have been one of many incarnations of God in human history betrays a complete failure to appreciate what the doctrine of the incarnation, in classical Christian faith, has been held to state. If God himself, in one of the modes of his being, has come into our world in person, to make himself personally known and to make himself vulnerable to the world's evil, in order to win our love and bind us to himself, we cannot suppose that he might have done so more than once. For only one man can actually *be* God to us, if God himself is one. We are to posit relation in God, yes, but not a split personality. Only one actual human person can be the vehicle and expression of the one God on earth (Hebblethwaite 1987, 189).

The nub of the matter, for Hebblethwaite, is thus apparently that because God's activity in the incarnation is personal, 'only one man can actually *be* God to us, if God himself is one'. But this is, surely, a *non sequitur*. Does the divine uniqueness prevent God from being in personal relationship with any number of human beings at once? Do not many people throughout the world simultaneously experience the personal presence of the one God? Why then is it in principle impossible for God to assume human nature on several occasions, revealing the divine nature to different sections of the human race, and becoming vulnerable to the world's evil in order to win the love and allegiance of people within those different groups? Such incarnations would be distinguishable by their human differences – different personalities and histories, presumably in different places and at different times and within different cultural contexts. If there were such a plurality, would it follow that one was personal and the others not personal? Or would all be rendered non-personal by the fact of there being more than one? There does not appear to be any path of sound reasoning leading to these conclusions. Hebblethwaite has simply asserted magisterially that the personal and unitary nature of God precludes more than one divine incarnation. In doing so he must I think be moved, not by conceptual or logical considerations, but by the motive of Christian absolutism. For the thought that the Jesus incarnation might not be the only one opens the door to the possibility of Christianity not being uniquely superior to all other religions; and I suspect it is this door that he wants to keep shut.

However, I propose at this point to go back behind these modern discussions to one of the clearest-minded of the classical theologians, Thomas Aquinas, who asked himself in a spirit of intellectual curiosity whether Christian theology permits the possibility of more than one incarnation of the eternal Word.

His discussion occurs in Part IIIa of the *Summa Theologica*, particularly in some of the articles of Questions 3 and 4. Starting from the fact of God the Son having become incarnate, he asks whether either of the other two persons, the Father and the Spirit, could have done the same. His answer is Yes, 'what the Son can do, the Father can do, for otherwise the three persons would not be equal in power. The Son had the power to become incarnate. So then did the Father and the Holy Spirit' (IIIa, 3,5). A little later (3,8) he argues that, given this possibility, it was nevertheless fitting that the Son, rather than the Father or the Spirit, should have been the one to become incarnate – mainly because it was the Son who had originally created human nature.[2]

Aquinas next asks whether two of the persons of the Trinity can 'assume the same human nature' (3,6), and he answers that they can; for 'three persons can subsist in the one divine nature. Therefore they could also subsist in one human nature in such a way that the one human nature would be taken by the three persons' (3,6). Does he mean here 'one human nature' generically, so that the two divine persons would become two different individuals who share the one human nature; or that they would both become incarnate in the same human individual? Quentin Quesnell takes Thomas to mean the latter – so that the two members of the Trinity would have to take 'one and the same concrete instance of human nature, i.e., to take one and the same human body-soul combination' (Quesnell 1987, 35). However, Aquinas adds something that seems incompatible with this interpretation: 'It would be impossible that they assume one hypostasis or person; as Anselm notes, Many persons cannot assume one and the same man' (3,6). But it does not greatly matter, in view of

[2]Anselm had previously treated this question in *Cur Deus Homo?* Book II, Chapter 9.

what comes later in Aquinas' text, which interpretation we adopt at this point.

Thomas now comes to the question – which promises interesting implications – whether the divine Son might subsequently become incarnate as another, different human being. Here he is clearly concerned with individual human natures – one nature for each human person. 'It seems [he says] that after the Incarnation the Son has the power to take up another human nature distinct from the one he actually did.' Again, 'we must hold that beside the human nature actually assumed a divine person could take up another numerically distinct' (3,7). It seems, then, that the second person of the Trinity could take human nature again, and if twice, then presumably three or four, or indeed any number of times, and could presumably have done so before the Jesus incarnation as well as after it. (Such a series of successive incarnations would be in some ways analogous to the Hindu conception of the *jiva* or, roughly, soul, becoming repeatedly incarnate, each incarnation forming a new and different psycho-physical individual. A major difference, however, is that on the Hindu scheme each later incarnation is influenced by the *karma* of the previous ones.)

One might well ask, then, from an orthodox Christian point of view, why there have not been other incarnations in addition to the one witnessed to in the New Testament. Aquinas is not afraid to raise this question. The only hypothesis that he considers, however, is the extreme one of God assuming human nature in *all* human individuals. The other and surely more serious possibility is that of a limited number of incarnations in various places and at various times in order to do for others what Jesus, as an influence within human history, has done for some.

Aquinas rejects the hypothesis of a universal incarnation in which every man and woman is God incarnate on the ground that this would 'take away the multitude of individuals human nature requires' (4,5); for there 'would only be one person having human nature, namely the person assuming', i.e. the second person of the Trinity (4,5). In other words, he is arguing that there would be no human race as we know it, consisting of a varied multitude of different unique individuals. Instead of a created race of free creatures who could (and did) fall, there would be a race of beings each of whom is God the Son taking a different individual human nature. Aquinas' imagined interlocutor accordingly raises this possibility: 'the divine incarnation flows from divine love. But love makes us give ourselves as far as possible to our friends. Since, then, the Son of God could have assumed many human natures, as we have noted, and by the same token all human natures, then he should have assumed it in all its supposits [i.e., individual persons]' (4,5). However, if there was – as we must presume – a reason for the creation of the actually existing human race, the interlocutor's hypothesis would leave that reason unsatisfied. This seems to be an acceptable argument. Aquinas seems, given his premises, to have a reasonable ground for his rejection of the idea of universal human incarnation.

But his argument does not apply to the other possibility of a limited number of such incarnations. If we grant that a universal incarnation would go too far by, in effect, abolishing humanity as we know it, we can nevertheless appeal to the motive of divine love as a reason for a limited number of incarnations. For the Jesus incarnation occurred at a particular point in history, after a number of civilizations had existed without its benefit; and it occurred in one particular part of the world, being unknown for over a millennium in most of the vast regions of China, the rest of Asia, the Americas, Australasia and the Arctic and Antarctic regions. It was in effect an incarnation for the inhabitants of the late Roman empire and its successor in our modern Western civilization and its colonial extensions. But given that the historical influence of Christ, as the visible expression of divine love, is of benefit to humanity, would it not have been much more beneficial if the Logos had also become incarnate in the other great centres of human civilization?

Aquinas did not, as we have seen, consider this possibility. His response to the suggestion that divine love should have been expressed in a universal incarnation is that 'the love of God toward man is manifested not only in taking on human nature, but above all through the things he suffered in human nature for all men . . . This would not have been the case had he assumed human nature in all its supposits [i.e., individual instances]' (4,6). Restated in relation to the idea of a limited series of incarnations, the argument would be that God incarnate could only die once to atone for the sins of the world, and therefore that there could only be one incarnation. But does this 'therefore' really hold? Aquinas himself would have had to say No; for he has already affirmed that there *could* be a plurality of divine incarnations. We might imagine him to grant that only one of these could die the atoning death that, according to the Anselmic-type satisfaction theory with which Aquinas worked, was necessary if sinful humanity was to receive God's forgiveness. But there are other things that divine incarnations could have done that would have been of inestimable value. They could have taught the true way of life, bringing many to accept God's rule in their hearts; they could have sought to purify nations, bringing justice and peace to the world; they could have healed the sick; and they could, and in many societies would, have been persecuted as suffering servants of the truth which they embodied.

St Thomas also takes up the matter of the timing of the Jesus incarnation. He does so, however, once again, in a needlessly extreme form. He asks whether God should have become incarnate at the beginning of human history. His answer is No, because the incarnation was a response to sin, and at the beginning (i.e. before the Fall) sin had not yet occurred. But neither, he adds, was it appropriate for God to become incarnate immediately after sin had begun. For as a good doctor does not (he says) give medicine to one who is ill at the beginning of the sickness, so likewise 'the Lord does not immediately provide the Incarnation to the human race as a remedy lest it be spurned out of pride, before men had recognized their own weakness' (1,6). He likewise asks whether Christ should have come only at the end of history and again answers No, but for various reasons which are not likely to appeal to the modern reader. In short, then, Christ came neither at the beginning nor at the end, but at the most appropriate moment. Aquinas establishes this, to his own satisfaction, *a priori*: 'God . . . determines all things in his wisdom. Therefore God became incarnate at the most suitable time' (1,5).

Some modern theologians have attempted a less *a priori* response to the question of timing. The incarnation required, it has been said, the Roman empire with its widely spread common language, its rule of law and its system of road and sea communications, for the gospel to be able to spread rapidly. Prior to that the conditions were not in place for the birth of the great world religion. The fourth-century church historian Eusebius was probably the first to point to 'the providential coincidence of the incarnation and the establishment of world peace under Augustus' (Young 1983, 5). However, Eusebius' line of thought is not at all plausible from an historical point of view. For centuries before the time of Jesus there were literate civilizations with sufficiently developed urban centres and networks of communication for great spiritual teachers to emerge and to exert a powerful spreading influence which has continued to this day – Confucius and the author(s) of the *Tao Te Ching* in China, Gautama the Buddha and Mahavira in India, Zoroaster in Persia, the great Hebrew prophets in Palestine, as well as Pythagoras, Socrates and Plato in Greece. There was also an advanced civilization in ancient Egypt, although this did not in fact become the cradle of an enduring new world faith. Thus it remains a legitimate question why the divine love did not manifest itself within other ancient civilizations as well as within the Graeco-Roman. Further, in many areas before the time of Jesus human life was fragmented into small tribal groups. It could perhaps be argued that these did not each warrant a divine incarnation to reveal God's love to them. But such reasoning would be uncomfortably arbitrary. It is far from self-evident that small tribal groups should be, or are, less the objects of divine love than large civilized nations.

Quentin Quesnell has spelled out something of what it would mean for there to be incarnations other than the Jesus incarnation. In each case it would mean the divine Word

becoming incarnate in another, different human body and soul, born of another mother, with another human father, of a different sex and race, in a different country, speaking a different language, and using different imagery in which to preach and explain God's relation to the human family. Each of these incarnations would indeed be the same divine person; but each would have a different human mind, a separate human will, and a distinct human consciousness. Each would have to know only as much as necessary to carry out the work for which that one incarnation took place. This would not necessarily include each knowing about the others. Each such individually assumed human nature, each such incarnation of the Word of God, would have a different name. Each would look at things differently, in the light of quite different cultures, educations, native talents, human experiences of infancy, childhood and youth (Quesnell 1987, 36-7).

If, then, we grant with St Thomas the possibility of such other incarnations of the eternal Word, the natural next question is whether, from a Christian point of view, such epoch-making spiritual leaders as Moses, Gautama, Confucius, Zoroaster, Socrates, Mohammed, Nanak may not in fact have been such divine incarnations. From their own point of view, of course, none of these great figures would have accepted such an identification. To some

(Gautama, Confucius, possibly Socrates) this would have been conceptually out of the question, whilst to others (Moses, Zoroaster, Mohammed, Nanak) it would have been blasphemous. But we have already seen that modern New Testament scholarship has jettisoned the idea that the historical Jesus taught or thought that he was God incarnate. It is believed that he saw himself as the eschatological prophet or, less probably, as the Danielic son of man or as the long-awaited Messiah, in each case heralding the end of the present age and the imminent coming of God's kingdom; but not, as later Christian thought came to see him, as the incarnate second person of a divine Trinity, or as son of God in other than the familiar Hebraic sense of a man close to God, an instrument of the divine purposes, acting as God's agent on earth. If, then, the one clear instance, from a Christian point of view, of divine incarnation was unaware that he was God incarnate, might not other instances have shared a like human ignorance? For it seems, in the light of the New Testament, that we should not expect a divine incarnation to be aware, or even necessarily to be able to believe, that he or she is in fact a divine incarnation.

The idea of divine incarnations additional to the Jesus incarnation seems dangerous to many Christians. It may be instructive to ask why this is so. Conceptually, the hypothesis of a number of incarnations – always supposing the idea of divine incarnation itself to be viable – is, as we have seen, logically and theologically permissible. If the holy Trinity wanted, in one or other of its persons, to become incarnate on earth more than once, it would be within the Deity's power to do this. In the light of St Thomas' arguments it would be difficult to deny this. But different theological standpoints will find this possibility either enlightening or threatening. St Thomas points to what will count to many as a threat when, against the hypothesis of a universal incarnation, he says that 'this would take away from the dignity of the incarnate Son of God, who is first born among many brethren (Romans 8.29) according to his human nature, just as he is the first born of all creatures (Colossians 1.15) according to the divine' (4,6). But as an argument this begs the question. On the assumption that there is only one divine incarnation it would of course infringe its uniqueness for there to be others. But we have to ask for the grounds of that assumption. The answer, I suggest, lies in a basic commitment to the superiority of the Christian religion as the only point in history at which God has assumed human nature. For if each of the great world faiths looks to its own divine incarnation – even though neither the divine/human individuals themselves nor the traditions which have formed around them thought in such terms – then the dogma of the unique salvific superiority of Christianity would collapse.

If we pursue the multiple incarnation concept a little further we may arrive at some such picture as this. When God became incarnate as Jesus he was humanly conscious of that aspect of the divine which can be conceived in Jewish terms, namely as the personal heavenly Father. And by following Jesus, and responding in faith to the heavenly Father, men and women can find salvation. But incarnated as Gautama Siddhartha, the Buddha, the Logos was humanly conscious of that aspect of the divine which could be conceived in quite different terms, as the eternal reality of *nirvana* or of the universal Buddha nature with which we can attain a blessed unitary consciousness as we transcend the false perspective of the self-enclosed ego. One could proceed to interpret along analogous lines each of the other major options represented by the different world religions. There would thus emerge a theology of religions which stresses the infinite nature of the Godhead, exceeding the scope of all our concepts, and the salvific efficacy of the variety of ways formed around the different incarnations that have occurred throughout human history. Such a view might be welcomed by Christians who accept the traditional incarnation doctrine and who yet at the same time recognize the salvific validity and effectiveness of the other major world faiths.

However, if understood in terms of a literal concept of divine incarnation, this path is blocked by the fact that no such concept has yet been shown to be viable. But if, as I am recommending, we understand the idea of divine incarnation metaphorically, it becomes entirely natural to say that all the great religious figures have in their different ways 'incarnated' the ideal of human life lived in response to the divine Reality.

10

Divine Incarnation as Metaphor

During the last thirty or so years metaphor has been one of the more intensively studied aspects of language, giving rise to a voluminous literature.[1] However, I do not propose to rehearse here the various rival theories of the nature of metaphor, from Aristotle to the present day, because the point that I want to make does not depend upon any of them. Instead I shall start from some broadly agreed conclusions from the widespread discussion which are relevant to my proposal.

The metaphorical stands in contrast to the literal use of language. The latter is simply standard use within a given linguistic community, employing words to convey agreed meanings, which may be recorded in a dictionary. Thus the literal meanings of a word are, roughly, its dictionary meanings, and to speak literally is to intend one's utterance to be understood in this standard or dictionary sense. In distinction from this, metaphor is a form of non-literal or figurative speech – along with metonymy, irony, synecdoche, hyperbole, simile, idiom and meiosis. Thus metaphorical speech is a use of language in which speaker-meaning differs from dictionary-meaning. The precise way in which it differs has proved hard to locate, and has in fact never been defined in any generally acceptable way. But the central idea is indicated by the derivation of the word from the Greek *metaphorein*, to transfer. There is a transfer of meaning. One term is illuminated by attaching to it some of the associations of another, so that metaphor is 'that trope, or figure of speech, in which we speak of one thing in terms suggestive of another' (Soskice 1985, 54). Metaphorical meaning is thus generated by the interaction of two sets of ideas. This is what is

[1]This includes, as some of the more important items, Monroe Beardsley 1962 and 1978; Colin Turbayne 1962; Philip Wheelwright 1962; Max Black 1962; William Alston 1964 and 'Irreducible Metaphors in Theology' in Alston 1989; Paul Ricoeur 1978; Andrew Ortony 1979; Sheldon Sacks 1979; George Lakoff and Mark Johnson 1980; Sallie McFague 1983; Janet Martin Soskice 1985; David E. Cooper 1986.

happening when one speaks, for example, of 'a running nose', or 'a rhetorical smoke-screen', or 'food for thought', or 'a sharp retort', or of 'our heavenly Father', 'Rock of Ages', 'lamb of God', or when we say that 'the chairman ploughed through the agenda' or 'the Father begat the Son before all ages'.

If, for example, I speak of the journey of life, I am applying some of the associations of 'journey' in most of our minds to the experience of living and am thereby highlighting aspects of this experience. Like a journey, life is a process through time, with a beginning and an end; as on a journey, one moves on from stage to stage; new and unexpected experiences can occur; one can proceed on a planned route, or one can get lost; and so on. In spelling out these similarities, or analogies, I have been translating the metaphor into literal speech. But this does not exhaust the metaphor. For such translation can never be complete and definitive, both because there is no fixed boundary to the range of similarities that may occur to different people, and because these similarities can activate an indefinite range of varied associations and feelings. There is thus an ineliminable and indefinable aura of meaning to metaphor. A metaphor's central thrust can be literally translated, but its ramifying overtones and emotional colour are variable and changing and thus are not translatable without remainder into a definitive list of literal propositions. The use of metaphor is accordingly a different kind of speech-act from the listing of identifiable similarities. Metaphorical speech is indeed akin to poetry, and shares its non-translatability into literal prose.[2]

It is for this reason that the effectiveness of metaphor as a form of communication depends upon a common reservoir of shared associations – what Max Black called a 'system of associated commonplaces' (Black 1962, 40). Indeed it is a very plausible view of the function of metaphor that it serves to promote community:

---

[2]It has become fashionable today in some circles to deny any distinction between the literal and the metaphorical and to say that all speech is metaphorical. This is a recommendation to use 'metaphorical' in a new and different way. But if all speech is metaphorical, the term no longer has any meaning, since it no longer marks any distinction. It seems to me more useful to retain the two terms, with their different meanings. It should, however, be noted that sometimes a phrase has both literal and metaphorical meaning – as in the Ford automobile advertisement, 'Everything we do is driven by you'.

I might add that metaphor is fairly close to analogy, in that both arise from similarities between different things; but 'incarnation' is clearly a case of metaphor rather than analogy, and I shall not pursue the subject of analogy further here.

'metaphorical talk effects a familiarity or "intimacy" between speakers, and between them and their world', so that 'the utterance of a metaphor may be viewed as a signal that the speaker takes his hearers to belong to a subset distinguished by a bond of intimacy' (Cooper 1986, 140, 158). And within a community of people who largely understand one another communication is greatly enhanced by a liberal use of metaphor, so that ordinary speech is usually saturated with it. This last sentence is itself an instance; and in the previous paragraphs I have spoken of one term 'illuminating' another, of the central 'thrust' of a metaphor, of its 'aura' of meaning, of its 'emotional colour', of the 'spelling out' of similarities. I did not plant these examples (this being yet another metaphor) to make a point; they all occurred quite naturally in the course of trying to say what I wanted to say. We speak metaphorically almost as much as literally; language is highly plastic and its use is an art.

Nor is the boundary between the literal and the metaphorical permanently fixed. 'Dead' metaphors become literal usages, being now so common and well established as to have acquired dictionary status. 'Pig-headed', for example, means, according to the *Oxford English Dictionary*, 'obstinate'. Whether, or when, a metaphor has become established as literal usage is a matter for judgment, and makers of dictionaries are paid to exercise their judgment about this on behalf of the rest of us.

Let us now move from these generalities to 'incarnation'. Prior to the theological settlement reached at Nicaea (325) and Chalcedon (451), Christian language exalting Jesus as Lord, Saviour, Son of God and God seems generally to have been devotional, or ecstatic, or liturgical (or all three), rather than an exercise in precise theological formulation. It was analogous to the language of love, in which all manner of extravagances and exaggerations are entirely appropriate but are not intended to be taken with strict literality. But within the more formal language of theology 'incarnation' began as a technical term, prompted by the prologue to the Fourth Gospel, 'And the Logos was made flesh' (John 1.14), *sarx egeneto*, Latinized as *incarnatus*. Thus the original home of 'incarnation' was in the official language of the church. And here it was not intended as metaphor but as shorthand for the doctrine that Jesus was God the Son living a human life, being both 'truly God' and 'truly man', *vere Deus, vere homo*. He was literally (not metaphorically) God and literally (not metaphorically) human. In earlier centuries the main stress was often upon Jesus' deity, although during the last hundred years or so more often upon his humanity; but despite this varying stress the church has always, in its official pronouncements, insisted upon both and has dismissed as heretical any christology which fails to follow suit. The essence of the doctrine has always been that the man Jesus of Nazareth 'was in some literal sense God' (Brown 1985, 102).

The doctrine was clearly assumed to have a meaning capable of being described in literal terms. The terms used in the definitive Chalcedonian definition were *hypostasis*, 'being' (treated in this instance as equivalent to *prosopon*, person), and *phusis*, 'nature'. Jesus was one *hypostasis* and *prosopon*, one being and person, *en duo phusesin*, in two natures. In other words, the one person, Jesus, had two natures, divine and human. However this was – deliberately – a rather general or vague statement, intended more to rule out errors than to explain the approved dogma in any philosophically satisfactory way. As G.L. Prestige says, the achievement of the fathers at Chalcedon 'was only negative; they defined what was false but provided no positive and convincing rationalization of the right faith' (Prestige 1936, 279). Their pronouncement did not pretend to spell out what it is for a person to have these two different natures. And yet there is an obvious puzzle as to how the same being can jointly embody those attributes of God and of humanity that are apparently incompatible. God is eternal, whilst humans have a beginning in time; God is infinite, humans finite; God is the creator of the universe, including humanity, whilst humans are part of God's creation; God is omnipotent, omniscient, omnipresent, whilst humans are limited in power and knowledge and have a bounded spatial location; and so on. Let us call this the incompatible-attributes problem. And so the general statement that Jesus had both a divine and a human nature needed to be explicated in a way that could solve or avoid this problem. This is what the various theories produced during the christological controversies from about the fourth to about the seventh century were attempting to do. They try to spell out the idea of divine incarnation in ways which avoid or resolve the incompatible-attributes problem.

We see how difficult the task is if we begin with the simplest possible concept of divine incarnation. If we assume a body/mind dichotomy, and say that a person's, X's, body is a human body but that X's mind is the mind of God, we should have one possible literal meaning for the statement that X is God incarnate. (This was in fact the conception of incarnation used by St Athanasius in his *De*

Incarnatione.)[3] This is the most basic possible such meaning; for it employs a minimum number of terms, and these terms, 'body' and 'mind', are used in their ordinary or literal sense – though it must be added that one of these, 'mind', has become problematic in much modern philosophical discussion. It is true that we might on further reflection have misgivings about whether the infinite divine consciousness could be stored in a finite system of human brain cells. We might even conclude that divine incarnation, so defined, is impossible. But at least we would know precisely what it is that we are declaring to be impossible.

Such an account of incarnation, whilst using language literally, could also be described as metaphysical, in that it refers to the divine mind. But given the concepts of divine mind and human body, and the notion of a mind being embodied, we seem to have about as clear and intelligible a literal sense of divine incarnation as is possible. However, at this point we recall that one of the conditions for a religiously acceptable explication of Jesus as God incarnate is that as well as showing how he is genuinely and unambiguously God it must also show how he is genuinely and unambiguously a human being. And our simplest possible model fails the second part of this test. A human body inhabited by the mind of God would not count as a genuine human being. Or rather, in order to regard him as such we should have to make a stipulation about what it is to be human that would have unacceptable implications in other directions. For is it not a presupposition of our personal and moral relationships with one another that we all have human minds as well as human bodies? And, specifically in relation to Jesus, must he not have had a human mind as well as a human body if he is to be (amongst other things) the exemplar whose basic attitudes to others we seek to imitate? And do not the Synoptic Gospels (as distinguished from much of the Fourth Gospel) depict Jesus as having a human consciousness? Thus whilst there is no law against radically redefining humanity so as to include a divine mind in a human body, nevertheless there would be a very heavy cost in

---

[3]In the *De Incarnatione* (which predates his controversy with the Arians) the only meaning that Athanasius gives to 'incarnation' is that of the Word of God taking a human body: 'He took to Himself a body, a human body even as our own' (para. 8), 'He assumed a body capable of death' (9), 'the Word submitted to appear in a body' (16), 'He takes to himself an instrument . . . a human body' (43), 'He manifested Himself by means of a body' (54). See also 13, 14, 18, 44, 45. Quotations from St Athanasius 1989.

other ways. Indeed the acceptance or rejection of proposed christologies always depends upon this kind of theological 'cost-benefit' analysis. It is logically permissible to believe anything that is not self-contradictory; nevertheless, not everything that is not self-contradictory makes good religious sense.

Previous chapters dealing with the contemporary two-minds form of traditional orthodoxy and with the divine self-emptying idea (kenosis) have led to the conclusion that a Chalcedonian-type christology cannot be spelled out as a literal theory in any religiously acceptable way. Indeed the more philosophically ingenious christologies have become the less religiously realistic they seem to be. This conclusion can never of course be final, for it must always be theoretically possible for a new theory to be conceived that is free from serious objection. However, an immense intellectual effort has been put over the centuries into what must be regarded as unsuccessful attempts to formulate the incarnation dogma as a literal assertion. I do not think that the theoretical possibility of a successful theory in the future should now be allowed to hold up the development of theologies which are compatible with the growing contemporary acceptance of Christianity as one valid way among others of conceptualizing and responding to the divine.

Such theologies will not see the idea of God's incarnation in the life of Jesus as having a literal physical or psychological or metaphysical meaning. But this does not entail that it has no meaning. Let us consider the alternative possibility that 'incarnation' in its theological use is a metaphor. It is an unusual kind of metaphor, since it began as literally intended language. The more usual transition is in the opposite direction, a metaphor 'dying' as metaphor to become literal speech. But in the case of divine incarnation the initial idea has proved to be devoid of literal meaning and accordingly identified as metaphor, functioning in a way that is continuous with its non-religious uses.

The metaphor of incarnation is a familiar one. We meet it, for example, in 'the qualities incarnated in a hero', or 'great men are incarnations of the spirit of their age'. Recently General Eva Burrows of the Salvation Army said in a BBC radio programme (1 July 1990), 'we want to be an incarnation of Christ in the world'. She did not mean that we want be 'of one substance with God the Father', but to be Christ's dedicated servants, carrying out God's purposes on earth. Again, if we say that Joan of Arc incarnated the resurgent spirit of France in 1429, or that George Washington incarnated the spirit of American Independence in 1776, or that Winston Churchill incarnated the British will to resist Hitler in 1940, we are using a natural and effective metaphor which communicates something important about the characters and historical roles of St Joan, Washington and Churchill. It says something that is capable of being true or false – true or false in the sense that the metaphor is appropriate and illuminating or inappropriate and misleading.

In the case of the metaphor of divine incarnation, what was lived out, made flesh, incarnated in the life of Jesus can be indicated in at least three ways, each of which is an aspect of the fact that Jesus was a human being exceptionally open and responsive to the divine presence: (1) In so far as Jesus was doing God's will, God was acting through him on earth and was in this respect 'incarnate' in Jesus' life; (2) In so far as Jesus was doing God's will he 'incarnated' the ideal of human life lived in openness and response to God; (3) In so far as Jesus lived a life of self-giving love, or *agape*, he 'incarnated' a love that is a finite reflection of the infinite divine love. The truth or the appropriateness of the metaphor depends upon its being literally true that Jesus lived in obedient response to the divine presence, and that he lived a life of unselfish love.

It is worth noting at this point that metaphor can readily develop into myth in the sense of a powerful complex of ideas, usually in story form, which is not literally true but which may nevertheless be true in the practical sense that it tends to evoke an appropriate dispositional attitude to its subject-matter. A myth, so defined, is a much extended metaphor. Metaphors operate to change our way of seeing something and thus our stance in relationship to it; and myths, as multi-dimensional metaphors, do this in a larger and more comprehensive way. Thus there is a myth of the Maid of Orleans, and a Washington myth, and a Churchill myth, in which these are seen and revered in their own contexts as saviour figures. The historical reality was in each case more complex and ambiguous; but the myths nevertheless have their degree, perhaps a high degree, of validity and truthfulness.

The myth of God incarnate is the story of the pre-existent divine Son descending into human life, dying to atone for the sins of the world, thereby revealing the divine nature, and returning into the eternal life of the Trinity. The mythic story expresses the significance of a point in history where we can see human life lived in faithful response to God and see God's nature reflected in that human response. The author of the *Theologia Germanica* captured this when he wrote that the Christian (or indeed 'every enlightened man') should be able to say 'I would fain be to the Eternal Goodness what his own hand is to a man' (Winckworth 1937, 32). To the extent that a man or a woman is to God what one's own hand is to oneself, to that extent God is 'incarnate' in that human life. The idea of the incarnation of God in the life of Jesus, so understood, is thus not a metaphysical claim about Jesus having two natures, but a metaphorical statement of the significance of a life through which God was acting on earth. In Jesus we see a man living in a startling degree of awareness of God and of response to God's presence.

The essential difference, then, between the literal and metaphorical ways of speaking of divine incarnation is that whereas the first can (at least in intention) be spelled out as a physical or psychological or metaphysical hypothesis (or a mixture of these), the second cannot be so translated without destroying its metaphorical character. And my thesis concerning the Christian doctrine of incarnation is that as a literal hypothesis it has not been found to have any acceptable meaning. Every content that has been suggested has had to be rejected as mistaken or, in traditional ecclesiastical language, heretical. Indeed the basic heresy has always been to treat religious metaphor as literal metaphysics. But on the other hand, as religious metaphor or myth the idea of incarnation communicates something of momentous importance about Jesus, something that forms the basis of distinctively Christian experience and faith.

In recent times this type of christology (or, better, this type of understanding of Jesus) has been developed by a number of writers, of whom I shall refer to two. One is Donald Baillie, a Presbyterian theologian whose book *God Was in Christ*[4] was described by Rudolf Bultmann as 'the most significant book of our time in the field of Christology' (Bultmann 1957, 35). Not only the title but the entire tone of Baillie's book shows that his intention was wholly orthodox. He was not criticizing the idea of divine incarnation in Jesus but was trying to make this intelligible to the modern mind. He did so by understanding incarnation in terms of what he called the paradox of grace. This is the paradoxical fact that when we do God's will it is

---

[4]Donald Baillie 1948. It is now ironic that one of the first articles that I published (Hick 1958) was a criticism of Baillie for his departure from Chalcedonian orthodoxy. I have, however, subsequently come to agree with Maurice Wiles about this (Wiles 1963, 1974 and 1977).

true both that we are acting freely and responsibly, and also that God, by divine grace, is acting in and through us. The paradox is summed up in Paul's words concerning his own labours, 'it was not I, but the grace of God which is with me' (I Corinthians 15.10). As Baillie says, the essence of the paradox

> lies in the conviction which a Christian man possesses, that every good thing in him, every good thing he does, is somehow not wrought by himself but by God. This is a highly paradoxical conviction, for in ascribing all to God it does not abrogate human personality nor disclaim personal responsibility. Never is human action more truly and fully personal, never does the agent feel more perfectly free, than in those moments of which he can say as a Christian that whatever good was in them was not his but God's (114).

Baillie now uses this paradox of grace as the clue to the yet greater paradox of the incarnation: that the life of Jesus was an authentically human life and yet that in and through that life God was at work on earth. He says:

> What I wish to suggest is that this paradox of grace points the way more clearly and makes a better approach than anything else in our experience to the mystery of the Incarnation itself; that this paradox in its fragmentary form in our own Christian lives is a reflection of that perfect union of God and man in the Incarnation on which our whole Christian life depends, and may therefore be our best clue to the understanding of it. In the New Testament we see the man in whom God was incarnate surpassing all other men in refusing to claim anything for himself independently and ascribing all the goodness to God. We see him also desiring to take up other men into his own close union with God, that they might be as he was. And if these men, entering in some small measure through him into that union, experience the paradox of grace for themselves in fragmentary ways, and are constrained to say, "It was not I but God", may not this be a clue to the understanding of that perfect life in which the paradox is complete and absolute, that life of Jesus which, being the perfection of humanity, is also, and even in a deeper and prior sense, the very life of God himself? If the paradox is a reality in our poor imperfect lives at all, so far as there is any good in them, does not the same or a similar paradox, taken at the perfect and

absolute pitch, appear as the mystery of the Incarnation? (117-
18).

In other words, the union of divine grace and human action which
occurs whenever God's grace works effectively in a man's or a
woman's life was operating to an absolute extent in the life of Jesus.
Jesus was not, on this view, the second person of a divine Trinity
living a human life and having both a divine and a human nature,
but was a man responding totally to divine grace and doing the will
of God. I shall return presently to these important qualifiers,
'absolute' and 'totally'.

A variant on essentially the same theme of humanity responsive
to God's grace sees Jesus as a man inspired by the divine Spirit. Such
a christology has been presented, for example, by Geoffrey Lampe,
an Anglican theologian and New Testament scholar who was
Regius Professor of Divinity at Cambridge University until his
death in 1980. In *God As Spirit*[5] he uses as his model the activity
within human life of the Spirit of God. The divine Spirit, however,
he says, 'is to be understood, not as referring to a divine hypostasis
distinct from God the Father and God the Son or Word, but as
indicating God himself as active towards and in his human creation'
(11). The principal activity in relation to humanity of God as Spirit
is inspiration; and accordingly the christology which Lampe presents is 'a Christology of inspiration' (96). For 'the concept of the
inspiration and indwelling of man by God as Spirit is particularly
helpful in enabling us to speak of God's continuing presence in
Jesus as the central and focal point within this relationship' (34).
Again, 'the use of this concept enables us to say that God indwelt
and motivated the human spirit of Jesus in such a way that in him,
uniquely, the relationship for which man is intended by his Creator
was fully realized' (11). I shall return to the qualifiers 'uniquely'
and 'fully'.

Using the conception of some of the Greek-speaking Fathers of
the church, such as Irenaeus, of the gradual creation of human
beings through their own freedom from an initial state of im-
maturity towards the finite 'likeness' of God (as distinguished from
the Augustinian picture of the fall of humanity from a state of
original righteousness), Lampe says that 'the Spirit transforms man
into that which he was not; yet this transformation is continuous

---

[5]Geoffrey Lampe 1977. For another version of a Spirit christology see Paul W.
Newman 1987.

with creation; it is the completion of creation' (18). On this view the Spirit of God has always been active within the human spirit, inspiring men and women to open themselves freely to the divine presence and to respond in their lives to the divine purpose. This continuous creative activity means that 'God has always been incarnate in his human creatures, forming their spirit from within and revealing himself in and through them' (23). We must accordingly 'speak of this continuum as a single creative and saving activity of God the Spirit towards, and within, the spirit of man, and of his presence in the person of Jesus as a particular moment within that continuous creativity' (100). For 'a union of personal deity with human personality can only be a perfected form of inspiration' (12).

It seems likely that this was in fact the earliest form of christology within the church. As Wolfhart Pannenberg says, 'Probably the oldest attempt to express God's presence in Jesus was characterized by the concept of the Spirit' (Pannenberg 1968, 116). He adds: 'At first the "Son of God" concept did not express a participation in the divine essence. Only in Gentile Christianity was the divine Sonship understood physically as participation in the divine essence. In the Jewish, also in the Hellenistic-Jewish, sphere, in contrast, the expression "Son of God" still retained the old meaning of adoption and of God's presence through his Spirit which was bestowed upon Jesus for a long time' (117).

This type of inspiration or paradox-of-grace christology seems to me a good rendering of the religious significance of Jesus, well expressed by the metaphor of divine incarnation. However, in the course of centuries the 'indefinable aura of meaning' attaching to the metaphor has been greatly inflated in the Christian mind by association with the literal Chalcedonian understanding of incarnation. For the realization is only now dawning on any wide scale that the belief in Jesus as God incarnate is a metaphorical rather than a literal physical, psychological or metaphysical affirmation. This realization involves the abandonment of something that Baillie and Lampe both assumed without question. For if, with them, we see in the life of Jesus a special instance of the fusion of divine grace/ inspiration and creaturely freedom that occurs in all authentic human response and obedience to God, we can ask how this particular instance compares with others. We are not speaking of something that is in principle unique, but of an interaction of the divine and the human which occurs in many different ways and degrees in all human openness to God's presence. Baillie assumed, as axiomatic for Christians, that Jesus' response to divine grace was uniquely 'complete' and 'absolute'; and Lampe that in Jesus we see 'a perfected form of inspiration', so that 'in him, uniquely, the relationship for which man is intended by his Creator was fully realized'. But neither of them seems to have noticed that the idea of the paradox of grace, or of divine inspiration, does not by itself entail this. It leaves open the further question of the relationship between the operation of God's grace/inspiration in Jesus and in other outstanding religious figures. In other words, whereas the Chalcedonian christology entailed the unique status of Jesus as the one and only person with both a human nature and a divine nature, a grace/inspiration christology does not by itself single him out in this way. It can no longer be an *a priori* dogma that Jesus is the supreme point of contact between God and humankind. This is now a matter of historical judgment, subject to all the difficulties and uncertainties of such judgments.

These difficulties and uncertainties have been emphasized by many New Testament scholars. How could we establish on historical grounds that Jesus was perfectly sinless, or that he always lived in perfect response to God, or that he was in all respects morally and spiritually superior to every other human being who has ever lived? The difficulty arises from the slight and fragmentary nature of the historical evidence available to us. In my own learning process it was Dennis Nineham who made this unmistakably clear. He recalls that 'B.H. Streeter once calculated that, apart from the forty days and nights in the wilderness (about which we are told virtually nothing), everything reported to have been said and done by Jesus in all four gospels would have occupied only some three weeks, which leaves the overwhelmingly greater part of his life and deeds unrecorded' (Nineham 1977, 188-9). He cites a number of passages from Christian writers (including one from myself before I had taken Nineham's point) to the effect that, in John A.T. Robinson's words, 'It is in Jesus, and Jesus *alone*, that there is *nothing* of self to be seen, but *solely* the ultimate, unconditional love of God. It is as he emptied himself *utterly* of himself that he became the carrier of the "name which is above every name"' (Robinson 1963, 74, italics added). Nineham asks, 'Is it, however, possible to validate claims of the kind in question on the basis of historical evidence? To prove an historical negative, such as the sinlessness of Jesus, is notoriously difficult to the point of impossibility . . . [T]he sort of claims for Jesus we are discussing could not be justified to the hilt by *any* historical records, however full or intimate or contemporary they might be, and even if their primary concern was with the quality and development of Jesus' inner life and character' (Nineham 1977, 188) – which of course the Gospels were not. This now opens up the questions of other intersections of divine grace/inspiration and human freedom lying at the origin of other religious traditions (to be discussed in Chapters 13 and 14), and of the difference that it will make as the realization of all this becomes more general within the churches (to be discussed in Chapter 15).

11

Atonement by the Blood of Jesus?

The term 'atonement' is so deeply embedded in Christian discourse that almost every theologian feels obliged to have a doctrine of some kind under this heading. And yet the word is so variously used that some of these doctrines have little in common except the name. In its broad etymological meaning, at-one-ment signifies becoming one with God – not ontologically but in the sense of entering into a right relationship with our creator, this being the process or state of salvation. But in its narrower sense atonement refers to a specific method of receiving salvation, one presupposing that the barrier to this is guilt. It is in this context that we find the ideas of penalty, redemption, sacrifice, oblation, propitiation, expiation, satisfaction, substitution, forgiveness, acquittal, ransom, justification, remission of sins, forming a complex of ideas which has long been central to the Western or Latin development of Christianity.

In this narrower sense, Jesus' crucifixion was an act of atoning, or making up for, human sin. On the other hand, in the broader sense in which atonement simply means salvation, or entering into a right relationship with God, Jesus' death may or may not be separated off from his self-giving life as a whole as having a special significance of its own. As a rough approximation we can say that the broader sense has been more at home in the Eastern or Greek development of Christianity and the narrower in its Western or Latin development.

In my view it would be best, in the interests of clarity, to restrict the term 'atonement' to its narrower and more specific meaning. The basic notion is then that salvation requires God's forgiveness and that this in turn requires an adequate atonement to satisfy the divine righteousness and/or justice. This atoning act is a transaction, analogous to making a payment to wipe out a debt or cancel an impending punishment. In the background there is the idea of the moral order of the universe which requires that sin, as a disruption of that order, be restored either by just punishment of the offender or a substitute, or by some adequate satisfaction in lieu of punishment.

I am going to argue that in this narrower sense the idea of atonement is a mistake; although of course the broader sense, in which atonement simply means salvation, is vitally important.

In so arguing I am, I think, reflecting a widespread contemporary perception. Indeed were it not for its recent revival by some Christian philosophers who, unlike most contemporary theologians, tend to see church doctrine as a set of immutable truths, one could easily think that the notion of atonement, in its narrower sense, had largely died out among thoughtful Christians. For modern treatments of salvation seldom centre upon Anselm's doctrine of a satisfaction to cancel the insult to God's majesty caused by creaturely disobedience, or the penal-substitutionary idea of an imputed justification won by Christ's taking upon himself the punishment due for human sin.

However, as with other traditional doctrines, it is important to try to go back in historical imagination to the original experience out of which it grew. It is evident that the profound and all-absorbing experience of the early post-Easter Christian community was of a living spirit, which they identified as the spirit of the risen Jesus, welling up within them, individually and corporately, and drawing them into a new, joyous and exhilarating form of life, full of positive meaning and free from the besetting fears of the ancient world – of demons, of fate, of sin, and of death. This new liberated life, overflowing with meaning and hope, was the religious reality that was to be expressed, first in what seem to us today a cluster of bizarre images, and later, within medieval Latin Christianity, in various sophisticated theories of a transactional atonement. However, we in the Western churches today, both Catholic and Reformed, may well feel that none of these inherited theories retains any real plausibility and that we should look again at the alternative development within Eastern Christianity of the idea of a gradual transformation of the human by the divine Spirit, called by the Orthodox theologians deification (*theosis*).

These two conceptions do not of course exclude each other. Latin theology has also held that the justification won by Jesus' death leads to sanctification, which is the gradual transformation of the sinner into a saint. And Orthodox theology also holds that Jesus' death was somehow crucial in bringing about human 'deification'. And since both traditions use the same stock of biblical images, one can find much the same language somewhere within each. Nevertheless, their basic tendencies move in different directions, one guided by a transactional-atonement conception and the other by a transformational conception of salvation.

We shall come back later to the Eastern tradition and its transformation conception, but in the meantime let us look more closely at the transactional model.

Before the division between the Eastern and Western churches the earliest attempt to conceptualize the Christian experience of liberation and new life fastened upon the Markan saying of Jesus, that 'the Son of man also came not to be served but to serve, and to give his life as a ransom (*lutron*) for many' (Mark 10.45). Ransom had a poignant meaning in the ancient world, when a considerable proportion of the population lived in a state of slavery, and free citizens were liable to become slaves if their tribe, city or nation was defeated in war. Being ransomed, and thus made free, was accordingly a vivid and powerful metaphor whose force most of us can only partially recapture today.

But, making the perennial theological mistake of taking metaphorical language literally, the early Christian theologians asked themselves to whom Jesus was, by his death, paying a ransom; and the inevitable answer was the devil – who else? In the words of Origen, 'To whom gave he his life "a ransom for many"? It cannot have been to God. Was it not then to the evil one? For he held us until the ransom for us, even the soul of Christ, was paid to him' (Grensted 1962, 38). And so for many centuries – indeed virtually until Anselm introduced his satisfaction theory in the eleventh century – it was generally accepted by Christian writers and preachers that the human race had fallen through sin under the jurisdiction of the devil and that the cross of Christ was part of a bargain with the devil to ransom us. Within this literature there is also, as a sub-plot reminiscent of fairy-story themes, the idea that in this bargain God outwitted the devil, transforming a situation in which he had a just claim over humanity into one in which he had put himself in the wrong by taking a greater ransom, namely God the Son, than was his due. Thus Gregory of Nyssa said that 'in order to secure that the ransom in our behalf might be easily accepted by him who required it, the Deity was hidden under the veil of our nature, that so, as with ravenous fish, the hook of the Deity might be gulped down along with the bait of the flesh' (Gregory of Nyssa 1892b, 494). St Augustine even more picturesquely suggested in one of his sermons that 'As our price he [Christ] held out his cross to him like a mouse trap, and as a bait set on it his own blood' (Grensted 1962, 44). Such imagery is only embarrassing today. But whilst the ransom theory was never elevated to credal authority, it was very widely used, occurring in the writings of Irenaeus, Origen, Gregory of Nyssa, Ambrose, Rufinus, Gregory the Great, Augustine and Chrysostom. Nevertheless it is impossible today to make any good sense or use of it. As Anselm later asked, Why should we accept that the Devil has any valid legal rights over against the infinite Creator? (Anselm 1962, 187-9). The wonder is that such a notion lasted so long. As Grensted says, 'That such a theory could stand for nine hundred years as the ordinary exposition of the fact of the Atonement is itself a sufficient proof that the need for serious discussion of the doctrine had not as yet been felt.'[1]

When the need for serious discussion did begin to be felt, the theories that were produced were premised on the belief in original sin as an inherited guilt affecting the entire human race and requiring an adequate atonement to expunge it. To attack this idea is today, for most of us, to do battle with an extinct monster. Nevertheless the ecclesiastical reluctance to abandon traditional language is so strong that even today there is point in being clear why we should cease to think and speak in terms of original sin – except as a mythological way of referring to the fact of universal human imperfection. For the original sin idea presupposes the wilful fall from grace of the first humans and the genetic inheritance by the whole species of a guilty and sinful nature. This is something that only doctrinal fundamentalists can accept today. But prior to the Enlightenment of the eighteenth century it was a seriously entertained idea. Thus the Catholic Council of Trent (1545-63) pronounced that 'If anyone does not profess that the first man Adam immediately lost the justice and holiness in which he was constituted when he disobeyed the command of God in the Garden of Paradise; and that, through the offence of this sin, he incurred the wrath and the indignation of God, and consequently incurred the

[1] L.W. Grensted 1962, 33. What Gustav Aulen called the 'classic' theory of atonement, according to which Christ was victor over the devil, seems to me to be a variation on the ransom model – a variation in which the ransomer is attacked and defeated instead of being paid off – rather than a radically alternative theory. 'Its central theme,' says Aulen, 'is the idea of the Atonement as a Divine conflict and victory; Christ – Christus Victor – fights against and triumphs over the evil powers of the world, the "tyrants" under which mankind is in bondage and suffering . . .' (Aulen 1953, 20).

death with which God had previously threatened him . . . And if anyone asserts that Adam's sin was injurious only to Adam and not to his descendants . . . or that . . . he transmitted to the whole human race only death and punishment of the body but not sin itself which is the death of the soul: let him be anathema' (Abbott 1966, 158-9: Denzinger 788-9); whilst the Presbyterian Westminster Confession (1647) declared that 'Our first parents being seduced by the subtilty and temptation of Satan, sinned in eating the forbidden fruit . . . By this sin they fell from their original righteousness, and communion with God, and so became dead in sin, and wholly defiled in all the faculties and parts of soul and body. They being the root of all mankind, the guilt of this sin was imputed, and the same death in sin and corrupted nature conveyed to all their posterity, descending from them by ordinary generation' (ch. 6).

However, today the idea of an actual human fall resulting in a universal inherited depravity and guilt is totally unbelievable for educated Christians. Instead of the human race being descended from a single specially created pair, we see the species as having evolved out of lower forms of life over an immensely long period of time. Instead of the earliest humans living in perfect communion with the God of Judaeo-Christian monotheism, we see them as probably having a primitive animistic outlook. Instead of them living in harmony with nature and with one another we see them as engaged in a struggle to survive in competition with other animals and probably with other human groups within an often harsh environment. If out of piety towards the traditional language we wish to retain the term 'The Fall', we can say that the earliest humans were, metaphorically speaking, already 'fallen' in the sense of being morally and spiritually imperfect. That is to say, they can be said to be as though they had fallen from an ideal state. But since that state never existed, would it not be better to abandon the concept of the Fall altogether? For if we believe that there never was a human fall from an original paradisal state, why risk confusing ourselves and others by speaking as if there were?

I take it that our endemic individual and corporate self-centredness, from which the many forms of moral evil flow, is an aspect of our nature as animals engaged in the universal struggle for survival; and that this self-centred propensity exists in tension with a distinctively human capacity for ego-transcendence in response to the felt claim upon us of moral values. In this tension we have a genuine, though limited, freedom and responsibility; and in so far as we are free we are guilty for our own wrong choices. There is thus a genuine problem of guilt. I shall return to this presently. But at the moment we are concerned with the ancient notion of original sin. For it is this that has fed the traditional conceptions of atonement. In the light of a typical contemporary ethic the idea of an inherited guilt for being born as the kind of being that we are is a moral absurdity. We cannot be guilty in the sight of God for having been born, within God's providence, as animals biologically programmed for self-protection and survival within a tough environment. And even if we discount our modern awareness of the continuity between *homo sapiens* and the rest of animal life, the moral principle behind the traditional doctrine is still totally unacceptable. Although evidently believable in the age in which it was propounded, the idea of a universal inherited guilt was losing plausibility by the end of the eighteenth century and had entirely lost it, for many, by the end of the nineteenth.

We have already seen in the ransom idea the way in which theology has drawn its soteriological models from the structures of contemporary society – originally the pervasive fact of slavery and the life-giving possibility of being ransomed from it. The next model to dominate the Christian imagination was proposed by St Anselm in his *Cur Deus Homo?* (completed in its present form in 1098), which together with his *Proslogion* was among the most influential theological books ever written. Anselm took over the concept of satisfaction which had long operated in both church and society. This was the idea that disobedience, whether to God or to one's feudal lord, was a slight upon his honour and dignity, and required for its cancellation an appropriate penance or gift in satisfaction. In the medieval penitential system a sinner's prescribed act of penance was believed to be accepted by God as restoring the moral balance and likewise, when one did something to undermine the dignity and authority of one's earthly overlord, one had either to be punished or to give some sufficient satisfaction to appease the lord's injured dignity. This notion, reflecting a strongly hierarchical and tightly-knit society, evidently made sense within the culture of medieval Europe.

Against this background Anselm defined sin as 'nothing else than not to render to God his due' (Anselm 1962, 202; Part I, chapter 11). What is due to God is absolute obedience: 'He who does not render this honour which is due to God, robs God of his own and dishonours him; and this is sin . . . So then, everyone who sins ought to pay back the honour of which he has robbed God; and this is the satisfaction which every sinner owes to God' (Part I, chapter 11). Further, 'Even God cannot raise to happiness any being bound at all by the debt of sin, because he ought not to' (Part I, chapter 21). However, it is impossible for humanity to make the necessary satisfaction; for even if we were perfectly obedient in the future, we would only be giving to God what is already due to him, and a satisfaction requires something extra that was not already due. Further, because God is the lord of the whole universe the adequate satisfaction for a slight upon the divine honour 'cannot be effected, except the price paid to God for the sin of man be something greater than all the universe besides God' (Part II, chapter 6). And, to add to the difficulty, since it is humanity who has offended God, it must be humanity that makes the restitution. Thus, since the needed satisfaction is one which 'none but God can make and none but man ought to make, it is necessary for the God-man to make it' (Part II, chapter 6). The God-man can give something that was not already owing to God, namely his own life: 'For God will not demand this of him as a debt; for, as no sin will be found, he ought not to die' (Part II, chapter 11). Accordingly, Christ's voluntary death on the cross constituted a full satisfaction for the sins of the world. This is the Anselmic theory.

However, in our own more democratic age it is virtually impossible to share Anselm's medieval sense of wrongdoing as a slight upon God's honour which requires a satisfaction to assuage the divine dignity before even the truly penitent can receive forgiveness. The entire conception, presupposing as it does a long-since vanished social order, now makes little sense to us; and in my view it would be best to cease altogether to use it in our contemporary theologies and liturgies.

Yet another emphasis was introduced by the Reformers in the sixteenth century. They made the originally Pauline idea of justification central, understanding it in a legal sense, defined by Melanchthon as follows: 'To justify, in accordance with forensic usage, here signifies to acquit the accused and to pronounce him righteous, but on account of the righteousness of another, namely of Christ, which righteousness of another is communicated to us by faith' (Grensted 1962, 193). The concept of justification, and hence of salvation as being counted innocent in the eyes of God, emerged from the background of an understanding of law that had changed since Anselm's time. In the medieval world, law was an expression of the will of the ruler, and transgression was an act of personal disobedience and dishonour for which either punishment or satisfaction was required. But the concept of an objective justice, set over ruled and ruler alike, had been developing in Europe since the Renaissance. Law was now thought to have its own eternal validity, requiring a punishment for wrongdoing which could not be set aside even by the ruler. It was this new principle that the Reformers applied and extended in their doctrine that Christ took our place in bearing the inexorable penalty for human sin – a powerful imagery that has long gripped the Christian imagination:

> He died that we might be forgiven,
>   He died to make us good,
> That we might go at last to heaven
>   Saved by his precious blood.
>
> There was no other good enough
>   To pay the price of sin;
> He only could unlock the gate
>   Of heaven and let us in.

It is hardly necessary today to criticize this penal-substitutionary conception, so totally implausible has it become for most of us. The idea that guilt can be removed from a wrongdoer by someone else being punished instead is morally grotesque. And if we put it in what might at first sight seem a more favourable light by suggesting that God punished Godself, in the person of God the Son, in order to be able justly to forgive sinners, we are still dealing with the religious absurdity of a moral law which God can and must satisfy by punishing the innocent in place of the guilty. As Anselm pointed out long ago, through his interlocutor in *Cur Deus Homo?*, 'it is a strange thing if God so delights in, or requires, the blood of the innocent, that he neither chooses, nor is able, to spare the guilty without the sacrifice of the innocent' (Anselm 1962, 200; Book I, chapter 10).

Richard Swinburne, in his *Responsibility and Atonement*, has recently made an impressive attempt to retrieve a transactional conception.[2] His understanding of salvation can be summarized as follows:

---

[2]Richard Swinburne 1989. Another different such attempt is that of Eleanor Stump 1988 and 1989.

(1)   Guilt in relation to God is the great barrier to salvation, i.e. to receiving God's gift of eternal life. (This is assumed throughout Swinburne's discussion.)

(2)   In the case of wrong done by one human being to another, reconciliation requires four things: repentance, apology, whatever reparation (i.e. undoing of the harm done) is possible, and penance, i.e. some additional act – such as the giving of a costly gift – which is not part of the reparation but is an expression of the reality of one's regret and sorrow at having done the wrong (Chapter 5).

(3)   God is a personal being – though absolutely unique in nature – with whom we exist in the same kind of moral relationship as to our fellow human beings, and the same general conditions for reconciliation apply. (This is assumed throughout Part II, though not explicitly stated.)

(4)   All wrong-doing to fellow humans is also wrong-doing done to God. For, 'Man's dependence on God is so total that he owes it to him to live a good life. Hence when a man fails in any objective or subjective duty of his fellows, he also fails in his duty towards God, his creator' (124).

(5)   We can repent and apologize to God for our sins, but we cannot on our own offer adequate atonement, i.e. reparation and penance. For, 'Since what needs atonement to God is human sin, men living second-rate lives when they have been given such great opportunities by their creator, appropriate reparation and penance would be made by a perfect human life' (157).

(6)   That 'perfect human life' is provided by Christ, who lived without sin and voluntarily endured a death which he openly intended as a sacrifice that we, accepting it from him, can offer to God as atonement for our sins, both individual and corporate. Christ's death is thus 'an offering made available to us men to offer as our reparation and penance'. 'There is no need,' Swinburne adds, 'to suppose that life and death [of Christ's] to be the equivalent of what men owe to God (or that plus appropriate penance), however that could be measured. It is simply a costly penance and reparation sufficient for a merciful God to let men off the rest' (154).

(7)   To be sanctified and thus finally saved is only possible to those who (as well as repenting and apologizing) participate in the Christian worship of God and plead the atoning death of Christ, thereby throwing off their guilt. To be saved we must thus be

joined – either in this life or hereafter – to the Christian church, which is the Body of Christ (173).

I think it must be granted that all this is possible; and indeed those of us who were once fundamentalist Christians, 'washed in the blood of the Lamb', are likely to feel an emotional tug towards this set of ideas. The question is not, however, whether such a schema is logically possible, but whether it is religiously plausible; and to many of us today it is likely to seem highly implausible, even though also with elements of truth within it. I shall comment from this point of view on the seven points listed above.

1. That the idea of salvation revolves around the issues of guilt and atonement is a central theme of the Latin theological tradition, launched above all by St Augustine. The Greek tradition, on the other hand, stemming from the early Hellenistic fathers of the church and preserved within Eastern Orthodoxy, thinks of salvation as deification or (perhaps better) transformation. Forgiveness is, of course, an element within this, but does not have the central place that the Latin tradition, followed by Swinburne at this point, gives to it. Swinburne prefers the Greek to the Latin development on a number of issues; nevertheless, he does not seem to have considered the radical alternative which the Eastern theological projectory offers. If one sees salvation/liberation as the transformation of human existence from self-centredness to a new orientation centred in the ultimate divine Reality, the transaction theories of salvation then appear as implausible answers to a mistaken question.

2. Swinburne's analysis of guilt and reconciliation between human beings is excellent; this is one of the 'elements of truth', as it will seem to more liberal Christians, within his total theory.

3. That God is another person, with unique attributes but subject to the same moral requirements as ourselves, and thus with obligations and duties and possibilities of supererogatory deeds; that God's probable procedures can be predicted by means of a human analogy; and that this leads to the belief that God's saving work is confined in its fullness to the Christian strand of history – this strikes me as anthropomorphic, parochial and unimaginative to a degree that renders it massively implausible. But I shall say more under point 5 about Swinburne's transfer of the conditions for reconciliation with a fellow human being to reconciliation with God.

4. That our relationship to fellow human beings involves our

relationship to God, so that in all that we do we are also ultimately having to do with God, is from a more liberal point of view another 'element of truth' within Swinburne's theory.

5.   When we do wrong the kind of reparation required is that we do what we can to nullify or reverse the consequences of our action. Thus when we contribute – as we do almost all the time – to the common evils of the world, we can do something to counter this by contributing to the common good of the world. When we wrong an individual we can usually do something to recompense the person wronged. And, as Swinburne points out, in such a case it is also appropriate to do something extra, which he calls penance, by offering some additional service or gift to express the reality of our regret and sorrow at having wronged that other person. But the question that has to be asked is whether this four-fold schema – repentance, apology, reparation and penance – can be carried over unchanged into our relationship with God. Swinburne's fundamental error, in my view, is in assuming that it can. Repentance, and apology as an expression of repentance, still apply; the sinner should truly and deeply repent and ask God's forgiveness. But is there also scope, specifically in relation to God, for reparation and the extra that Swinburne calls penance? I suggest that when we have offered reparation-plus-penance to the human beings whom we have injured, there is no further reparation-plus-penance to be made solely for God's benefit. In doing all we can to repair matters with our wronged neighbour we are doing what genuine repentance requires. For God cannot be benefitted, and thus recompensed and atoned to, by any human acts in addition to those that benefit God's creation. In relation to God the truly penitent person, genuinely resolving to do better in the future, can only accept forgiveness as a free gift of grace, undeserved and unearned. It may well be Jesus' life and teaching that prompt someone to do this. But it is not, in my view, appropriate to express that fact by depicting his death as an atoning sacrifice that benefits God and so enables God to forgive humanity.

Swinburne emphasizes that 'One man can help another to make the necessary atonement – can persuade him to repent, help him to formulate the words of apology, and give him the means by which to make reparation and penance' (149). True; and likewise the divine Spirit may prompt us to a true repentance which wants to make reparation to the human individual or community that we have wronged, and to offer any additional service or gift that may be appropriate. But what the Spirit will thus prompt us to do is some act in relation to those human neighbours. It is this that satisfies the principle, which Swinburne rightly stresses, that to take a wrongdoer and his or her wrongdoing seriously entails the need for whatever restitution, and whatever additional gift or service, may be appropriate. But the idea that something further, corresponding to this reparation-plus-penance towards our human neighbour, is required by God for Godself, seems to me groundless. It rests upon a category mistake in which God is treated as another individual within the same moral community as ourselves. For a moral relationship with another person presupposes the possibility of actions that can benefit or injure that other person; but we cannot benefit or injure our creator over and above our actions in benefitting and injuring our fellow creatures.

Further, even if, despite this, a benefit solely to God were possible and required, Swinburne's unargued assumption that a perfect human life would constitute it is, surely, illogical. A perfect life, fulfilling every 'objective and subjective duty', is already, according to Swinburne, owed by all of us to God, and therefore could not constitute a reparation-plus-penance for not having lived a perfect life in the past. And yet again, even if *per impossible* it could, how would one single perfect human life, namely that of Jesus, count as all human beings having led perfect lives? Swinburne's answer at this point is that God was free to accept whatever God wished as an atonement for human sin. 'God could,' he says, 'have chosen to accept one supererogatory act of an ordinary man as adequate for the sins of the world. Or he could have chosen to accept some angel's act for this purpose' (160). This is a deeply damaging admission, rendering it truly extraordinary that God should require the agonizing death of God's Son. For on Swinburne's view there was no necessity for the cross, such as was provided in their own way by the satisfaction and penal-substitutionary theories. Swinburne is abandoning the idea of a moral law that could only be satisfied by Jesus' death. For it was, according to him, entirely within God's free choice to establish the conditions for human salvation. But in that case God's insistence on the blood, sweat, pain and anguish involved in the crucifixion of God's innocent Son now seems even to cast doubt on the moral character of the deity.

6. Swinburne says several times that Jesus openly intended his death as 'an offering to God to make expiation in some way for the sins of men' (122). There is in fact no consensus among New

Testament scholars as to how Jesus understood his own death. To what extent did he think of it as having religious significance? There is a range of possibilities. A theologically minimalist view is expressed by E.P. Sanders. He lists it as 'conceivable' (Sanders 1985, 326) or even 'possible' (332) – in distinction from 'probable', 'highly probable', or 'virtually certain' – that Jesus 'may have given his own death a martyrological significance' (326). Acknowledging, indeed emphasizing, the historical uncertainties, he notes that 'the idea that a martyr's death is beneficial for others and that his cause will be vindicated is attested in Judaism . . . It is not necessary to assume that Jesus indicated to his followers that they should think in this way. Once he died, it probably seemed entirely natural to attribute benefit to his death and look for vindication' (324-5).

At the other end of the scale is the older view of Joachim Jeremias, developed in his influential treatment of the last supper. He recalls that a lamb was killed at the original passover and its blood smeared, at Jahweh's command, on the Israelites' doors: 'As a reward for the Israelites' obedience to the commandment to spread blood on their doors, God manifested himself and spared them, "passing over" their houses. For the sake of the passover blood God revoked the death sentence against Israel; he said: "I will see the blood of the passover and make atonement for you". In the same way the people of God of the End time will be redeemed by the merits of the passover blood. Jesus describes his death as this eschatological passover sacrifice: his vicarious death brings into operation the final deliverance, the new covenant of God' (Jeremias 1965, 226). And Jeremias concludes, 'This is therefore what Jesus said at the Last Supper about the meaning of his death: his death is the vicarious death of the suffering servant, which atones for the sins of the "many", the peoples of the world, which ushers in the beginning of the final salvation and which effects the new covenant with God' (231).

On Jeremias' interpretation we have to suppose that Jesus, in E. P. Sanders' words, 'conceived in advance the doctrine of atonement' (Sanders 1985, 332), a supposition which Sanders regards as historically highly improbable. 'Aspects of Jeremias' view, for example that Jesus identified himself with the Suffering Servant of Isaiah, have,' he says, 'been disproved, but there are general objections to the whole line of thought that has Jesus intending to die for others, rather than just accepting his death and trusting that God would redeem the situation and vindicate him' (332). However, let us nevertheless suppose, for the sake of argument, that Jesus did understand his coming death as a sacrifice to God, analogous to the original passover sacrifice, and that he thought of this as required to inaugurate God's coming kingdom. Such a self-understanding could only occur within the context of Jesus' apocalyptic expectation, which was itself a variation on contemporary Jewish restoration eschatology. But Jesus' expectation, confidently taken up by the early church, was not fulfilled, and had faded out of the Christian consciousness before the end of the first century. The identification of Jesus as the eschatological prophet inaugurating God's kingdom went with it, being progressively superseded by his exaltation to a divine status. This in turn made possible the various atonement theories which presuppose his divinity, eventually seeing the cross as (in the words of the Anglican liturgy) 'a full, perfect, and sufficient sacrifice, oblation, and satisfaction, for the sins of the whole world'. However, as we saw in Chapter 3, even conservative New Testament scholarship today does not suggest that Jesus thought of himself as God, or God the Son, second person of a divine Trinity, incarnate; and so we cannot reasonably suppose that he thought of his death in any way that presupposes that. It is much more believable, as a maximal possibility, that Jesus saw himself as the final prophet precipitating the coming of God's rule on earth, than that he saw it in anything like the terms developed by the church's later atonement theories.

It is incidentally noteworthy that Swinburne departs from the traditional view that the value of Jesus' death was equal to, or exceeded, the evil of human sin, so as to be able to balance it. Swinburne says that 'It is simply a costly penance and reparation sufficient for a merciful God to let men off the rest' (154). But if a merciful God can properly 'let men off the rest' without a full punishment having been inflicted or a full satisfaction exacted, why may not God freely forgive sinners who come in genuine penitence and a radically changed mind? The traditional atonement theories explained *why* God could not freely forgive penitent sinners. But what was intelligible – whether or not morally acceptable – on those theories becomes unintelligible, and doubly morally questionable, on Swinburne's view.

7. Swinburne also modifies the traditional exclusivist doctrine that salvation is confined to Christians, so that *extra ecclesiam nulla salus*, by adding that non-Christians may have an opportunity to be converted beyond this life. This epicycle of theory, although

departing from established teaching about the finality of death, is the only refuge left for one who is in general doctrinally fundamentalist but who does not wish to have to defend a manifestly morally repugnant position.

I thus do not find at all attractive or convincing this latest attempt to rehabilitate the conception of salvation as being brought about by Jesus' death as an atonement to God for human sin.

12

Salvation as Human Transformation

The basic fault of the traditional understandings of salvation within the Western development of Christianity is that they have no room for divine forgiveness! For a forgiveness that has to be bought by the bearing of a just punishment, or the giving of an adequate satisfaction, or the offering of a sufficient sacrifice, is not forgiveness, but merely an acknowledgment that the debt has been paid in full. But in the recorded teaching of Jesus there is, in contrast, genuine divine forgiveness for those who are truly penitent and vividly conscious of their utter unworthiness. In the Lord's Prayer we are taught to address God directly as our heavenly Father and to ask for forgiveness for our sins, expecting to receive this, the only condition being that we in turn forgive one another. There is no suggestion of the need for a mediator between ourselves and God or for an atoning death to enable God to forgive. Again, in the Lukan parable of the prodigal son, the father, when he sees his penitent son returning home, does not say, 'Because I am a just as well as a loving father, I cannot forgive him until someone has been duly punished for his sins', but rather he 'had compassion, and ran and embraced him and kissed him. And the son said unto to him, Father, I have sinned against heaven, and before you; I am no longer worthy to be called your son. But the father said to his servants, Bring quickly the best robe, and put it on him and put a ring on his hand, and shoes on his feet: and bring the fatted calf and kill it, and let us eat and make merry: for this my son was dead, and is alive again; he was lost, and is found' (Luke 15.20-24). And again, in the story of the Pharisee and the tax collector, the latter 'standing far off, would not lift up his eyes to heaven, but beat his breast, saying, God, be merciful to me a sinner.' Jesus says, 'I tell you, this man went down to his house justified' (Luke 18.13-14). And yet again, there is his insistence that he came to bring sinners to a penitent acceptance of God's mercy: 'Go and learn what this means, "I desire mercy, and not sacrifice." For I came not to call the righteous, but sinners' (Matthew 9.13).

This was fully in accord with contemporary Jewish understanding. E.P. Sanders, in his authoritative work on Jesus' Jewish background, says that 'The forgiveness of repentant sinners is a major motif in virtually all the Jewish material which is still available from the period' (Sanders 1985, 18); and it continues today in the prayers on the Day of Atonement. For Judaism sees human nature as basically good and yet also with an evil inclination that has continually to be resisted. However, God is aware of our finitude and weakness, and is always ready to forgive the truly penitent. In Islam there is an essentially similar view. God is always spoken of in the Qur'an as *Allah rahman rahim*, God the gracious and merciful. God knows our weakness and forgives those who, in the self-surrender of faith, bow before the compassionate Lord of the universe. Again, in the most widely influential of the Hindu scriptures, the *Bhagavad Gita*, we read,

Therefore I bow,
I prostrate myself,
I beg your grace,
For you are the Lord to be worshipped.
Please, God, be patient with me
As a father with his son, a friend with his friend,
A lover with his beloved (*Bhagavad Gita* 1979, 141; XI, 44).

This sense of divine mercy is indeed found throughout the world's theistic faiths, with our Latin belief in the need for an atoning human death standing out as exceptional. However, within contemporary Protestant thought there has come to be a widespread acceptance of the idea of a free divine forgiveness for those who truly repent. In an attempt to reconcile this with the traditional language about Jesus' death as the instrument of our salvation, various 'moral influence' theories have been proposed in the modern period. Their essence is admirably expressed in the old preachers' story about the tribal chief who urges his people to abandon cannibalism. When his urgings are ineffective he tells them that if they must kill someone they should go to a certain clearing the next day at dawn and kill the man they find there wrapped in a red blanket. They do so, and on opening the blanket they find that they have killed their own beloved chieftain; and they are so struck with remorse that they are at last motivated to give up their cannibalism. Likewise, it is suggested, remorse at having crucified the Son of God can lead to repentance and hence God's forgiveness.

Thus Auguste Sabatier wrote that Jesus' passion and death 'was the most powerful call to repentance that humanity has ever heard, and also the most operative and fruitful in marvellous results. The cross is the expiation of sins only because it is the cause of the repentance to which remission is promised' (Sabatier 1904, 127). This is no longer a transactional conception of atonement, and indeed no longer a conception of atonement, in the sense of expiation, at all. It is rather a suggestion about how Jesus' death may have helped to make salvation possible. The limitation, however, of this suggestion is that remorse at humanity having collectively killed God the Son can only be felt by that minority of human beings who believe that Jesus of Nazareth was indeed the second person of a divine Trinity. The notion, which the older satisfaction and penal-substitutionary theories made possible, of an atonement offered on behalf of all humanity, is here lost. The moral influence conception of atonement is in fact one of those theological epicycles by which it is sought to abandon an untenable traditional idea – in this case the transactional conception of salvation – whilst at the same time retaining the traditional language.

We can now move from a critique of the Western/Latin understanding of salvation as hinging upon sin and guilt, and as requiring the atoning sacrifice of Jesus, to build upon the work of the Hellenistic fathers, treating this, however, not as a fully developed theological option but as a movement of thought which can be continued today.

For Christianity is richer and more varied than most Christians, immersed within their own particular strand of it, have commonly been aware. Those of us formed by Western Christianity or its missionary extensions are often ignorant of the rather different eastern development of Christian thought. The Orthodox churches themselves, which are guardians of this tradition, have remained for many centuries more or less moribund both theologically and ecclesiastically – though recently there has been some interesting new activity. However, I am not advocating acceptance of the total Orthodox theological package. But buried within its history there is the groundwork of a profound and attractive alternative to the mediaeval theology of the Roman church as well as that of the sixteenth-century Reformers and their successors. The difference is between salvation as hinging upon an atoning transaction that enables God to forgive the fallen human race, and salvation as the gradual transformation of human beings, who already exist in the 'image' of God, into what the Hellenistic fathers, on the basis of Genesis 1.26, called the 'likeness' of God. Thus the eighth-century John of Damascus wrote in his *On the Orthodox Faith* (II.12) that 'The expression "according to the image" indicates rationality and freedom, whilst the expression "according to the likeness" indicates assimilation to God through virtue' (Ware 1963, 224). This 'assimilation to God' was also frequently called *theosis* (deification). In the words of the seventh-century Maximus the Confessor, 'A man who becomes obedient to God in all things hears God saying: "I said: you are gods" (John 10.34); he then is God and is called "God" not by nature or by relation but by [divine] decree and grace' (Meyendorff 1987, 164). This is the gradual transformation of the person from human animal into the finite 'likeness' of God; and it is this actual human change that constitutes salvation. Thus whilst on the Latin view to be saved is to be justified, i.e. relieved of guilt, by Christ's sacrificial death, on the Orthodox view to be in process of salvation is to be responding to the presence of the divine Spirit and thus gradually moving towards a radical new re-centring within the divine life. It should be noted that this Eastern understanding largely coincides with the modern 'liberal' approach initiated in the nineteenth century by Friedrich Schleiermacher, who viewed the saving influence of Christ in the context of God's total creative work, so that Christ's 'every activity may be regarded as a continuation of that person-forming divine influence upon human nature' (Schleiermacher 1956, 427).

In Orthodox thought the deification theme is embedded in a comprehensive theology in which the ideas of incarnation and Trinity are central elements and in which the resurrected Christ plays a vital role in the process of transformation. That role was, however, only described in broad metaphorical terms. Thus Athanasius said that humans 'could not become sons, being by nature creatures, otherwise than by receiving the Spirit of the natural and true Son. Wherefore, that this might be, "The Word became flesh" that He might make man capable of Godhead' (Athanasius 1957, 380); and again, 'He, indeed, assumed humanity that we might become God' (Athanasius 1989, 93). But the way in which God becoming human enables humans to become divine was not spelled out. Indeed it perhaps cannot be spelled out intelligibly except in terms of the experience, known within all religious traditions, of being influenced and changed by the life and words of a great exemplar. There is perhaps a continuity here with what

Adolf Deissmann called St Paul's 'mysticism' (Deissmann 1926, 193f.), with humans undergoing a transformation (*metamorphosis*) in Christ; for we 'are being changed into [Christ's] likeness from one degree of glory to another' (II Corinthians 3.18). We are to be transformed from the state of slavery into the state of sonship (Romans 8.15-17); or again, conformed (*symmorphosis*) to the image of Christ (8.29). 'Do not be conformed to the world,' Paul urges the Christians in Rome, 'but be transformed by the renewal of your mind' (12.2). And indeed we may say that to be a Christian is to be one in whose life Christ is the major, the largest single, influence (often among a variety of influences) for salvific transformation.

Jesus' death has indeed played no small part in this influence. Although the meaning of that death was pictured during most of the first Christian millennium in the bizarre ransom imagery, and during most of the second millennium in terms of the morally questionable satisfaction and penal-substitution theories, the cross has continued throughout as our central Christian symbol because it stirs deeper and more complex emotions than are captured by any of these official doctrines. It is for many people a self-evident intuition that an authentic religious leader is willing, if necessary, to be martyred by those who reject the challenging truths that he or she embodies. It is indeed because true prophets and gurus embody, or live out, or incarnate, their teachings that to oppose the message is to oppose the messenger; and the most emphatic form of rejection is by inflicting death. To illustrate this from recent history, in the moral and political conflicts of India and the United States there was a certain tragic appropriateness in the fact that Mahatma Gandhi and Martin Luther King, teaching the universal requirements of love and justice, were assassinated by fanatics motivated by religious and racial prejudice. There was likewise a tragic appropriateness in the death of Jesus. He taught the way of life of God's kingdom and the imminent coming of that kingdom on earth. This was to the ruling Roman power a potential incitement to rise up against it in the name of God, as was to happen in 66-70 and again in 135 C E. He also prophesied the destruction of the Jerusalem temple, thus deeply antagonizing its priestly guardians, who collaborated in his arrest and trial. But these historical factors were soon submerged in the Christian consciousness by a religious interpretation of the crucifixion. The acceptance of Jesus' death as having a positive meaning inevitably evoked, in the thought-world of that time, the universal language of sacrifice. In the Judaism of Jesus' period a sacrifice made as a sin offering to God involved the shedding of blood as a giving of the life essence. However, as a cumulative result of the teaching of Jesus, as well as of Hosea and Amos before him and many others after him, can we not now see that the sacrifice of animal or human blood pointed, in a crude and inadequate way, to the much deeper sacrifice of the ego point of view in becoming a channel of divine grace on earth? The real meaning of Jesus' death was not that his blood was shed – indeed crucifixion did not involve a great deal of bloodshed – but that he gave himself utterly to God in faith and trust. His cross was thus a powerful manifestation and continuing symbol of the divine kingdom in this present world, as a way of life in which one turns the other cheek, forgives one's enemies 'unto seventy times seven', trusts God even in the darkness of pain, horror and tragedy, and is continually raised again to the new life of faith.

And yet even this does not exhaust the felt impact of Jesus' death. For the voluntary acceptance of death by a holy person has a moral power that reverberates beyond any words that we can frame to express it. Even on a much lower level, when someone knowingly gives his or her life for the sake of another – say, in a rescue from fire or avalanche or bomb or an oncoming train or car, or in some other way – something has happened that is awe-inspiring and, in an indefinable way, enriching and enhancing to the human community. And so it was, in a much greater way, with the death of Jesus. This is no doubt why the mythological pictures of a ransom paid to the devil, or of a sacrifice to appease the divine honour or justice, were able to last so long; for since we cannot fully articulate the impression made by the crucifixion of one who was so close to God, no ecclesiastical language about it has been ruled out as too strange or extravagant.

Nevertheless we have to insist that these ecclesiastical theories are all misleading. It is misleading to think that there is a devil with legitimate rights over against God. It is misleading to think of the heavenly Father on the model of a feudal lord or a stern cosmic moralist. And it is misleading to see an acceptance of the Christian mythology of the cross as the only way to salvation for all human beings. Let the voluntary sacrifice of a holy life continue to challenge and inspire us in a way that transcends words. But let us not reduce its meaning to any culture-bound theological theory.

To summarize and conclude: Jesus' death was of a piece with his life, expressing a total integrity in his self-giving to God; and his cross continues to inspire and challenge us on a level that does not involve the atonement theories developed by the churches. Those theories have no doubt helped people in the past to rationalize the immense impact upon them of the crucifixion, and they did so in ways that cohered with the plausibility structures of their own time. But our own intellectual world is so different, both within the church and without, that those traditional atonement theories can no longer perform any useful function.

13

Salvation/Liberation as a World-wide Process

The previous chapters have suggested an understanding of Jesus and of the salvation that he has made possible for many that can enable Christianity to contribute, in co-operation with the other great world faiths, to the common welfare of humankind. For whilst a claim to be the one and only 'true religion' is, as we have seen, dangerously open to exploitation in ways that exacerbate human conflicts, a religion that accepts the other great traditions as equally authentic can join with them to promote international peace and to solve the problems of planetary ecology and two-thirds world poverty, malnutrition and disease, and the vast periodic disasters of war and famine.

But how are the world religions to arrive at such a mutual acceptance? For each presents itself, implicitly or explicitly, as in some important sense absolute and unsurpassable. The problem of the relationship between these different streams of religious life has often been posed in terms of their divergent belief-systems. For whilst there are various overlaps between their teachings there are also vast and radical differences: is the divine reality (let us refer to this as the Real) personal or non-personal; if personal, is it unitary or triune; is the universe created, or emanated, or itself eternal; do we live only once on this earth or are we repeatedly reborn? and so on and so on. When the problem of religious plurality is approached through these rival truth-claims it appears particularly intractable.

I want to suggest, however, that it may more profitably be approached from a different direction, in terms of the claims of the various traditions to provide, or (better) to be effective contexts of, salvation. 'Salvation' is primarily a Christian term; but I shall use it here to include its functional analogues within the other major world religions. In this broader sense we can say that Christianity and these other great traditions are alike paths of salvation. For whereas pre-axial religion was (and is) centrally concerned to keep life going on an even keel, the post-axial traditions, originating or rooted in the 'axial age' of the first millennium BCE – principally Hinduism (including for our present purpose Jainism and Sikhism), Judaism, Buddhism, Taoism, Christianity, Islam – are centrally concerned with a radical betterment or transformation of the human situation.

It is of course possible to define salvation in such a way that it becomes a necessary truth that only one particular tradition can provide it. If, for example, from within Christianity we define salvation as being forgiven by God because of Jesus' atoning death, and so becoming part of God's redeemed community, the church, then salvation is by definition Christian salvation. If on the other hand, from within Mahayana Buddhism, we define it as the attainment of *satori* or awakening, and so becoming an ego-free manifestation of the eternal Dharmakaya, then salvation is by definition Buddhist liberation. And so on. But if we stand back from these different conceptions to compare them we can, I think, very naturally and properly see them as different forms of the more fundamental conception of a radical change from a profoundly unsatisfactory state to one that is limitlessly better because rightly related to the Real. Vernon White has well expressed this in Christian language: 'In Gospel terms, this entails dying to self and living to God. It requires a turning away from all self-centredness which excludes others, and freely relating with love, worship, and respect to God, humankind, and our environment, in due proportion' (White 1991, 54). Each tradition conceptualizes in its own way the wrongness of ordinary human existence – as a state of fallenness from paradisal virtue and happiness; or as a condition of moral weakness and alienation from God; or as the fragmentation of the infinite One into false finite individualities; or as a self-centredness which pervasively poisons our involvement in the world process, making it to us an experience of anxious, unhappy unfulfilment. But each at the same time proclaims a limitlessly better possibility, again conceptualized in different ways – as the joy of conforming one's life to God's law; as giving oneself to God in Christ, so that 'it is no longer I who live, but Christ who lives in me' (Galatians 2.20), leading to eternal life in God's presence; as a complete surrender to God, and hence peace with God, leading to the bliss of paradise; as transcending the ego and realizing oneness with the limitless being-consciousness-bliss (*satchitananda*) of Brahman; as overcoming the ego point of view in the serene selflessness of *nirvana*. I suggest that these different conceptions of salvation are specifications of what, in a generic formula, is the transformation of human existence from self-centredness to a new orientation centred in the divine Reality. And in each case the good news is that this limitlessly better possibility is actually available and can be entered upon, or begin to be entered upon, here and now. Each tradition sets forth the way to attain this great good: faithfulness to the Torah, discipleship to Jesus, obedient living out of the Qur'anic way of life, the Eightfold Path of the Buddhist dharma, or the three great Hindu *margas* of mystical insight, activity in the world, and self-giving devotion to God.

The great world religions, then, are ways of salvation. Each claims to constitute an effective context within which the transformation of human existence can and does take place from self-centredness to Reality-centredness. How are we to judge such claims? We cannot directly observe the inner spiritual quality of a human relationship to the Real; but we can observe how that relationship, as one's deepest and most pervasive orientation, affects the moral and spiritual quality of a human personality and of a man's or a woman's relationship to others. It would seem, then, that we can only assess these salvation-projects in so far as we are able to observe their fruits in human life. The inquiry has to be, in a broad sense, empirical. For the issue is one of fact, even though a kind of fact that is hard to define and difficult to measure, rather than being settleable by *a priori* stipulation.

The word 'spiritual' which I have just used is notoriously vague; but I am using it to refer to a quality or, better, an orientation which we can discern in those individuals whom we call saints – a Christian term which I am using here to cover such analogues as arahat, bodhisattva, jivanmukta, mahatma, and in varying degrees all who approach these spiritual heights. In these cases the human self is variously described as becoming part of the life of God, being 'to the Eternal Goodness what his own hand is to a man' (Winckworth 1937, 32); or being permeated from within by the infinite reality of Brahman; or becoming a conscious manifestation of the universal Buddha nature. In each case there is a transformation from natural self-concern to a new centring in the Real as experienced within the saint's own tradition. One is conscious in the presence of such a person that he or she is, to a startling extent, open to the Transcendent, so as to be largely free from self-regarding concerns and anxieties and empowered to live as an instrument of God/ Truth/Reality.

It is to be noted that there are two main patterns of this transformation. There are saints who withdraw from the world into prayer or meditation, and saints who seek to change the world – in the mediaeval period a contemplative Julian of Norwich and a political Joan of Arc, or in our own century a mystical Sri Ramakrishna and a political Mahatma Gandhi. In our present age of sociological consciousness, when we are aware that our inherited political and economic structures can be analysed and purposefully changed, saintliness is more likely than in earlier times to take social and political forms. But, of whichever type, the saints are not a different species from the rest of us: they are simply much more advanced in the process of inner transformation.

The ethical aspect of this consists in observable modes of behaviour. But how do we identify the kind of behaviour which, to the degree that it characterizes a life, reflects a corresponding degree of reorientation to the divine Reality? Should we use Christian ethical criteria, or Buddhist, or Muslim . . .? The answer, I suggest, is that on the level of their most basic moral insights the great traditions use a common criterion. For they agree in giving a central and normative role to the unselfish regard for others that we call love or compassion. This is commonly expressed in the principle of valuing others as we value ourselves, and treating them accordingly. Thus in the ancient Hindu *Mahabharata* we read that 'One should never do to another that which one would regard as injurious to oneself. This, in brief, is the rule of Righteousness' (*Anushana parva*, 113.7). Again, 'He who . . . benefits persons of all orders, who is always devoted to the good of all beings, who does not feel aversion to anybody . . . succeeds in ascending to Heaven' (*Anushana parva*, 145.24). In the Buddhist *Sutta Nipata* we read, 'As a mother cares for her son, all her days, so towards all living things a man's mind should be all-embracing' (149). In the Jain scriptures we are told that one should go about 'treating all creatures in the world as he himself would be treated' (*Kitanga Sutra*, I.ii.33). Confucius, expounding humaneness (*jen*), said, 'Do not do to others what you would not like yourself' (*Analects*, xxi, 2). In a Taoist scripture we read that the good man will 'regard [others'] gains as if they were his own, and their losses in the same way' (*Thai Shang*, 3). The Zoroastrian scriptures declare, 'That nature only is good when it shall not do unto another whatever is not good for its own self' (*Dadistan-i-dinik*, 94.5). We are all familiar with Jesus' teaching, 'As you wish that men would do to you, do so to them' (Luke 6.31). In the Jewish Talmud we read, 'What is hateful to yourself do not do to your fellow man. That is the whole of the Torah' (*Babylonian Talmud*, Shabbath 31a). And in the Hadith of Islam we read the prophet Muhammad's words, 'No man is a true believer unless he desires for his brother that which he desires for himself' (*Ibn Madja*, Intro. 9). Clearly, if everyone acted on this basic principle, taught by all the major faiths, there would be no injustice, no avoidable suffering, and the human family would everywhere live in peace.

When we turn from this general principal of love/compassion to the actual behaviour of people within the different traditions, asking to what extent they live in this way, we realize how little research has been done on so important a question. We do not have much more to go on than general impressions, supplemented by travellers' tales and anecdotal reports. We observe among our neighbours within our own community a great deal of practical loving-kindness; and we are told that a remarkable degree of self-giving love is to be found, for example, among the Hindu fishing families in the mud huts along the Madras shore; and we hear various other similar accounts from other lands. We read biographies, social histories and novels of Muslim village life in Africa, Buddhist life in Thailand, Hindu life in India, Jewish life in New York, as well as Christian life around the world, both in the past and today, and we get the impression that the personal virtues (as well as vices) are basically much the same within these very different religio-cultural settings and that in all of them unselfish concern for others occurs and is highly valued. And, needless to say, as well as love and compassion we also see all-too-abundantly, and again apparently spread more or less equally in every society, cruelty, greed, hatred, selfishness and malice.

All this constitutes a haphazard and impressionistic body of data. Indeed I want to stress, not how easy it is, but on the contrary how difficult it is, to make responsible judgments in this area. For not only do we lack full information, but the fragmentary information that we have has to be interpreted in the light of the varying conditions of human life in different periods of history and in different economic and political circumstances. And I suggest that all that we can conclude at present is that we have no good reason to believe that any one of the great religious traditions has shown itself to be more productive of love/compassion than another.

The same is true when we turn to the large-scale social outworkings of the different salvation-projects. Here the units are not individual human lives, spanning a few decades, but religious cultures spanning many centuries. For we can no more judge a civilization than a human life by confining our attention to a single temporal cross-section. Each of the great streams of religious life has had its times of flourishing and its times of recession. Each has produced its own distinctive kinds of good and its own distinctive kinds of evil. But to assess either the goods or the evils cross- culturally is difficult, to say the least. How do we weigh, for example, the lack of economic progress, and consequent widespread poverty, in traditional Buddhist cultures against the endemic violence and racism of Christian civilization, culminating in the twentieth-century Jewish holocaust? How do we weigh what the West regards as the hollowness of arranged marriages against what the East regards as the hollowness of a marriage system that leads to such a high proportion of divorces and broken families? From within each culture one can see clearly enough the defects of the others. But an objective ethical comparison of such vast and complex totalities is at present an unattainable ideal. And the result is that we are not in a position to claim an over-all moral superiority for any one of the great living religious traditions. From a traditional Christian point of view the growing realization of this has proved extremely challenging. Vernon White, a defender of the unique centrality of Christ in the salvific process, has spoken candidly of the 'empirical shock of tasting and seeing *so much* "reconciliation" outside Christ, and so little in Christ' (White 1991, 17).

Let us now see where we have arrived. I have suggested that if we identify the central claim of each of the great religious traditions as the claim to be an effective context of salvation; and if we see salvation as a progressive change in human beings from self-centredness to a new orientation centred in the ultimate divine Reality; and if this new orientation has both a more elusive 'spiritual' character and a more readily observable moral aspect – then we arrive at the modest and largely negative conclusion that, so far as we can tell, no one of the great world religions stands out as more salvific than the others. Certainly the onus of proof lies upon anyone who wishes to claim that one particular tradition (presumably their own) stands out as uniquely superior.

What, then, in view of this is the relationship between the great world religions?

14

Christian Truth and Other Truths

What are we to make of the often mutually contradicting doctrines of the different traditions? In order to make progress at this point, we must distinguish various kinds and levels of doctrinal conflict.

There are, first, conceptions of the ultimate as Yahweh, or as the Holy Trinity, or Allah, or Shiva, or Vishnu, or as Brahman, or the Dharmakaya, Sunyata, the Tao, and so on.

However, if 'salvation' is taking place, and taking place to much the same extent, within the religious systems presided over by these various deities and absolutes, this suggests that they are different manifestations to humanity of a yet more ultimate ground of all salvific transformation. Let us then consider the possibility that an infinite transcendent reality is being differently conceived, and therefore differently experienced, and therefore differently responded to from within our several religio-cultural ways of being human.

Such a conception is readily capable of philosophical support. For we are familiar today with the ways in which all human experience is partly formed by the conceptual and linguistic frameworks within which it occurs. The basically Kantian insight that the mind is active in perception, and that we are always aware of our environment as it appears to a consciousness operating with our particular conceptual resources and procedures, has been amply confirmed by work in cognitive psychology and the sociology of knowledge and can now be extended with some confidence to the analysis of the various forms of religious awareness. If, then, we proceed inductively from these, adopting a religious as distinguished from a naturalistic interpretation of them, we are likely to find ourselves making two moves. The first is to postulate an ultimate transcendent reality (which I am referring to as the Real) which, being beyond the scope of our human concepts, cannot be directly experienced by us as it is in itself but only as it appears in terms of our various human thought-forms. And the second is to identify the many thought-and-experienced deities and absolutes as different manifestations of the Real within different historical modes of human consciousness. In Kantian terms, the divine noumenon, the Real *an sich*, is experienced through different human receptivities as a range of divine phenomena in the formation of which different sets of religious concepts have played an essential part.

These varying 'receptivities' consist of conceptual schemas within which a range of personal, communal and historical factors have produced yet further variations. The most basic concepts in terms of which the Real has been humanly thought-and-experienced are those of (personal) deity and of the (non-personal) absolute. But the Real is not of course actually experienced either as deity in general or as the absolute in general. Each basic concept becomes (to continue with the Kantian terminology) schematized in more concrete forms. It is at this point that individual and cultural factors enter into the process. The religious tradition of which we are a part, with its unique history and ethos, and its great exemplars, its scriptures feeding our thoughts and emotions, and perhaps above all its devotional, sacramental or meditative practices, constitutes an uniquely shaped and coloured 'lens' through which we are concretely aware of the Real as the personal Adonai, or as the Heavenly Father, or as Allah, or Vishnu, or Shiva . . . or again as the non-personal Brahman, or the Tao, or Dharmakaya, or Emptiness, or the Ground . . . Thus, one whose spiritual life is formed by Christian prayer and sacrament is led to experience the Real as the divine Thou, whereas one who practises advaitic yoga, or Buddhist zazen, is thereby brought to experience the Real as the infinite being-consciousness-bliss of Brahman, or as the limitless emptiness of *sunyata*, which is at the same time the fullness of immediate reality as 'wondrous being'.

Three explanatory comments at this point before turning to the next level of doctrinal disagreement. First, to suppose that the experienced deities and absolutes which are the intentional objects of worship, or foci of religious meditation, are appearances or manifestations of the Real, rather than each being itself the Real *an sich*, is not to suppose that they are illusions – any more than the varying ways in which a mountain appears to a plurality of differently placed observers are illusory. That the same reality may be variously experienced and described is true even of physical objects. But in the case of the infinite divine reality there must be much greater scope for the use of different human conceptual schemas, producing varying modes of phenomenal experience. Whereas the concepts in terms of which we are aware of mountains and rivers and houses are largely (though by no means entirely) standard throughout the human race, the concepts in terms of which we become aware of the Real have developed in widely different ways within the different cultures of the earth.

As a second comment, to say that the Real is beyond the range of our human concepts is not intended to mean that it is beyond the scope of purely formal, logically generated concepts – such as the concept of being beyond the range of (other than purely formal) concepts! We could not refer at all to that which cannot be conceptualized in any way, not even by the concept of being unconceptualizable. But the other than purely formal concepts by which our experience is structured must be presumed not to apply to its noumenal ground. The characteristics mapped in thought and language are constitutive of our *human* experience. We have no warrant to apply them to the noumenal ground of the phenomenal (i.e. experienced) realm. We should not therefore think of the Real *an sich* as singular or plural, substance or process, personal or non-personal, good or bad, purposive or non-purposive; for these alternatives do not apply to it. The ineffability of the Ultimate has long been a basic theme of religious thought. For example, within Christianity, Gregory of Nyssa declared that:

> The simplicity of the True Faith assumes God to be that which He is, namely, incapable of being grasped by any term, or any idea, or any other device of our apprehension, remaining beyond the reach not only of the human but of the angelic and all supramundane intelligence, unthinkable, unutterable, above all expression in words, having but one name that can represent His proper nature, the single name being 'Above Every Name' (Gregory of Nyssa 1892a, 99: Book I, chapter 42).

Augustine said that 'God transcends even the mind' (Augustine 1953, 259) and Aquinas that 'by its immensity, the divine substance surpasses every form that our intellect reaches' (Aquinas 1955, 96: I.14.2). In Islam the Qur'an affirms of God that 'No eyes can penetrate Him' and that God is 'beyond what they describe' (6.103 and 37.80). The Kena Upanishad declares of Brahman, 'There the eye goes not, speech goes not, nor the mind' (Radhakrishnan 1953, 582), and Shankara wrote that Brahman is that 'before which words recoil, and to which no understanding has ever attained' (Otto 1932,

28). The religious mind is led to this conclusion by a sense of the limitless greatness of the Ultimate as, in Anselm's formula, not only 'that than which a greater cannot be thought' but also 'greater than can be thought' (Anselm 1965, 81: chapter 15). I suggest that the idea is also required by a religious interpretation of the multiple forms of religion; for this cannot identify the ultimately Real exclusively with any one of its manifestations to human consciousness.

But, third, we might well ask, why postulate an ineffable and unobservable divine-reality-in-itself? If we can say virtually nothing about it, why affirm its existence? The answer is that the reality or non-reality of the postulated noumenal ground of the experienced religious phenomena constitutes the difference between a religious and a naturalistic interpretation of religion. If there is no such transcendent ground, the various forms of religious experience are purely human projections. If on the other hand there is such a transcendent ground, then these phenomena may be joint products of the universal presence of the Transcendent and of the varying sets of concepts and images operating within the religious traditions of the earth. To affirm the Real is thus to affirm that religious experience is not solely a construction of our human imagination but is a response – though always a culturally conditioned response – to the Real.

Those doctrinal conflicts, then, that hinge upon different conceptions of the Real, arise, according to the hypothesis I am proposing, from the variations between different sets of human conceptual schemata and spiritual practices. But it seems that each of these varying ways of thinking-and-experiencing the Real has been able to mediate Its transforming presence to human life. For the different major concepts of the ultimate do not seem – so far as we can tell – to result in one religious totality being soteriologically more effective than another.

The second level of doctrinal difference consists of sets of metaphysical beliefs which cohere with, although they are not exclusively linked to, a particular conception of the ultimate. These are beliefs about the relation of the material universe to the Real: creation *ex nihilo*, emanation, an eternal universe, an unknown form of dependency or groundedness . . . ? And about human destiny: reincarnation or a single life, eternal self-identity or transcendence of separate selfhood . . . ? Again, there are questions about the existence of heavens and hells and purgatories and angels and devils, and many other subsidiary states and entities. Out of this mass of disputed religious issues let me select two major examples: is the universe created *ex nihilo*, and do human beings reincarnate?

I suggest that we would do well to apply to such questions a principle that was taught by the Buddha two and a half millennia ago. He listed a series of 'undetermined questions' (*avyakata*) – whether the universe is eternal, whether it is spatially infinite, whether (putting it in modern terms) mind and brain are identical, and what the state is of a completed project of human existence (a Tathagata, or Buddha) after bodily death. He refused to answer any of these questions, saying that we do not need to have knowledge of such matters in order to attain liberation or awakening; and indeed that to regard such information as soteriologically essential would only divert us from the single-minded quest for liberation. I think that we can at this point profitably learn from the Buddha, even extending his conception of the undetermined questions further than he did himself – for together with almost everyone else in his own culture he regarded one of our examples, reincarnation, as a matter of assured knowledge. Let us, then, accept that we do not *know* whether, e.g., the universe was created *ex nihilo*, or whether human beings are reincarnated; and further, that it is not necessary for salvation to hold a correct opinion on either matter.

I am not suggesting that such issues are unimportant. On their own level they are extremely important, being both of great interest to us and also having widely ramifying implications within our belief-systems and hence for our lives. The thought of having been created out of nothing can nourish a salutary sense of absolute dependence. (But other conceptions can also nurture that sense.) The idea of reincarnation can offer the hope of future spiritual progress; though, combined with the principle of karma, it can also serve to validate the present inequalities of human circumstances. (But other eschatologies also have their problems, both theoretical and practical.) Thus these – and other – disputed issues do have a genuine importance. Further, it is possible that some of them may one day be settled, or more nearly settled, by empirical evidence. It might become established, for example, that the quantity of matter in the universe is such that its gravitational pull will eventually reverse the present expansion of the galaxies, an outcome that would cohere well with the model of a beginninglessly and endlessly expanding and contracting universe. Again, it might become established, by an accumulation of evidence, that reincarnation does indeed occur in the case of either some or all people. On the other hand it is possible that we shall never in this world achieve finally agreed knowledge in these areas. Certainly, at the present time, whilst we have theories, preferences, hunches, inherited convictions, we cannot honestly claim to have secure knowledge. And the same is true, I suggest, of the entire range of metaphysical issues about which the religions dispute. They are of intense interest, properly the subject of continuing research, discussion and debate, but are not matters concerning which absolute dogmas are appropriate. Still less is it appropriate to maintain that salvation depends upon accepting any one particular opinion or dogma concerning them. For we have seen that the transformation of human existence from self-centredness to Reality-centredness seems to be taking place within each of the great traditions to a more or less equal extent despite their very different answers to these debated questions. It follows that a correct opinion concerning them is not required for salvation.

The third level of doctrinal disagreement concerns historical questions. Each of the great traditions includes a larger or smaller body of historical beliefs. In the case of Judaism these include at least the main features of the history described in the Hebrew scriptures; in the case of Christianity, these plus the main features of the life, death and resurrection of Jesus as described in the New Testament; in the case of Islam, the main features of the history described in the Qur'an (much of it overlapping with the Jewish and Christian scriptures); in the case of Vaishnavite Hinduism, the historicity of Krishna; in the case of Buddhism, the historicity of Gautama and his enlightenment at Bodh Gaya; and so on. But although each tradition thus has its own record of the past, there are very few instances of direct disagreement between these. For the strands of history cherished by these different historical memories do not generally overlap; and where they do overlap they do not generally involve significant differences. The overlaps are mainly within the ancient Near Eastern history common to the Jewish, Christian and Muslim scriptures; and within this I can only locate two points of direct disagreement – the Torah's statement that Abraham nearly sacrificed his son Isaac at Mount Moriah (Genesis 22) versus the Muslim interpretation of the Qur'anic version (in Sura 37) that it was his other son Ishmael; and the New Testament witness that Jesus died on the cross versus the Qur'anic teaching that 'they did not slay him, neither crucified him, only a likeness of that was shown them' (Sura 4.156). (This latter, however, would seem to be a conflict between an historical report, in the New Testament, supported by the non-Christian writers Josephus and Tacitus, and a theological inference – that God would not allow so great a prophet to be killed – in the Qur'an.)

All that one can say in general about such disagreements, whether between two traditions or between any one of them and the secular historians, is that they could only properly be settled by the weight of historical evidence. However, the events in question are usually so remote in time, and the evidence so slight and uncertain, that the question cannot be definitively settled. We have to be content with different communal 'memories', enriched as they are by the mythic halo around all long-lived human stories about events with transcendent significance. Once again, then, I suggest that differences of historical judgment, although having their own proper importance, do not prevent the different traditions from being effective, and so far as we can tell more or less equally effective, contexts of salvation. Evidently, then, it is not necessary for salvation that we should have correct historical information. (It is likewise not necessary for salvation, we may add, that we should have correct scientific information.)

Putting all this together, the picture that I am suggesting can be outlined as follows: our human religious experience, variously shaped as it is by our sets of religious concepts and practices, is a cognitive response to the universal presence of the ultimate divine Reality that, in itself, exceeds human conceptuality. This Reality is manifested to us in ways formed by a variety of human ideas, as the range of divine *personae* and metaphysical *impersonae* witnessed to in the history of religions. Each major tradition, built around its own distinctive way of thinking-and-experiencing the Real, has developed its answers to the perennial questions of our origin and destiny, constituting more or less comprehensive and coherent cosmologies and eschatologies. These are human creations which, by their association with living streams of religious experience, have become invested with a sacred authority. However, they cannot all be wholly true; probably none is wholly true; perhaps all are partly true. But since the salvific process has been going on through the centuries despite this unknown distribution of truth and falsity in our cosmologies and eschatologies, it follows that it is not essential for salvation to adopt any one of them. We would therefore do well to learn to tolerate unresolved, and at present unresolvable, differences concerning these penultimate matters.

One element, however, to be found in the belief-systems of most of the traditions raises a special problem, namely that which asserts the sole salvific efficacy of that tradition. I shall discuss this problem in terms of Christianity because it is particularly acute for those of us who are Christians. I have already referred (in Chapter 8) to the historical side-effects of the dogma; but what of the theological merits of the dogma itself?

We are all familiar with such New Testament texts as 'there is salvation in no one else [than Jesus Christ], for there is no other name under heaven given among men by which we must be saved' (Acts 4.12), and with the Catholic dogma *Extra ecclesiam nulla salus* (no salvation outside the church) and its Protestant equivalent – never formulated as an official dogma but nevertheless implicit within the eighteenth- and nineteenth-century Protestant missionary expansion – no salvation outside Christianity. This differs from other elements of Christian belief in that it is not only a statement about the potential relationship of Christians to God but at the same time about the *actual* relationship of non-Christians to God. It says that the latter, in virtue of being non-Christians, lack salvation. Clearly such a dogma is incompatible with the observation that the salvific transformation of human existence is going on, and so far as we can tell going on to a more or less equal extent, within all the great traditions. In so far, then, as we accept that salvation is not confined to Christianity we must reject the old exclusivist dogma.

This has in fact now been done by most thinking Christians, even though exceptions remain within the large fundamentalist constituencies. The *extra ecclesiam* dogma, although not explicitly repealed, has been outflanked by the work of such influential Catholic theologians as Karl Rahner, whose new approach was in effect endorsed by Vatican II. Rahner expressed his more inclusivist outlook by suggesting that devout people of other faiths may be accepted as 'anonymous Christians' – within the invisible church even without knowing it, and thus within the sphere of salvation. And a number of Protestant theologians have advocated an essentially similar position. They are undeterred by the thought that if devout Muslims, Hindus, etc. can be seen as anonymous Christians, so likewise can devout Christians be seen as anonymous Muslims, Hindus, etc.; and that in all its uses the idea is a way of subordinating the faith of others to one's own.

The feature that particularly commends this kind of inclusivism to many Christians is that it recognizes the spiritual values of other religions, and the occurrence of salvation within them, and yet at the same time implicitly affirms the final superiority of their own religion over all others.[1] For it maintains that salvation, wherever it occurs, is Christian salvation, and Christians are those who alone know and preach its true source in the atoning death of Christ.

This again, like the old exclusivism, is a statement not only about the ground of salvation for Christians but also for Jews, Muslims, Hindus, Buddhists and everyone else. But we have seen that it has to be acknowledged that the immediate ground of their transformation is the particular spiritual path along which they move. It is by living in accordance with the Torah or the Qur'anic revelation that Jews and Muslims find a transforming peace with God; it is by one or other of their great *margas* that Hindus attain to *moksha*; it is by the Eightfold Path that Theravada Buddhists come to *nirvana*; it is by *zazen* that Zen Buddhists attain to *satori*; and so on. The Christian inclusivist is, then, by implication, declaring that these various spiritual paths are efficacious, and constitute authentic contexts of salvation, in virtue of the fact that Jesus died on the cross; and, by further implication, that if he had not died on the cross they would not be efficacious.

This is a novel and somewhat astonishing doctrine. How are we to make sense of the idea that the salvific power of the *dharma* taught five hundred years earlier by the Buddha is a consequence of the death of Jesus in approximately 30 C E? Such an apparently bizarre conception should only be affirmed for some very strong reason. It was certainly not taught by Jesus or his apostles. It has emerged only in the thought of twentieth-century Christians who have come to recognize that Jews are being salvifically transformed through the spirituality of Judaism, Muslims through that of Islam, Hindus and Buddhists through the paths mapped out by their respective traditions, and so on; but who nevertheless wish to retain their inherited sense of the unique superiority of the Christian path. The only outlet left for this sense, once one has acknowledged the salvific efficacy of the various great spiritual ways, is the arbitrary and contrived notion of their metaphysical dependency upon the death of Christ. But the theologian who undertakes to spell out this invisible causality is not to be envied. The problem is one not of

---

[1]For a recent example see Dupuis 1991, ch.6.

logical possibility – it only requires logical agility to cope with that – but of religious or spiritual plausibility. It would be a better use of theological time and energy, in my opinion, to develop forms of trinitarian, christological and soteriological doctrine that are compatible with our awareness of the independent salvific authenticity of the other great world faiths. Such forms are already available in principle in conceptions of the Trinity, not as ontologically three but as three ways in which the one God is humanly thought and experienced; conceptions of Christ as a man so fully open to and inspired by God as to be, in the ancient Hebrew metaphor, a 'son of God'; and conceptions of salvation as an actual human transformation which has been powerfully elicited and shaped among his disciples by the influence of Jesus.

There may indeed well be a variety of ways in which Christian thought can develop in response to our acute late-twentieth-century awareness of the other world faiths, as there were of responding to the nineteenth-century awareness of the evolution of the forms of life and the historical character of the holy scriptures. And likewise there will no doubt be a variety of ways in which each of the other great traditions can rethink its inherited assumption of its own unique superiority. But it is not for us Christians to tell people of other traditions how to do their own business. Rather, we should attend to our own. It is to this task that I have been trying to contribute in this book.

15

New Anglican Thinking

As I said in the preface to this new edition, I am adding something about new christological thinking, but instead of making a wide survey of all the very numerous contributions I shall concentrate on one major Protestant and one major Catholic theologian who have been breaking new ground. In the first category I select the Anglican John Macquarrie, formerly Professor of Divinity at Oxford, but still active in his retirement. I referred to him in chapter 6, but now want to take the discussion further. When *The Myth of God Incarnate* was published in 1977 he was one of the five authors of the 'rapid response' published later that year as *The Truth of God Incarnate*. He joined in the general ecclesiastical reaction against the word 'myth' in the title, and pointed to a lack of consistency in its use among the book's seven authors. Others also concentrated, in their attacks on the book, on what they saw as the scandal of calling divine incarnation a 'merely' mythological idea. However Macquarrie himself said in his same article, 'It may at once be agreed that the story of a divine being who descends to earth as man is technically a "myth" and not straightforward history . . .' (Macquarrie 1977, 140; repeated, with other material, in 2002, Ch. 7. Unless otherwise indicated all further quotations in this chapter are also from Macquarrie's writings).

There was, as Macquarrie and others noted, nothing much new in the *Myth* book. Its central theme, that the historical Jesus did not claim to be God (or God the Son) incarnate, had long been familiar and accepted among mainstream New Testament scholars. But it had not been passed on through the priests and ministers of the churches to the people in the pews, and the longer this was delayed the harder it became to make it known and to begin to adapt the church's formulae and preaching accordingly. This is why we chose our provocative title and why it succeeded in getting the issue into the public consciousness.

In a subsequent major work, *Jesus Christ in Modern Thought,* one of the most thorough and authoritative books that we have on the subject, Macquarrie is also clear that the familiar centrepiece of popular Christian discourse – that Jesus was (and is) the Son of God – must be understood metaphorically, not literally. He writes:

> To speak of Jesus as 'Son of God' is to use a metaphor. It is certainly an important metaphor and affirms a close relation to God, but it does not imply deification . . . [The metaphor] arises within a long traditional usage, in which a person close to or considered to be an agent of God might be called his son . . . God's metaphorical 'sending' of his metaphorical 'son' can be understood in ways that do not imply pre-existence, once we accept that the language is metaphorical and not literal.' (1990, 42 and 56).

This is half of the central message of *The Myth of God Incarnate*. The other half is the contention that it is a vital preliminary question whether Jesus himself, the historical individual, thought of himself as having a unique divine status. Until within approximately the last 150 years it was taken for granted within the churches that Jesus had explicitly taught his own deity. Did he not say 'I and the Father are one' (John 10.30), 'He who has seen me has seen the Father' (John 14.9), and did he not proclaim his sole saviourhood for all humanity when he declared 'I am the way, and the truth, and the life; no one comes to the Father but by me' (John 14.6)? However there is now a broad consensus among New Testament scholars and theologians, including Macquarrie, that these sayings cannot be attributed to the historical Jesus but were put into his mouth by a Christian writer some sixty or seventy years after Jesus' death, expressing the developing faith of the church at that time. Jesus himself, the historical individual, did not claim to be God incarnate, or God the Son, second person of a divine Trinity incarnate. This position is also supported by Macquarrie: 'What the disciples came to believe was that Jesus *is* the Christ, and also Lord, Son of God and so on, not that *he said he was* Christ, Lord, etc.' (1990, 354). Even this may be an overstatement. It is unlikely that any of the original twelve disciples regarded Jesus as divine. We see the beginnings of his deification in the New Testament, none of which however was written by any of the original apostles. We find it particularly in St John's Gospel written towards the end of the first century, with St Paul as a major influence having already led the growing church in that direction. But it was not fully formalized and promulgated as Christian orthodoxy until the Council of Chalcedon in 451, declaring that Jesus had two complete natures, one human and the other divine: a single person 'recognized in two natures, without confusion, without change, without division, without separation'. We maintained in the *Myth* book that this is a piece of human philosophizing, although long enjoying orthodox status, and is properly open to critical scrutiny and, if necessary, revision. And in fact very many modern theologians, Macquarrie prominent among them, have sought for better ways of expressing what they regard as essentially the same faith. But Macquarrie goes further than many others in holding that Jesus 'differs from other human beings in degree, not in kind' (1990, 359) and 'I would argue that the potentiality for becoming a Son of God belongs to humanity as such' (1990, 43).

Given then that Jesus did not claim to be God the Son, second person of a divine Trinity incarnate, how is the church's conviction to the contrary supported? Three lines of argument have been developed.

One is the mainly Catholic belief that the development of doctrine within the church, including its ecumenical Councils (particularly Nicaea and Chalcedon), has been, and still is, divinely inspired and thus protected from taking a wrong direction. If offered as an argument this is clearly circular. Who says that the church has been divinely inspired? The church says so, and says that it is divinely inspired in saying so!

Because the church's claim to divine guidance *may* nevertheless be correct we must ask if its history shows it to be a truly holy community, evidencing signs of divine inspiration. I suggest that any unbiased moral judgement must conclude that the church – including the Catholic church as the largest component of organized Christianity, but including the other main branches also – has done about as much harm as good in the course of human history. On the one hand, to its credit, are its provision of a framework of meaning for life for hundreds of millions of men and women; the nourishing of human goodness in innumerable ordinary people through the ages; the work of its great thinkers and the lives of its great saints (including some but by no means all of those officially canonized); its founding of universities and hospitals; its inspiration of painting, music, architecture, drama and much else. But to its discredit have been the centuries long persecution of the Jews;

the Crusades; the burning of heretics and witches; its embodiment of the systemic and still largely continuing subordination of the female half of the human race; its function in many areas of history as an instrument of the hierarchical control of the rich over the poor; its validation of innumerable wars and imperial aggressions; the support of significant parts of the church for slavery in North America and apartheid in South Africa; its resistance to the growth of the sciences when they contradicted the biblical narrative – all in the name of God and with the conviction of divine authority. I cannot think that a divinely guided institution would be responsible for so much evil, or that a guiding God would be concerned only with the church's theology and not with its behaviour in the world. I therefore conclude that if Jesus himself did not claim a uniquely divine status, the history of the church does not endow it with the moral or spiritual authority to claim to know better than he did who he was.

But, second, the basic idea of a divinely guided tradition is reformulated in a way that appeals to Protestants as well as some Catholics, namely in terms of the 'Christ-event' as God's revelation in history. This is a path that Macquarrie takes, and I quoted him on this at length on p. 35. It is the belief that the whole vast complex continuing 'event' that began with the historical Jesus and has continued down to today through the history of the church, including its theology, is God's initiative in human history – not of course in every detail, but taken as a whole. And so when the gospel is proclaimed today, with its exaltation of Jesus to a divine status, this is itself part of the continuing 'Christ event'.

This is a truly spectacular piece of theological spin-doctoring! In one bold stroke it sets aside as irrelevant all the weaknesses that modern scholarship has revealed in the structure of traditional orthodoxy. I argued in Chapters 5-7 that the doctrine of a literal, or ontological, divine incarnation has not been and cannot be spelled out in any coherent and intelligible way – something that Macquarrie also seems to hold when he describes incarnation as 'a paradox beyond the powers of the human mind to resolve' (1998, 25). Further, all the reasons mentioned above for doubting the true holiness and hence the divine authority of the church apply equally to the extended 'Christ-event'. For this too must include all the horrors as well as all the blessings of Christian history.

The third line of argument is that although Jesus' deity was not explicit in his teaching, it was nevertheless implicit in some of his words and actions. This is also favoured by Macquarrie. He lists the points at which we see in the Gospels the 'something more' that 'makes the difference between the devout Jew at the beginning of the story and the metaphysical Christ at the end' (1998, 110). Earlier in his book, indicating what he hopes to achieve in it, he says that while incarnation will remain a mystery, unexplained and un-understood, 'at least we shall have seen some of the compelling reasons that have led to the church's claims for Christ' (1998, 25). What, according to him, are these compelling reasons?

As he lists them, the first is the boy Jesus remaining behind when his parents returned from Jerusalem to Nazareth, 'to listen to the doctors in the Temple and to ask them questions', this showing that 'even in the so-called "hidden years" of his boyhood, his divine vocation was stirring within him' (1998, 110). Elsewhere however he says that the story 'may be legend' (1995, 105). But even if it is historically true, two questions immediately arise. Might it not just show that he was an unusually intelligent and religiously concerned youngster? Or, if his divine vocation was indeed stirring within him, why suppose that this vocation was to be God the Son incarnate? Further, Macquarrie rejects Adoptionism, the idea that God selected the human Jesus and called him to be his Son (1998, Ch. 4). But if Jesus was from the beginning God the Son incarnate, could this properly be described as a 'vocation'?

Macquarrie lists, second, Jesus' baptism by John the Baptist when 'behold, the heavens were opened and he saw the Spirit of God descending like a dove, and alighting on him; and lo, a voice from heaven, saying, This is my beloved Son, with whom I am well pleased' (Matthew 3.16). I doubt whether Macquarrie, deploying expertly as he does the full range of modern New Testament scholarship, regards the story as history rather than legend. This is hinted at when he gives the story the status of, 'as narrated by the evangelists' (1998, 110). If it were historical it would certainly have great significance. But this is one of the disputed questions in New Testament scholarship in which however the historical value of the narrative (beyond the fact of Jesus having been baptized by John) has proved to be generally unconvincing.

Third is the disciples' recognition of Jesus as the messiah. Macquarrie comments, 'Mark places this in the middle of his ministry, some modern scholars argue that such recognition came only after the death and resurrection, but the dating does not matter much. The point is that at some time the disciples recognized Jesus as Messiah, the anointed one sent by God to deliver the people' (1998, 110), although 'We cannot say that [Jesus] thought of himself as messiah or under any of the other titles that came to be applied to him' (1990, 353). But it is also important to remember that the Jewish messiah was never thought of as God incarnate but always as a human agent sent by God to deliver his chosen people. To attribute deity to the messiah would have been regarded by Jews as blasphemy.

Fourth is the transfiguration story (Mark 9.2-8), in which the divine voice is heard saying 'This is my beloved Son; listen to him'. Here Macquarrie has no hesitation in saying that 'It is a legendary story . . . [But, he adds,] Could we say that it was a numinous moment in [the disciples'] experience, briefly revealing something eternal and indestructible in Jesus, the disciples' first glimpse of the eternal Word, the metaphysical Christ?' (1998, 110-11). Macquarrie poses this as a question apparently expecting the answer 'Yes'. But if the story is legendary, as he believes, surely the more natural answer is 'No'.

The fifth is St John's report that Jesus, before his crucifixion, said, 'I, when I am lifted up from the earth, will draw all men to myself' (John 12.32). Macquarrie comments, 'This is the "absolute paradox" in its strongest form' (1998, 111). But does he really differ from most modern scholarship in its conclusion that such Fourth Gospel sayings as this cannot responsibly be attributed to the historical Jesus? They are words of the Christ of faith created by the Christian imagination and expressed two or three generations later in a theological treatise in the form of a life of Jesus.

Sixth, and finally, there is Jesus' resurrection. Here Macquarrie rejects the traditional belief in its physical character. In common with many New Testament scholars today he regards the resurrection stories in Matthew and Luke (written some fifty years later) as unhistorical. (The Gospel of Mark, in its original ending, has no appearances of the risen Jesus.) He appeals to Paul's distinction between the physical body and the spiritual body (1 Corinthians 15.44), and says, 'I think a little reflection, and also Paul's arguments, make it clear that what is resurrected is not the dead body that has been laid in the grave, not the body of flesh and blood and carbon chemistry by which human beings live on earth' (1990, 408). And in his more recent book he adds, 'There may have been several reasons for the rise of the belief that Jesus had been raised from the dead. The reports of an empty tomb may have been one;

visions of the risen Lord granted to some of the disciples may have
been another; and perhaps a pondering of the Hebrew prophets was
a third' (1998, 113).

Does all this, then, amount to 'compelling reasons' to believe
that Jesus was God the Son incarnate? I cannot see that it does.
Indeed, I suspect that Macquarrie does not either, and that his use
of the phrase 'compelling reasons' reflects a momentary triumph
of ecclesiastical commitment over scholarly intellect – something
that happens to most church theologians. It is this that has made
the traditional belief-package offered by the churches, embodied in
its liturgies, hymns and sermons, so unappealing to the majority of
the now only nominally Christian population of this country and
much of western Europe.

In his scholarly mode, Macquarrie shows little enthusiasm for
most of traditional Christian doctrine other than the one dogma
of the incarnation. He holds that the idea of Christ's divine pre-
existence 'does not imply a personal pre-existence of Jesus Christ'
(1990, 389). As he says at one point (in connection with this same
doctrine), 'we are dealing with language that is metaphorical or
even mythological, and the language and logic of common sense
may not be directly applicable' (1990, 56). On the other hand, in
his later *Christology Revisited* he seems to revert, in his ecclesiastical mode, to at least an echo of the doctrine of pre-existence, saying that 'from the beginning Christ the incarnate Word was there
in the counsels of God' (1998, 114).

He also holds that the doctrine of the virgin birth, or more precisely Jesus' virginal conception, cannot be understood as literal
biological fact, for 'if we suppose Jesus to have been conceived
and born in an altogether unique way, then it seems that we have
separated him from the rest of the human race and thereby made
him irrelevant to the human quest for salvation or for the true life'
(1998, 393); that his birth in Bethlehem, together with the beauti-
ful Christmas story of the wise men following a star in the east and
the shepherds in the field hearing the angel chorus, are not historical (1998, 393); that the traditional doctrine of Jesus' sinlessness
needs to be carefully qualified (1998, 397-8); that all ideas of Jesus'
death as an atoning sacrifice to satisfy God's righteous wrath, or as
a substitute for humanity in bearing God's just punishment for the
sins of the world, should be rejected (1998, 401-2); that the idea of
Jesus' descent into hell in the period between his crucifixion and
resurrection is 'purely mythological' (1998, 405); and in his 1990

book he refers to the doctrine of the Trinity only as it is used by other theologians, while in his 1998 book it is barely mentioned at all.

The question, then, is why Macquarrie continues, having abandoned all its supporting substructure, to insist on the doctrine of the incarnation, for he criticizes all the available theological explanations of it. He does not accept the orthodox two-natures dogma of Chalcedon, or by implication its contemporary restatement in terms of two minds, which I discussed in Chapter 5. He rejects the idea widely held among the early theologians of the church that while Jesus shared human nature in general he did not have an *individual* human personal nature (*anhypostasia*), which would entail that, as Macquarrie puts it, 'the directive principle in Jesus Christ was not human but divine' (1998, 53). He likewise rejects the traditional alternative to this, that Jesus did have an individual human nature but that this was taken up and subsumed into the divine nature of the eternal Logos (*enhypostasia*), which would mean that his humanity was not our humanity but that of a new and unique kind of being. Against this Macquarrie says, 'we must understand the difference between Christ and the rest of humanity as one of degree, rather than of kind' though, he adds, 'a difference of degree may be so great that for all practical purposes it counts as a difference of kind' (1998, 59).

Despite recommending the difference in degree rather than in kind Macquarrie nevertheless strongly affirms 'the absolute paradox – that this humble crucified man is also the eternal Word of God' (1998, 114). He affirms Jesus as 'the God-man, and his closeness to God, indeed, his unity with God', although this 'does not annul his true humanity' (1998, 59). Indeed, he says, 'I do not think that, if we remain Christian, we can ever escape the fundamental paradox, that Jesus Christ is both human and divine' (1998, 17). But it seems to remain for him a bare paradox. In view of his lack of reliance on the gospel stories he might well concur with Kierkegaard's famous statement, 'If the contemporary generation had left behind them nothing but the words, "We have believed that in such and such a year God appeared among us in the humble form of a servant, lived and taught among us, and then died" – this is more than enough' (Kierkegaard 1985, 104).

It is evident that Macquarrie is thinking within the parameters of an inherited belief system. This makes it possible for him to see Jesus' God-Manhood as a given fact. It is however for him a mystery, the absolute paradox, which cannot be understood; for 'we can understand only in part, and even so we have to help ourselves out by the use of myth, metaphor, paradox and other figures of speech' (1998, 108). But why accept Jesus' deity as a given fact? The 'compelling reasons' that Macquarrie has listed are far from compelling, either individually or collectively. Presumably the answer is that he sees an affirmation of Jesus' deity (as well as humanity) as required of a devout practising member of the church, committed to its life and liturgy.

Many theologians today still continue to do their work as though Christianity were the only religion in the world, the other great world faiths being simply ignored. But it is greatly to Macquarrie's credit that, beginning earlier than most other British theologians, he has taken seriously the question of Christ's place in the global religious scene. He depicts that scene as follows. The world religions have in common:

> the recognition of what I shall call a 'holy reality'. In some cases this holy reality may be called God, but this particular word suggests a personal being, and in some religions the holy reality is conceived as an impersonal Absolute or in other ways for which God-language would not be appropriate . . . In general, the religions of the West and also of the Middle East think of the holy reality as God (personal), while the religions of the further East think rather in terms of an impersonal (perhaps suprapersonal) Absolute. (1990, 418)

This is in a final chapter on 'Christ and the Saviour Figures' in *Jesus Christ in Modern Thought*; and later, in *The Mediators,* he includes Jesus along with Moses, Zoroaster,[1] Lao-tzu, the Buddha, Confucius, Socrates, Krishna and Muhammad. In the light of this he asks, 'Does [Jesus Christ] have an absolutely unique and incomparable status? Does he provide the only way to a right relationship with God, so that other ways and those who have taught them must be accounted mistaken?' (1990, 115). His implicit answer seems to be 'No', for all of these figures, like Jesus, mediated 'an understanding of holy Being to their followers' and 'sought to bring about the enhancement of human life' (1990, 115). 'In their several ways, they pursued justice, righteousness, love, compassion, peace

---

[1]Current scholarship dates him six or more centuries earlier than Macquarrie's dates, but this does not affect Zoroaster's rightful place in the list.

and whatever else belongs to the well-being of the race. In them there is concentrated for us the greatest spiritual striving and aspirations that have been known on earth' (1990, 420). For the other saviour figures, like Jesus, 'had given themselves up to the service of a divine reality, who might work in them and through them for the lifting up of all creatures on earth' (1990, 115).

This last quotation, however, suggests a certain residual ambivalence in Macquarrie's mind. For 'a divine reality, *who* might work . . .' (my italics) must be a personal God, indicating a retreat from the recognition that the holy reality is conceived, and experienced, in some faiths as personal and in others as trans-personal. Such a retreat would exclude Buddhism, for the 'gods' (*devas*) which (as Macquarrie notes) Buddhism recognizes are not a plurality of gods, still less one god, in the monotheistic sense. They are more analogous to the angels and archangels of the western traditions. As thought and experienced within Buddhism, both Mahayana and Theravada, the holy reality is *not* a personal God. It is perhaps his ambivalence about accepting non-personal human awarenesses of the ultimate reality that enables Macquarrie to end his major book by quoting uncritically,[2] as though it came from Jesus, the famous Fourth Gospel words, so comforting to many in the pews, 'I am the way, the truth and the life; no one comes to the Father but by me' (1990, 422).

Further, to return finally to our central concern of christology, if what Macquarrie says about the other great world faiths were intended to accept a parity among the world religions, including Christianity, it would be incompatible with the conception of Jesus as the unique mediator between God and humanity. For if we affirm Jesus as 'the God-man . . . [and] his unity with God'(1998, 59), in other than a metaphorical sense, this means that in Christ God came into human history to found a new religion, which is thus God's own religion, to which he must presumably wish all human beings to adhere, and which thus has a uniquely central and normative place in the religious life of the world.

My conclusion, then, is that Macquarrie is well in the front rank of new Christian thinking today, but that his sense of responsibility within the church leads him to formulate his views in ways that deliberately soften their impact, and thus have less effect than they might have had in moving Christian thinking forward. Along,

[2]Elsewhere, on p. 416 of the same book, he has more responsibly quoted this as something that 'John's gospel . . . represents Jesus as saying'.

unfortunately, with most other theologians today he is more interested in the endless internal churning over of the traditional ideas and language than in attempts to free Jesus and his message from the ecclesiastical wrappings of the past. And yet only that can hope to make sense to the 85-90 per cent of the population who seldom or never go to church. Jesus, his person and life and teachings, *is* relevant today and is as valuable as anything else that religion can offer us, but this will never become evident to the modern world by learned tinkering with the traditional formulae.

16

New Catholic Thinking

I have already discussed, and found wanting, the traditionally orthodox Catholic christology, based on the Chalcedonian definition. But I am far from being the only person to see the two-natures formula as no longer coherently intelligible or useful. I also discussed and rejected two modern attempts to reformulate it in terms of either two minds (instead of two natures), and of *kenosis* or self-emptying. But going beyond this, all sorts of creative new approaches have been proposed in recent decades by such major Catholic theologians as Karl Rahner, Edward Schillebeeckx, Hans Küng, Jacques Dupuis, Roger Haight and others. They have explored new ways of thinking, partly because they have taken seriously the reality of the other world religions, which was not a factor in the minds of those who created the traditional dogma. Here I am selecting for special attention the proposals of Roger Haight, S.J., in his recent very important book *Jesus Symbol of God* (1999). Except when otherwise indicated my quotations are from this book.

Haight is open to the possibility of deep-going change: it may, he says, be that 'christological beliefs are on the verge of passing into a new configuration' (27). He believes, however, that he is nevertheless going to offer a 'high' christology that can be accepted as orthodox. It is therefore very regrettable for the world of Christian scholarship that the Vatican is trying to stifle engagement with his work: the Congregation for the Doctrine of the Faith, then headed by Cardinal Joseph Ratzinger before his election as Pope, has notified Father Haight that his book is under investigation for unorthodoxy and that he can no longer teach as a Catholic theologian. As a result he has left the Jesuit seminary in Boston where he had long been teaching and has moved to the ecumenical Union Theological Seminary in New York.

Haight's book begins with the priority of soteriology over christology, which means in effect that we should start with the

Christian experience of salvation, as it occurs in this life, and from this develop our understanding of Jesus Christ. For 'Salvation cannot be understood as merely a promise or as an exclusively future reality' but as 'a symbol pointing to a reality that is existentially actualized in a person's life' (355). In other words, instead of working downwards from on high, beginning with a fixed authoritative formula, we should work 'from below' (as advocated by Karl Rahner), starting from the realities of human experience. This point is further emphasized by Haight's distinction between faith and belief, reminiscent of that drawn by Wilfred Cantwell Smith in his classic *The Meaning and End of Religion*, although he differs from Smith at some other points. For Haight, faith 'is a universal form of religious experience . . . that entails an awareness of and loyalty to an ultimate or transcendent reality . . . Faith in its primary sense is an intentional human response, reaction, act, or pervasive and operative attitude' (4).

Epistemologically, faith 'is cognitive' but is not knowledge in the sense of perceptual or scientific knowledge, for 'the object of faith is precisely that which transcends the finite world we know' (4-5). Beliefs on the other hand are historical expressions of faith, and as such can develop through time. For 'faith can retain a measure of autonomous identity within different expressions of belief . . . [This] allows for development and change in a religious tradition . . . Beliefs may change while faith at its deepest level remains constant, even as it is modified' (5). Accordingly, even a 'new configuration' of christology 'would not necessarily mean that the core of Christian faith would also change, for faith is distinct from belief, and its fundamental commitment has continually undergone changing beliefs through the centuries' (27).

Faith, Haight emphasizes, is not acceptance of a theory, but a practical response to awareness of God. Religious symbols point to transcendence, and they 'work' when their meaning is actively participated in, both intellectually and in the living of our lives. They then mediate the most fundamental meaning of our existence. But they are themselves natural phenomena as well as signals of transcendence, and they are often multivalent, bearing more than one meaning.

Haight points to two main types of Catholic christology today, Logos christologies and Spirit christologies, both of which he believes are viable although his own preference is for the latter. And both make central use of the notion of the symbol, which 'mediates awareness of something beyond itself. Sometimes the only way this "other" can be known is through some symbolic mediation' (8). Symbols, as he makes clear later, are metaphors, so that he can speak of 'metaphors or symbols' (465). For the ultimate can only be conceptualized or communicated indirectly through symbols, and 'Because theology deals with transcendent reality, and the data of faith is received through revelation, theology is a symbolic discipline' (9). Revelation here does not mean revealed propositions but 'faith being met by, even stimulated and initiated by, the ultimate. Revelation is the encounter in faith with the transcendent. In Christian terms, the core revelation is the presence of God encountered in faith' (5-6).

Haight regards Logos christology as an approach that makes it possible for the Christian to appreciate the reality and salvific value of other religions, but he nevertheless has certain reservations about it in the form in which it has been influentially presented by Karl Rahner. Principally, 'despite [Rahner's] intentions and his strong affirmations of Jesus' real humanity, the suspicions arise at several points. Jesus is not like us in so far as God is present to Jesus as Logos and God is present to us as Spirit. In other words, God's presence as Logos to Jesus is a qualitatively different mode of presence than God's union with human beings generally' (432). In contrast to this, Haight believes that 'Just as [Jesus] was inspired by God as Spirit, so in an analogous way are members of the Christian community' (456). The qualification suggested by 'an analogous way' presumably reflects the belief that 'God as Spirit was present to Jesus in a superlative degree' (464). For 'Jesus of Nazareth was a human being with a human existence and identity consubstantial with us. But Jesus, as the religious symbol that constitutes Christian faith, makes God present in the world' (298).

A further point of difference occurs when Rahner gives a unique and once-for-all salvific significance to Jesus. 'But a consciousness of historicity makes this difficult to hold. Rahner's position rests on the speculative premise that Jesus does not only represent and reveal the saving love of God, but constitutes and causes it for all people, even when there is no historical contact with Jesus . . . But why is not this transcendental love of God sacramentally actualised in history in many instances? Why is Jesus not one of many symbolic actualisations of God's loving presence to humankind?' (433).

Haight's alternative Spirit christology sees 'Jesus Christ as symbol of God' (12); 'for Christians, Jesus is the concrete symbol of God . . . Jesus is a mediation of the experience of God in history' (14). 'This structure [of christology] revolves around Jesus and his being the historical mediation of God to human existence. This is the structure of Christian faith, of the faith of each individual Christian and of the community as it moves through history' (40). It reflects the distinctively Christian experience of God's presence: 'Jesus is the historical mediation of God for the Christian imagination' (112), 'the revealer of God to the Christian imagination' (358). 'Jesus as symbol participates in God as Spirit, mediates God, and makes God present' (458), the function of a religious symbol being, as Haight has said, to mediate awareness of something else, namely the presence of God. 'The foundational metaphor for understanding Jesus Christ that underlies Logos christology', he says, 'is "incarnation" . . . The language of incarnation, of God as Logos assuming human flesh, is not literal language of which the referent is an object of this worldly knowledge and definition . . . The foundational metaphor of incarnation cannot appear credible when it is reduced to digital, empirical, or literal non-symbolic language' (438).

Like any other christology this has implications for the doctrine of the Trinity, for 'trinity is a function of christology . . . Trinity is thus logically derivative from the place that Jesus Christ plays in the Christian life and imagination. Consideration of the divinity of Jesus Christ generates the question of differentiation within the Godhead' (479). But if, as Haight proposes, Jesus was symbolically, or metaphorically, God the Son, this provides no basis for the traditional idea of an 'immanent' Trinity of three distinguishable persons within the Godhead – the Father, the Son, and Holy Spirit. Further:

> one finds no doctrine of an immanent trinity in the New Testament, that is, a doctrine depicting the inner reality of God as differentiated . . . The language of the New Testament represents God at work in the world for human salvation in 'economic' terms such as 'Word', 'Wisdom', 'Angel of the Lord', 'Spirit', 'Son of Man', and so on. This language is often described as functional, experiential, relational, and narrative; it recounts the experience of God's saving action for us in history. (474)

And he reminds us that 'Jewish tradition was quite familiar with the personification of various symbols representing God's action in the world. A most influential example of this is the personification of God's wisdom or *Sophia*. But whereas personification is recognized as figurative speech, hypostatization represents a certain literalization of it . . . the making of an idea or a concept or a figure of speech into a real thing, or entity' (475). Haight comments, surely correctly, that 'much of trinitarian theology today does precisely this, despite the intentions and disclaimers of its authors. Notions of God as a community, ideas of hypostatizing the differentiations within God and calling them persons in such a way that they are in dialogical intercommunication with one another, militate against the first point of the doctrine itself' (483) – namely the unity of God. On the other hand, wanting to leave the traditional language in place, Haight adds that 'One cannot quite conceive of fully Christian language about God that does not also employ the symbols of Christ and the Spirit' (484). He further supports the need for trinitarian language with an appeal to the experience of all who, in being open to divine revelation, 'experience transcendence as an internal presence' (484), this being symbolized as the Holy Spirit. But, as a critical comment on Haight's work, surely there can be no *need* to add the symbol of the Holy Spirit, except that the church has traditionally built it into its liturgies. But this should not be decisive for theologians who are aware that much of our traditional liturgical language has become meaningless to very many in the west and who are trying to make the central Christian message meaningful again in today's world.

Haight faces the questions that, in the light of the modern historical study of the New Testament and Christian origins, confront all who work in the field of christology. However he proceeds cautiously. For example, 'The particular historicity of the events behind the miracle stories is simply not known. But this is not really important. In principle, miracle stories of themselves can tell us nothing of the divine origin of Jesus . . . Although it is historically certain that Jesus cared for the sick and those who suffered, exactly how this was manifested is secondary' (82). But when we come to the supposed supreme miracle of Jesus' physical resurrection, his position is more clear-cut. He speaks of 'this symbol of Jesus being resurrected' (123). And, contrary to such theologians as Wolfhart Pannenberg and such New Testament scholars as N.T. Wright, writes:

it is better to say that Jesus' resurrection is not an historical fact, because the idea of an historical fact suggests an empirical event which could have been witnessed and can now be imaginatively construed . . . But this resurrection need not entail the assumption of his physical corpse . . . The bodily resurrection of Jesus thus means that Jesus in his whole integral integrity has been assumed into God's life. But the resurrection may be conceived as a meta-historical and meta-physical happening at the moment of death, and does not require the disappearance of Jesus' corpse. (124-5)

And concerning the stories of the empty tomb, 'these stories are symbolic: they give expression to the faith of the community that Jesus is risen' (135). Accordingly, 'the stories of appearances and the empty tomb are ways of expressing and teaching the content of a faith already formed' (145). As to Jesus' teaching, 'the centering characteristic of Jesus as a religious figure in first-century Palestine was his prophetic preaching of the kingdom of God for the restoration of Israel' (66), bearing in mind that 'The kingdom of God is a religious symbol' (97).

Haight stresses that there are a number of different christologies within the New Testament. 'But in all of its christologies at no point in the New Testament is Jesus identified with the transcendent God without ambiguity. The Prologue to John's Gospel, which seems to be the most straightforward statement of Jesus being divine, has to be read according to its genre as poetic, figurative language' (256). Concerning Jesus as Son of God, the term's metaphorical character is made clear by implication in Mark's Gospel:

After his baptism Jesus sees the Spirit descend upon him and hears the voice from heaven: 'Thou art my beloved Son; with thee I am well pleased'. This declaration is modeled upon Psalm 2:7 where, to the newly enthroned king of Israel, God says: 'You are my Son, today I have begotten you'. But the king is representative of the nation, and a more fundamental Jewish usage of Son of God describes the nation Israel as God's chosen people . . . The scene depicts Jesus as the one uniquely representing the obedience to God's will to which all Israel is being called by John [the Baptist]. (160)

Jesus then is a metaphorical, not literal Son of God, and the Lord's Prayer makes it clear that 'All should call God Father as Jesus himself does' (111). Thus 'One must recognize immediately that as a human being Jesus is Jesus, is not God, but points away from himself to God' (112).

Haight further recognizes that in the early development of christology there was 'the hypostatization of symbolic language about God . . . making an idea or a concept into a real thing' (257). As a result 'Wisdom is no longer a linguistic symbol referring obliquely to an attribute of God; Logos is no longer a figure of speech but a distinct being; Spirit is no longer a constructive exercise of the human poetic imagination that metaphorically depicts the effects of God as the invisible power of the wind, but a literal something' (257), for 'christology developed chiefly within the context of worship and cult' (139).

However despite, or beyond, all this Haight affirms the church's elevation of Jesus as a legitimate development. On the one hand, 'Surely Jesus did not display any consciousness that he had two natures and was hypostatically united to the divine Word' (39). But on the other hand, 'historical research into Jesus seems to impel the following thesis: later interpretations of Jesus may capture his intrinsic meaning and reality even though they may not have been part of Jesus' self-consciousness or self-understanding. In other words, one can affirm something to be the case about Jesus, especially in his relation to God or in his relation to ourselves, that was not necessarily part of Jesus' consciousness' (39). But a critical comment is called for here: how could *historical* research possibly require such a thesis, which goes beyond the historical to a faith interpretation of it? However Haight's move, which we find in many other theologians, is unavoidable if, as the Catholic church maintains, the beliefs gradually formed by the church in the development dominated by St Paul, and explicitly formulated during the next four centuries, were divinely guided and therefore authoritative. And Haight is a faithful Catholic believer who is not seeking to undermine this belief system but to make it more understandable and more credible in the world of today. For he recognizes that 'Christology must transcend fideism, that is, pure assertion of this faith, without any account of its inner logic or its coherence with what is known to be true from other sources' (29).

His criteria are 'faithfulness to the tradition, intelligibility in today's world, and empowerment of the Christian life' (47). We have seen that for him faithfulness to the tradition has to permit our modern historical questionings. He extends the second criterion to take account of:

> the unique and exalted character of Jesus Christ in face of the existence and vitality of other world religions, together with the generally positive evaluation of these religions in principle. The norms of intelligibility and coherence demand that one reconcile the universal relevance of Jesus Christ with the conviction that other religions have a role in world history under God's providence . . . Jesus has to be understood within the context of an understanding of and attitude to the larger portion of human beings who share other religious traditions. (50-1)

Before turning to this, however, a critical note. On the one hand, the conception of Jesus as the distinctively Christian symbol of God is a constructive proposal, which not only Haight's Catholic colleagues but also the wider Christian world should welcome with gratitude. That we have to proceed from the ground up rather than from traditional dogma downwards, and that the historical Jesus did not think of himself as divine, or teach anything like the later church doctrines about him, should become common ground. But, on the other hand, within his discussion there are still moments of the kind of ambiguity that almost inevitably characterize the present transitional phase of Christian thought. The central thrust of his christology is that Jesus' disciples encountered God *through* Jesus. In his presence God became utterly real to them, not in the sense that they thought that Jesus was himself God but in the sense that his overwhelmingly powerful God-consciousness and God-centred life mediated God's presence to them; and that this has continued and been renewed through the centuries in the life of the church. And so Haight speaks of 'a basic faith in God mediated *through* Jesus' (146, my italics); of 'a universally relevant revelation of God mediated *through* the particular person, Jesus Christ' (189, my italics). 'Jesus is the central *medium* and *focus* for Christian encounter with and faith in God' (195, my italics). But this is different from saying that God was ontologically *in* Jesus, with its implicit invoking of 'in him the whole fullness of deity dwells bodily' (Colossians 2.9). The misleading potential of *in* language here is acknowledged when Haight explains that 'people encountered God *in* Jesus' (my italics) 'is translated in more technical theological language as follows: Jesus is the historical mediation of God for

the Christian imagination' (112). However, that Jesus is the historical mediation of God for the Christian imagination is later elevated
by Haight into an ontological incarnation. He says, if perhaps
slightly unenthusiastically, 'No reason dictates why God as Spirit's
personal self-communication, presence, and activity in Jesus
should not be understood as an ontological incarnation, as long as
incarnation is not taken to mean that Jesus' consubstantiality with
us is negated' (459). I see this as a forgivable instance of accom-
modation to a conservative constituency. For that Jesus is the symbol, within the Christian imagination, of our awareness of God's
presence and God's love does not mean that God was *in* Jesus in
an ontological as distinguished from a symbolic or metaphorical
sense. The religious reality is that 'Jesus makes God present in a
saving way' (338). As Haight also puts it, 'the gospel records con-
tain a number of different actions performed by Jesus that are
considered more or less historically authentic, and they communicate something about *his conception of God* ' (104, my italics). But
Haight is tempted – understandably within his ecclesiastical context – to have it both ways by equating 'through' with 'in': 'Jesus
makes God present, and God is encountered *in or through him*'
(239, my italics), 'Jesus was one who *mediated* God, and people
encountered God *in* Jesus' (203, my italics). He is more consistent
to his own symbolic understanding of christology when he says that
Jesus mediated 'a presence of God, symbolized in a certain way,
and a manner of responding to this presence . . . Christology is
about Jesus of Nazareth. Yet Jesus is of interest because he mediates God and God's salvation. As the human mediator Jesus points
not to himself but at God and God's rule' (204). Or again, 'knowledge of God in Jesus or opened up by Jesus constitutes a sphere
of specifically Christian symbolic knowledge of God' (199). But
this does not require or authorize the traditional dogma of an ontological incarnation. Nor does it require or authorize the traditional
dogma that Jesus Christ had two natures, one human and the other
divine, as Haight nevertheless quasi-affirms when he says that 'The
doctrine of two natures corresponds to the dialectical structure of
Jesus as symbol of God' (205).

The other discernable stretching of his christology, as it seems
to me, to fit the dominant ecclesiastical framework occurs when
Haight discusses worship directed to Jesus. Christology, he
believes, must explain 'why [Jesus] is the object of Christian worship' (429), for 'This worship was the principal reason which led

to the clear and explicit affirmation of the divinity of Jesus in the patristic period' (429-30). However in Haight's Spirit christology Jesus' 'divinity' is not intended to attribute deity to him. He is not God but a symbol of God, and a mediator of God's grace. How then can it be appropriate to worship Jesus? Haight seems to justify it by arbitrarily equating mediation with worship-worthiness: 'Jesus mediates salvation from God and is therefore the object of Christian worship' (430). Later again, however, he takes a small step back when he says that 'one does not worship or pray to Jesus in insofar as Jesus is a human being and creature; rather, one worships and prays to God in and through Jesus' (457).

Turning now from criticism to appreciation, Haight's book is notable, and admirable, in seeing christology in a global context in which Christianity is one context of human salvation among others: 'Christian theology must be done within a pluralistic religious context.' (417). Usually a theologian's chapter on Christianity and the other world religions comes last, almost as an appendix. In Haight's book it comes before his chapters on the divinity of Jesus Christ and on the Trinity, for, 'An adequate Christology today must include an account of the relation of Jesus of other mediations of God' (395). It must accordingly 'show why Christians may regard Jesus as a normative revelation of God, while at the same time being convinced that God is also revealed normatively elsewhere' (395). 'I propose the thesis', Haight says, 'that the normativity of Jesus does not exclude a positive appraisal of religious pluralism, and that Christians may regard other world religions as true, in the sense that they are mediations of God's salvation' (411).

What, for Haight, does 'normative' mean? It seems to combine meanings. On the one hand, the normativity of Jesus means that for Christians he is the uniquely authoritative symbol of God: 'in so far as Jesus Christ is the central medium for Christianity's conception of ultimate reality, it is impossible by definition for Christ to be less than normative for a Christian appropriation of ultimate reality' (407); 'In sum, from a Christian theological standpoint Jesus is normative for the Christian imagination' (410). In this tradition-specific sense, 'Christians may regard Jesus as a normative revelation of God, while at the same time being convinced that God is also revealed normatively elsewhere' (395). But, for Haight, Jesus' normativeness also means his *universal* relevance: he is 'universally relevant, and thus normative' (456); 'Because of the nature of Christian revelation as encounter with a personal God, it is impossible that such an experience not be conceived as having a universal relevance' (406), so that 'Jesus represents normative truth for all humanity' (417). This normativity is not however unique, since 'because God is salvifically present to other religions, other representations of God can be universally normative, and thus, too, for Christians, even as Jesus Christ is universally normative (422).

So far Haight's position is coherent and consistent. However he also feels obliged to hold that 'Jesus is salvation bringer not for a certain group in history but for all human beings' (421). At first sight this suggests that Jesus is the sole saviour of all humanity. But Haight has himself argued 'against human salvation being universally caused by Jesus Christ' (412), claiming that 'there is little evidence that Jesus preached himself as the constitutive mediator of God's salvation for all human beings' (405), and he has argued in favour of the alternative position that:

> Jesus, therefore, is constitutive and the cause of the salvation of Christians because he is the mediator of the Christian awareness of life in the Spirit. But Jesus is not constitutive of salvation universally. Rather, a Spirit christology, by recognizing that the Spirit is operative outside the Christian sphere, is open to other mediations of God. The Spirit is spread abroad, and it is not necessary to think that God as Spirit can be incarnated only once in history. (456)

It therefore seems that, according to Haight, Jesus is potentially the saviour of all, in that he is saviour of all who take him as their saviour, but he is not in fact the saviour of all because many others are saved through different mediations of God. For 'other religions are mediations of God's grace, and thus not fundamentally in competition with God's action in Jesus' (420). Again, following Rahner, 'because such grace is necessarily mediated, and the religions are the historical and cultural media of transcendence, the religions are the de facto channels of God's saving grace' (412). And so Haight believes that 'Affirming the validity of other religions does not undermine the normativity of Jesus Christ. And affirming the normativity of Jesus Christ, not simply for Christians but for all human beings, does not undermine the validity and truth contained in other religions. Positively, one can and should affirm together the normativity of Jesus, the true and salvific character of other religions, and thus the positive character of religious pluralism' (421). Indeed, 'the recognition of God's universal saving influence transforms religious pluralism into a positive situation in which more can be learned about ultimate reality and human existence than is available in a single tradition . . . It is difficult to believe today that one single religion alone can possess the fullness of truth about transcendent reality' (422). And so Jesus' special position for Christians means that 'Jesus reveals something that has been going on from the beginning, before and outside of Jesus' own influence . . . [and so] no reason remains to design a meta-narrative that makes Jesus' historical life a cause of God's constant and ever-present salvific love' (422).

I, for one, warmly welcome Haight's work, seeing it as a very significant, if inevitably controversial, step forward in the Christian understanding of Jesus. But there is one further frontier that remains to be crossed. Haight hints at this when he uses the phrases 'ultimate reality' and 'transcendent reality' (422). The Christian experience of the ultimate reality has always been as a divine Thou. It is an experience of 'God, who is personal, who creates, who is friendly, who loves creatures and enters into an interactive relationship with them' (409). Accordingly, for him, 'religions are substantially true when they implicitly mediate God's love, whether or not they formally and explicitly represent it' (413). But is the assumption that the Ultimate is a person consistent with the recognition that 'more can be learned about ultimate reality and human existence than is available in a single tradition' (422) or presumably any single family of traditions, namely the 'western' monotheisms? For 'the goal [of dialogue] is not that one religion be converted to the religion of the other' (418). The global picture shows that the ultimate reality that is conceived in the 'Abrahamic' faiths as a personal God is conceived as trans-personal, beyond the distinction between the personal and the impersonal, in Buddhism, Taoism and some forms of Hinduism. And yet by the concrete criterion of salvation as the observable beginning of the transformation of human beings from natural self-centredness to a new orientation centred in the ultimate, these other great traditions are also authentic contexts of salvation. They too 'open the human spirit out of itself and turn it toward self-transcendence' (415). They too 'allow transcendence to press in upon them and, in turn, open human beings up to self-transcendence' (417). They too 'explicitly direct human freedom in the direction of self-transcendence and ultimacy' (421-2).

And so the next frontier that Christian thinking has to cross is from the general concept of 'other religions' as salvific to a positive religious interpretation of religion globally. Although Haight has not taken that further step, he has nevertheless taken a great stride forward in responsible globally conscious christology.

17

What Does This Mean for the Churches?

What, then, are our conclusions?

Concerning Jesus, it seems most likely that he thought of himself as called to fulfil the role of the final prophet before the imminent inbreaking of God's kingdom on earth. This was, as he must have understood it, an unique and critical human role. Accepting his eschatological vision, the early church waited in a state of urgent anticipation for him to come again as God's agent on the last day in glory and power. However, with the gradual fading of this expectation their faith in the lord Jesus transformed him from a prophet into a semi-divine Son of God and then ultimately into the fully divine God the Son, second person of a triune Deity. The New Testament documents, originating during the early stages of this transformation, include both flashbacks to the historical Jesus and anticipations of the fully divine Christ who was to be definitively proclaimed when Christianity became the religion of the empire.

Jesus' role as eschatological prophet ceased to be relevant as his expectation of an early end to ordinary human history proved to be erroneous. (This fact is not always fully faced by upholders of traditional orthodoxy. How could God the Son have been so massively mistaken?) But there was another side to Jesus' teaching that continued to be relevant. It arose from what must have been an extraordinarily powerful consciousness of God as the heavenly Father and of the new way of life that becomes natural in God's presence. This is the way of complete trust in God, of loving concern for one's fellows, of non-violence, forgiveness, and a service to others which in Jesus' case consisted in a career of healing and teaching. It is because he not only taught this way of life, but lived it, incarnated it, that Jesus' memory, enshrined in the church, is alive and powerful today.

But although Jesus, as the prophet of the imminent kingdom of God, did not intend to found a continuing church, or a new religion outside Judaism, what we know as Christianity nevertheless came into being, with the New Testament eventually becoming its foundation document. This reflects both memories of memories of Jesus and a stage in the church's progressive appropriation and deification of him. The New Testament's mixture of history and theology, memory and projection, can thus be used, according as one focusses on its more historical or its more doctrinal strands, to criticize or to support the developed belief in Jesus as God incarnate. Whether one sees the doctrine of the incarnation as already revealed implicitly in the words and actions of Jesus or as the gradual creation of the church, thus depends upon one's selection from the New Testament material. The most important single element guiding this selection is probably one's attitude to the church itself. Is the church and its continued life of such value that we should overlook the serious historical doubts concerning its claim to divine validation? Or is the church so ambiguous an institution, and its claim to religious preeminence so dubious, that one has no reason to overrule these doubts about its supernatural basis and character?

I have sensed again and again in theological discussions that this is the real determining 'gut' issue. What is at stake is the traditional belief in the unique superiority of Christianity as embodied in the church and in Western civilization. Those who are deeply committed to this are inclined to see within the ambiguous New Testament data the Jesus whose deity provides the church with a divine foundation. On the other hand those who have come to see the great religions and cultures of the world, including Christianity, as different but (so far as we can tell) more or less equally valuable forms of response to the Transcendent, are inclined to read the evidence of Christian origins differently.

However, I think it is fair to say that the burden of proof, or rather of justification, now lies heavily upon traditional orthodoxy. The earlier understanding of the New Testament, according to which Jesus himself clearly claimed a divine status, has been abandoned by responsible scholarship, and belief in the deity of Jesus has had to fall back upon the idea of an implicit claim. This is in the nature of the case a weaker ground than direct dominical authority would have been, and the broad picture is thus one of retreat from a certainty based on a divine pronouncement to a probability based on debateable historical evidences. Further, the growing number of attempts to meet the challenge to spell out the doctrine of the incarnation intelligibly – each proving persuasive only to some, and with the proponents of each type of theory criticizing the other types – has only added an air of confusion to the retreat.

The alternative to traditional orthodoxy need not be to renounce Christianity. Another more constructive possibility is to continue the development of Christian self-understanding in the direction suggested by the new global consciousness of our time. To what extent is this likely to happen? Will Christians come to see Christianity as one among several authentic ways of conceiving, experiencing and responding to the Transcendent; and will they come to see Jesus, in a way that coheres with this, as a man who was exceptionally open to the divine presence and who thus incarnated to a high degree the ideal of human life lived in response to the Real?

The true answer is probably both Yes and No. Some Christians are moving in this direction, and will continue to do so; and many others are not. At the moment (1993) there is still within most of the churches a general ideological swing to the right, and the majority mood is inhospitable even to the discussion of such issues. This is correlated with the resurgence of many forms and degrees of nationalistic us-against-them mentality, with the corresponding unpopularity of larger visions, both political and religious.

At the same time, though on a smaller scale, there is a continuing movement towards a global outlook, towards respect for other cultures and faiths and for minorities within one's own society, often associated with a revulsion against the hatred and violence of contemporary nationalism, and a concern for the earth and its atmosphere as our fragile environment and for all life as continuous with our own. Among Christians who share this global outlook it is often a commonplace that Christianity is one among a number of different perceptions of the divine and that Jesus was a great human prophet and servant of God.

To question the idea of Jesus as literally God incarnate is also, by implication, to question the idea of God as literally three persons in one. For the doctrine of the Trinity is derived from the doctrine of the incarnation. If Jesus was God on earth there must also have been God in heaven, so that Christian theology required at least a binity. When the Holy Spirit – not distinguished at first from the spirit of Jesus – was added as a distinct *hypostasis* the binity became a trinity. But for a non-traditional form of Christianity the trinitarian symbol does not refer to three centres of consciousness and will but to three ways in which the one God is humanly known –as creator, as transformer, and as inner spirit. We do not need to reify these ways as three distinct persons.

But before abandoning the older theological tradition let us ask, Is there not great religious value in the idea of divine incarnation, understood literally, which justifies us in retaining it? Yes and No. There are indeed senses in which a literal divine incarnation (assuming the idea to be viable) would have great religious value. But these various values are, in some cases, available in different ways within other traditions or, in other cases, carry with them a shadow side of unacceptable implications.

Thus in virtue of the doctrine of the incarnation (assuming this to be a viable idea) Christianity is a historical faith, firmly rooted in the soil of history and revealing God as present with us in the midst of human life. God is, in H.H. Farmer's phrase, 'inhistorized' (Farmer 1954, 195). And from a Western point of view at least, this constitutes a very positive value. But it should be noted that Christianity is not the only religion which sees God as active on earth and as participating in the historical process. Judaism, Islam and Sikhism also see God at work in this world, guiding a community, intervening miraculously at crucial moments in its history, and thus deeply involved in human affairs. The idea of divine incarnation in Jesus is thus one way, but not the only way, of picturing God's 'inhistorization'. In a different manner, and with much less concern for chronological history, Hindu faith also sees the divine as present in this world, in the depths of our own being. And in a different way again Mahayana Buddhism is concerned with the rediscovery of this ordinary world as extraordinary by awakening to the startling identity of *samsara*, the cycle of change, suffering and anxiety, when selflessly experienced, with the bliss of *nirvana*.

Again in the incarnation (still assuming this to be a viable idea) God has become known to us with a directness and fullness that would not otherwise be possible. There is, in Brian Hebblethwaite's words, a 'greatly increased potential for human knowledge of God and personal union with God introduced by God's own presence and acts, in human form, this side of the gap between Creator and creature. The character of Christ *is* for us the revealed character of God, and becomes the criterion for our understanding of the nature and will of God . . . God's love is communicated to us immediately by God's own incarnate presence here in our midst' (Hebblethwaite

1987, 35). For if Jesus was God incarnate, many men and women in first-century Palestine met God face to face, and subsequent generations continue to do so in imagination as they read the Gospels and partake of the eucharist. If we accept the doctrine of the incarnation we believe that the gracious and yet demanding love that we see in Jesus is, literally and identically, the love of God, expressed most fully in Jesus' atoning sacrifice on the cross. This would indeed be a great religious benefit.

Yet even this central value is haunted by its own shadow side in what has been called 'the scandal of particularity' or, better, the scandal of restricted access, or of limited revelation. For why is this great benefit limited to a minority of the human race? Why did it only occur so relatively recently in human history? And why only within one of the major streams of human life? Why not also in the great ancient civilizations of China and of India, and why not also in the many smaller tribal societies of Africa, the Americas, Australasia, northern Europe and Asia? We saw in Chapter 9 that from the point of view of so orthodox a theologian as Thomas Aquinas there could be no objection in principle to a plurality of divine incarnations. The greater, then, the benefit of the incarnation as a revelation of God's love, the greater the contradiction to that revelation in its restriction to a single manifestation affecting only a minority of human kind. For one implication of the traditional Christian belief in a single unique divine incarnation is the arbitrary limitation of divine saving concern to one particular section of the human race.

The only kind of theology that would render a plurality of divine incarnations pointless would be a strongly exclusivist one which holds that the main purpose of the incarnation was that Jesus should die for our sins, and that we can only receive salvation if we consciously plead his death as an atonement on our behalf. For only one atoning death is necessary, and in order to benefit from it anyone must know of it. This is, as Richard Swinburne says, 'an argument for one *final* major revelation, reporting that atonement' (Swinburne 1992, 76). But this exclusivism was rejected by the Roman Catholic Church at Vatican II and is mainly confined now to Protestant theological fundamentalists. For the large majority of Christian theologians, who today are inclusivists or pluralists, there is no basis for such an argument.

It is not an adequate response to this to say that the church has a duty to evangelize the world and that the incarnation is thus, through the church, an act on behalf of all humanity. For how could it be an expression of limitless love to 'contract out' the revelation of that love to a very inadequate human group, which can now be seen definitively to have failed in its project to convert the world? If the idea of a divine incarnation in human life is viable, why has God not become incarnate as often as might be necessary to reach the whole world? I am not aware that any convincing answer to this question has yet been offered. The scandal of restricted access, or of limited revelation, thus vitiates what would otherwise have been the supreme value of a divine incarnation.

Another great religious value of the incarnation (still assuming this to be a viable idea) would be that it reveals God as sharing, through Jesus' life and death, in our human suffering. Of course, if God is omniscient God knows all human suffering as it occurs, and if God is 'passible', capable of suffering (something, however, that the Council of Chalcedon emphatically denied),[1] then God is, in A.N. Whitehead's phrase, 'the fellow sufferer who understands' (Whitehead 1919, 496). But, says Brian Hebblethwaite, 'Only if we can say that God has *himself*, on the Cross, "borne our sorrows" can we find him universally present "in" the sufferings of others . . . This whole dimension of the Christian doctrine of the Incarnation, its recognition of the costly nature of God's forgiving love, and its perception that only a suffering God is morally credible, is lost if God's involvement is reduced to a matter of "awareness" and "sympathy"' (Hebblethwaite 1987, 36). The idea of divine suffering appeals to many today, even though until comparatively recent times it was officially regarded as dangerously mistaken: God was immutable and impassible, and it was in Jesus' human, not in his divine, nature that he suffered on the cross. The notion of a suffering God does indeed move uncomfortably close to anthropomorphism – an anthropomorphism which indeed haunts the whole conception of divine incarnation. (Jacob Neusner remarks that 'Anthropomorphism forms the genus of which incarnation constitutes a species', Neusner 1988, 11.) However, given the widespread contemporary approval of the idea, it has to be added that, as Frances Young has said, 'Jesus is not the only evidence of a suffering God' (Young 1977, 37). The Hebrew Bible points to God's suffering love for Israel. And looking further afield,

---

[1] In its preamble the Chalcedonian edict says that 'The Synod . . . deposes from the priesthood those who dare to say that the Godhead of the Only-Begotten is passible.' Divinity was taken in orthodox theology, until comparatively recent times, to entail immutability and impassibility.

there is no lack of expression of God's presence within human suffering. For example, the literature of Islam includes such vivid passages as Rumi's 'God said, "a favourite and chosen servant of mine fell sick. I am he. Consider well: his infirmity is My infirmity, his sickness is My sickness"' (Nicholson 1978, 65); and the contemporary Sikh mystic and social activist, Kushdeva Singh, has written:

> People go to their temples
> To greet Me;
> How simple and ignorant are my children
> Who think that I live in isolation.
>
> Why don't they come and greet me
> In the procession of life, where I always live,
> In the farms, the factories, and the market,
> Where I encourage those
> Who earn their bread by the sweat of their brow?
>
> Why don't they come and greet Me
> In the cottages of the poor
> And find Me blessing the poor and the needy
> And wiping the tears of widows and orphans?
>
> Why don't they come and greet Me
> By the road-side
> And find Me blessing the beggar asking for bread?
>
> Why don't they come and greet Me
> Among those who are trampled upon
> By those proud of pelf and power,
> And see Me beholding their suffering and pouring out
>   compassion?
> Why don't they come and greet Me
> Among women sunk in sin and shame
> Where I sit by them to bless and uplift?
>
> I am sure
> They can never miss Me
> If they try to meet Me
> In the sweat and struggle of life
> And in the tears and tragedies of the poor (Kushdeva Singh
> 1974, 31-2).

This particular value – the revelation of divine love in the crucified God – has of course traditionally been expressed in the doctrine of the atonement. In Chapters 11 and 12 I have argued that this doctrine has been a mistake, carrying unacceptable ethical implications and being contrary to Jesus' own teaching; and I need not repeat that argument here.

It is also said that by entering into and becoming part of the human experience of suffering, God confronts and takes ultimate responsibility for the presence of evil within the created universe. This is an appealing thought. As I expressed it myself in an earlier (1968) writing, 'it is part of the meaning of Christian monotheism that there is an ultimately responsible moral being, who is absolute goodness and love, whom we may trust amid the uncertainties and anxieties of the gradual unfolding of reality to us in time. We are led to this trust by seeing the divine responsibility at work on earth in the life of Christ. For there we see the Love which has ordained the long, costly soul-making process entering into it and sharing with us in its inevitable pains and sufferings' (Hick 1973, 69-70). And I think it must be freely granted that (assuming, of course, the viability of the idea of divine incarnation) it is a powerful thought that, in Vernon White's words, 'unless and until God himself has experienced suffering, death, and temptation to sin, and overcomes them, as a human individual, he has no moral authority to overcome them in and with the rest of humanity' (White 1991, 39).

However, even this idea, powerful though it is, also has its shadow side. For it, too, shares in the scandal of restricted access. If in the incarnation God is reconciling us to the creative process, with all its harsh as well as its welcome aspects, why is this salvific revelation only given to a minority of human beings? It can of course be said that 'in principle' it is available to everyone; for it is not deliberately hidden or withheld from anyone. But one can say that of any truth that is in fact only made available through certain limited media. And the idea that Jesus of Nazareth was God incarnate, and that in his atoning death we are shown the suffering love of God, has never been available in practice to more than a minority of human beings – the minority constituting Christendom and its colonial extensions, and indeed within this minority only that modern sub-minority that rejects the traditional Christian orthodoxy of divine impassibility. Thus the greater the benefit of being born into this divinely favoured segment of human history, the greater the injustice to those born outside it. This is the scandal of restricted access which unhappily undermines every religious value that we can attribute to the incarnation doctrine.

It is of course possible to try to remove this scandal by denying any religious advantage in being a Christian. One can hold that the knowledge of God's love, expressed in Jesus' atoning act, does not add anything to the fact of that love and atoning act. Thus Vernon White, advocating an inclusivist theology of religions, says that '*Knowledge* of the Saviour is not a necessary constituent of *being* saved' (White 1991, 39). Christ is secretly saving people within other religions and within no religion. White (more clear-minded than some inclusivists) asks, 'Does this then reduce the role and significance of the Christian Church to an inessential historical accident? Strictly speaking it is true that the logic of our position implies that, were there no historical knowledge of the Christ event and no human agency to transmit it, it would still have saving efficacy' (White 1991, 113-14) – presumably meaning that it would still have just as much saving efficacy as it now has. So far this sounds like an inclusivism that has the courage of its convictions. For if it really is the case that God has not, by the incarnation, given any privileged access to Christians, then there is no religious advantage in being a Christian and no reason to try to convert others to Christianity. But White almost immediately rebounds from this obvious conclusion. He says that 'this does not marginalize the role of the Church in God's purposes for the world . . . The event [of the incarnation] had its effect without knowledge; but gaining the knowledge of it is still a highly significant part of final fulfilment . . . Evangelism, far from being superfluous, becomes (at best) a profound act of sharing and generosity, bringing crucial elements of final fulfilment into the present' (White 1991, 114). So there *is* after all, according to White, a significant religious plus available to Christians that is not at present available to Jews, Muslims, Hindus, Sikhs, Buddhists, Taoists and others; and the scandal of restricted access is accordingly still with us. The dilemma that traditional orthodoxy has to face is that the greater the religious 'plus' attached by God to being a Christian rather than a Jew, Muslim, Buddhist, etc., the greater is the religious 'minus' ordained by God in being a Buddhist, Muslim, Jew, etc., rather than a Christian. This scandal of limited revelation can only be lessened by lessening that 'plus', and only removed entirely by entirely removing it. One cannot responsibly have it both ways, affirming both that there is an important religious advantage to a person's being a Christian, and yet that those who have been born or brought into the Christian world are not thereby divinely favoured in a way that is unjust to most of the remaining majority of the human race.

There is also a hint in Vernon White's pages of another way in which some seek to mitigate the scandal of restricted access, namely by affirming a 'second chance' to enter the privileged circle in the life to come. In saying that explicit knowledge of Christ is not necessary for salvation White adds, 'not, that is, in this life' (White 1991, 112). However he goes on to say that, 'Even if every knee shall ultimately bow at the name of Jesus (whether or not they heard it in Church), the anticipation of that now is a glorious privilege' (White 1991, 114). And so the scandal of (present) restricted access returns once more. Christians have a 'glorious privilege' which non-Christians lack; and this, combined with the fact that it is not (normally) the latters' fault that they lack it, is incompatible with a universal divine love.

This scandal, which vitiates what would otherwise be important religious values of the idea of Jesus as God incarnate, challenges us to enlarge our field of vision. When we do so we see not only the negative fact that most of the world is non-Christian, but also the positive fact that most who are not Christian are of faiths other than Christianity. This makes the scandal of restricted access doubly scandalous; for insistence upon the unique revelation of God's love and co-suffering with humanity in Jesus downgrades the other great world faiths to the status of derivative or lesser revelations and/or unconscious and secondary conduits of Christian salvation. I have argued in Chapters 13 and 14, in line with much contemporary thinking, that this traditional superiority-claim is religiously unrealistic; and indeed I think that scepticism and discomfort about it is very widespread today among thoughtful Christians.

The tension within the churches being created by the challenge of religious pluralism is similar to that felt in the second half of the nineteenth century as the fact of biological evolution was pressing upon Christian consciousness, setting up a painful conflict with the inherited orthodoxy. Evolution challenged the picture of the universe in terms of which Christians had long lived, with humanity as a special divine creation set apart from the rest of life; and, even more importantly, challenging its foundation in the Bible, literally construed and received as having direct divine authority. The reaction against this challenge was powerful and prolonged. But in the end, *magna est veritas et praevalebit*, the truth will out; and the churches have gradually had to change their theology and their use of the Bible in accordance with the new knowledge. *Homo sapiens* has thus far been successful because the human mind adjusts itself to reality, even if often only slowly and reluctantly. And I anticipate that a process analogous to the slow and painful acceptance of evolution will take place in the acceptance that Christianity is one among a plurality of authentic human responses to the divine reality. There will be powerful resistance; considerable inner turmoil and agony, sometimes expressed in anger against those who are recommending change; and a gradual, uneven, variegated development of Christian thought, leaving – as in the case of the controversies over science and the scriptures – a continuing and probably powerful fundamentalist wing.

The almost inevitable Christian acceptance of religious pluralism can take two different forms – providing scope, alas, for yet another internal division. One possibility, launched by Rudolf Bultmann and others more than a generation ago, is 'demythologization', stripping Christian belief of its mythological elements. This runs parallel with a movement going back to the Reformation of the sixteenth century, the 'Radical Reformation' embodied today mainly in the Unitarian movement. The other, and to many of us more attractive, possibility is to acknowledge the mythological character of myth and to affirm its positive value in touching the more poetic and creative side of our nature, and then allowing our imagination and emotion to resonate to myth as myth. Here we can learn from the Hindus, who delight in myth and are able to feed upon it spiritually without having to pretend that it is other than myth. To see, for example, the remains of the Elephanta temple near Bombay is to see a great mythic world that was, and is, consciously perceived and inhabited as such. The bare bones of its cognitive content can of course be expressed in literal terms. Thus the huge Trimurti showing the divine as having simultaneously the three faces of Brahma the creator, Vishnu the preserver, and Shiva the destroyer, speaks of the ultimate unity of the cosmic process, with its continual cycle of creation and dissolution or, in Christian language, of death and resurrection. But this is made vividly real to the imagination and powerfully evocative to the emotions by its mythic representation; and in the temple worship men and women came face to face with this deep structure of reality and were moved to accept both its gracious and its harsh aspects.

However, it must be admitted that the celebration of myth, which apparently comes so easily to the Indian mind, does not come so easily to the typical Western mind. When, for example, at Christmas we see the stable scene with the figures of Mary and Joseph, the haloed baby in the crib, the shepherds and the wise men kneeling before him, the cattle looking on and the miraculous star above, we have to suspend the historical questionings that would otherwise spoil the occasion. For we seem to have an ingrained tendency either to accept our myths as literally true or reject them as simply false. We need to learn to accept the idea of mythological truth in religion as a practical truthfulness consisting in a myth's evoking in us a dispositional response that is appropriate to its ultimate referent. The ultimate referent of religious mythology is the Transcendent, the eternally Real, experienced in different ways within the different religious traditions. And in so far as these different perceptions, formed by different sets of human concepts, are valid they are in soteriological alignment with the transcendent Reality, so that in living in right relationship to any one of these manifestations of the Real we are rightly related to the Real itself. For on a religious understanding of them the great world faiths are genuine (though not therefore perfect) human responses to the Transcendent, constituting contexts within which men and women are transformed from self-centredness to Reality-centredness. (The philosophical position that lies behind this brief statement is developed in my *An Interpretation of Religion*, Hick 1989.)

But for most modern Western Christians (including myself) it remains difficult to accept myth as myth. Returning to the crib, and the Christmas story as a whole, we know that it is historically unlikely that Jesus was born on 25 December (the date of a pre-Christian pagan winter festival which Christianity inherited), that the year of his birth was 1 C E (it was more probably about 5 B C E); unlikely that he was born in Bethlehem (which was probably adopted into the story to fulfil prophecy), that he had no human father (a mythic theme that became attached to a number of great figures in antiquity); and we have seen reasons to reject the dogma that he was God incarnate (a dogma that Jesus himself would probably have regarded as blasphemous). In view of all this, how does one participate in Christmas? Either one opts out, on the ground that the Christmas story is literally false; or one opts in, accepting the myth as evocative poetry, stirring the emotions, expanding the imagination, warming the heart – and all in the direction of an enhanced sense of the gracious, loving, benign character of the Ultimate in relationship to human life. But it must be admitted that for many of us this remains difficult; and unless and until sensibilities change we shall have to live with this unresolved problem. It is particularly difficult for those who are called to lead the worship of the church, knowing that many in their congregations regard the mythic story as literally true. It must have been equally difficult a hundred years ago when reading, for example, the story of Adam and Eve as the scripture for the day, and understanding it as truth in mythic form whilst knowing that many in the pews could only see it as literal history. The same words were being understood in different ways by different people. And so it is today. 'The Word was made flesh' entails for some that Jesus, uniquely, had two natures, divine and human, and is accordingly to be worshipped as God; whilst it means for others both that Jesus' life embodied a love that is a reflection of the divine love, and that the ideal of humanity living in response to God was, to a startling extent, embodied, incarnated, in his life, so that we may take him as our lord, guru, spiritual leader.

Why does it matter whether we think of the Christian story – the story of God the Son descending from heaven to earth to die in atonement for the sins of the world and to found the church – as literally or as mythologically true? It matters because, as we have seen, its literal understanding has unacceptable implications which the mythic construal does not have. If Jesus was literally and uniquely God incarnate, Christianity is thereby singled out as the only religion founded by God in person. It would then be strange if, having founded a new religion, God did not wish it to supersede all other religions. It would be strange if those who are incorporated into God's own religion (into 'the Body of Christ') were not in some important way thereby spiritually better off than those outside. It would be strange if the civilization based on God's religion were not qualitatively better than all others. In short, the dogma of the incarnation implies the unique superiority of Christianity and of Christian civilization. But that supposed superiority seems to many of us today to be very dubious. And when we look critically at its religious validation we find it to be shaky indeed. The idea lacks a secure historical basis in the teachings of Jesus; the attempts to make it conceptually intelligible have so far failed; and, further, it has been tainted by its use to justify enormous human evils.

The alternative is a Christian faith which takes Jesus as our supreme (but not necessarily only) spiritual guide; as our personal and communal lord, leader, guru, exemplar, and teacher, but not as literally himself God; and which sees Christianity as one authentic context of salvation/liberation amongst others, not opposing but interacting in mutually creative ways with the other great paths. But could such a Christian faith, no longer claiming to be final and universally normative, hope to survive? Does not a viable religious movement require the supercharged emotion of a close, warm, community formed around an absolute claim, and the security of a privileged insider knowledge over against an outside world? Does it not need evangelical fervour and dedication? And must it not therefore hold to a simple and doctrinally, even if not biblically, fundamentalist structure of belief?

The answer, again, is both Yes and No. Many people in this bewilderingly complex world do seek simple straightforward beliefs concerning the Ultimate and concerning the basic long-term meaning of their lives. And fundamentalist forms of belief can provide this. Indeed they can appeal not only to the relatively uneducated but also to people who are highly educated in fields other than the study of religion. In this connection, the sociologist Peter Berger says that 'there is some warrant for asserting that the propensity to believe evident nonsense increases rather than decreases with higher education' (Berger 1992, 126)! Conceptions, however implausible, accepted without criticism within a supportive community can have immense power.

However, it is not only the familiar traditional Christian picture that is simple and straightforward. Indeed as soon as this is pressed beyond the level of hymns and choruses and popular sermons it becomes far from simple and far from straightforward. The ideas of the Trinity and of the two natures of Christ are in fact incomprehensible to most people. In comparison a non-traditional Christian faith can be genuinely simple and yet profound. Consider the belief that there is an ultimate transcendent Reality which is the source and ground of everything; that this Reality is benign in relation to human life; that the universal presence of this Reality is reflected ('incarnated') in human terms in the lives of the world's great spiritual leaders; and that amongst these we have found Jesus to be our principal revelation of the Real and our principal guide for living.

This is basic religious faith in a Christian form. It is our human response to the mystery of the universe, powered by religious experience and guided by rational thought. But the sense of benign

Transcendence needs to be taken up into the stream of imaginative imagery and song and music which in our electronic age pervasively moulds the dispositions and attitude to life of very many people. The 'signals of transcendence' that are all around us need to be connected to our thoughts and emotions. This cannot be done by philosophers and theologians, whose work is more analogous to 'pure' scientific research in its relation to technology. The application to life must be the work of people creative in the arts of all kinds, including the art of living, responding to their experience of Transcendence and embodying it in the concrete mythic forms in terms of which human life is lived.

When will this happen? Will it happen? Is it perhaps already beginning to happen? The future will tell.

Reference Bibliography

Biblical quotations are from the New Revised Standard Version

Abbott, Walter M.
1966: *The Documents of Vatican II* (London and Dublin: Geoffrey Chapman, and New York: Association Press)

Akers, Charles Edmund
1930: *A History of South America*, 3rd ed. (London: John Murray, and New York: E.P. Dutton)

Alston, William
1964: *Philosophy of Language* (Englewood Cliffs, N.J.: Prentice-Hall)
1989: *Divine Nature and Human Language* (Ithaca, N.Y.: Cornell University Press)

Anderson, Norman
1978: *The Mystery of the Incarnation* (London: Hodder & Stoughton, and Grove, Illinois: Inter-Varsity Press)

Anselm, St
1962: *Cur Deus Homo?* trans. S.W. Deane in *Saint Anselm: Basic Writings* (La Salle, Illinois: Open Court)
1965: *Proslogion*, trans. M.J. Charlesworth (Oxford: Clarendon Press)

Aquinas, Thomas
1955: *Summa contra Gentiles*, Book I, trans. Anton Pegis (New York: Doubleday, Image)
1976: *Summa Theologica*, Blackfriars Latin/English ed. (London: Eyre & Spottiswoode, and New York: McGraw Hill)

Athanasius, St
1957: *Discourses Against the Arians*, in Philip Schaff and Henry Wace, eds., *The Nicene and Post-Nicene Fathers*, Second Series, Vol. IV (Grand Rapids, Michigan: Eerdmans)
1989: *On the Incarnation* (London: Mowbray, and Crestwood, N.Y.: St Vladimir's Orthodox Theological Seminary)

Augustine, St
1953: *Of True Religion*, trans. J.H.S. Burleigh, *Augustine: Earlier Writings* (Library of Christian Classics, Philadelphia: Westminster Press, and London: SCM Press)

Aulen, Gustaf
1953: *Christus Victor* (London: SPCK)

Baillie, Donald
    1948: *God Was in Christ* (London: Faber & Faber, and New York: Scribner's)
Baillie, John, ed.
    1957: *The Theology of the Sacraments* (New York: Scribner's)
Barr, James
    1988 a: 'Abba Isn't "Daddy"', in *Journal of Theological Studies*, Vol. 39
    1988 b: 'Abba, Father', in *Theology*, Vol. 91, No. 741
Beardsley, Monroe
    1962: 'The Metaphorical Twist', in *Philosophy and Phenomenological Research*, Vol.22, No.3
    1978: 'Metaphorical Senses' in *Nous*, Vol.12
Berger, Peter
    1992: *A Far Glory: The Quest for Faith in an Age of Credulity* (New York: Free Press, and London: Maxwell Macmillan International)
Bettenson, Henry, ed.
    1956: *Documents of the Christian Church* (London and New York: Oxford University Press)
Bhagavad Gita
    1979: Kees Bolle, trans. (University of California Press)
Black, Max
    1962: *Models and Metaphors* (Ithaca, N.Y.: Cornell University Press)
Bornkamm, Günther
    1960: *Jesus of Nazareth* (London: Hodder & Stoughton, and New York: Harper & Row)
Bowden, John
    1988: *Jesus: The Unanswered Questions* (London: SCM Press, and Nashville, Tennessee: Abingdon Press [1990])
Brown, David
    1985: *The Divine Trinity* (London: Duckworth, and LaSalle, Illinois: Open Court)
Brown, Judith
    1989: *Gandhi: Prisoner of Hope* (New Haven and London: Yale University Press)
Bultmann, Rudolf
    1955: *Essays Philosophical and Theological* (London: SCM Press, and New York: Macmillan)

Carey, George
    1977: *God Incarnate* (Leicester, England: Inter-Varsity Press)
Casey, Maurice
    1991: *From Jewish Prophet to Gentile God* (Cambridge: James Clarke, and Louisville: Westminster/John Knox)

Clarkson, John F. et al.
1955: *The Church Teaches: Documents of the Church in English Trans-lation* (St Louis and London: B. Herder)
Clement of Alexandria
1956: *Stromateis*, in Alexander Roberts and James Donaldson, eds., *The Ante-Nicene Fathers*, Vol. II (Grand Rapids, Michigan: Eerdmans)
Coakley, Sarah
1988: *Christ Without Absolutes* (Oxford: Clarendon Press)
Cohn-Sherbok, Dan
1992: *The Crucified Jew: Twenty Centuries of Christian Anti-Semitism* (London: Harper-Collins)
Cooper, David
1986: *Metaphor* (Oxford: Blackwell)
Crawford, Robert G.
1988: *The Saga of God Incarnate*, 2nd ed. (Pretoria: University of South Africa)

Daly, Mary
1973: *Beyond God the Father* (Boston: Beacon Press, and London: The Women's Press [1986])
Davis, Stephen
1983: *Logic and the Nature of God* (London: Macmillan, and Grand Rapids, Michigan: Eerdmans)
Davis, Stephen, ed.
1988: *Encountering Jesus* (Atlanta: John Knox Press)
Deissmann, Adolf
1926: *The Religion of Jesus and the Faith of Paul* (London: Hodder & Stoughton)
Driver, Tom
1981: *Christ for a Changing World* (New York: Crossroad, and London: SCM Press).
Dunn, James
1980: *Christology in the Making* (London: SCM Press, and Philadelphia: Westminster Press)
Dupuis, Jacques
1991: *Jesus Christ at the Encounter of World Religions* (Maryknoll, N.Y.: Orbis)

Eliade, Mircea
1982: *A History of Religious Ideas*, Vol. 2 (Chicago and London: University of Chicago Press)

Erskine, Noel Leo
   1981: *Decolonizing Theology: A Caribbean Perspective* (Maryknoll, N.Y.: Orbis)
Eusebius
   1952: *Ecclesiastical History* in Philip Schaff and Henry Wace, eds., *The Nicene and Post-Nicene Fathers*, Vol. I (Grand Rapids, Michigan: Eerdmans)

Farmer, H.H.
   1941: *The Servant of the Word* (London: Nisbet)
   1954: *Revelation and Religion* (London: Nisbet, and New York: Harper)
Feenstra, Ronald J. and Plantinga, Cornelius, Jr. eds.
   1989: *Trinity, Incarnation and Atonement* (University of Notre Dame Press)
Feenstra, Ronald J.
   1989: 'Reconsidering Kenotic Christology', in Feenstra & Plantinga 1989
Forsyth, P.T.
   1910: *The Person and Place of Jesus Christ*, 2nd ed. (London: Hodder & Stoughton)
Flusser, David
   1991: 'Jesus, His Ancestry, and the Commandment of Love', in James H. Charlesworth, ed., *Jesus' Jewishness* (New York: Crossroad)
Fredricksen, Paula
   1988: *From Jesus to Christ* (New Haven and London: Yale University Press)

Gandhi, Ramchandra
   1984: *I am Thou* (Poona: Indian Philosophical Quarterly Publications)
Geach, Peter
   1977: *Providence and Evil* (Cambridge University Press)
Gore, Charles
   1907: *Dissertations on Subjects Connected with the Incarnation* (London: John Murray)
Goulder, Michael, ed.
   1979: *Incarnation and Myth: The Debate Continued* (London: SCM Press, and Grand Rapids, Michigan: Eerdmans)
Grant, Robert
   1971: *Augustus to Constantine* (London: Collins, and New York: Harper)
Green, Michael, ed.
   1977: *The Truth of God Incarnate* (London: Hodder & Stoughton)
Gregory of Nyssa
   1892 a: *Against Eunomius* in Philip Schaff and Henry Wace, eds., *The*

Nicene and Post-Nicene Fathers, Second Series, Vol. V. (Grand Rapids, Michigan: Eerdmans)
1892 b: *The Great Catechism,* ditto
Grensted, L.W.
1962: *A Short History of the Doctrine of the Atonement* (Manchester University Press)

Haight, Roger
1999: *Jesus Symbol of God* (Maryknoll, N.Y.: Orbis)
Hanson, A.T.
1984: 'Two Consciousnesses: the Modern Version of Chalcedon', in *Scottish Journal of Theology,* Vol. 37, No. 4
Harvey, A.E., ed.
1981: *God Incarnate: Story and Belief* (London: SPCK)
Hebblethwaite, Brian
1987: *The Incarnation* (Cambridge University Press)
Hengel, Martin
1975: *The Son of God* (London: SCM Press, and Philadelphia: Fortress Press)
Herbert, R.T.
1979: *Paradox and Identity in Theology* (Ithaca, N.Y.: Cornell University Press)
Hick, John, ed.
1977: *The Myth of God Incarnate* (London: SCM Press, and Philadelphia: Westminster Press) [2nd edition, 1993]
Hick, John
1958: 'The Christology of D.M. Baillie', in *Scottish Journal of Theology,* Vol. 11
1973: *God and the Universe of Faiths* (London: Macmillan, and New York: St Martin's Press)
1989: *An Interpretation of Religion* (London: Macmillan, and New Haven: Yale University Press) [2nd edition, 2004]
1993: 'The Non-Absoluteness of Christianity' and 'The Logic of God Incarnate' in *Disputed Questions in Theology and the Philosophy of Religion* (London: Macmillan, and New Haven: Yale University Press)
Houlden, Leslie
1992: *Jesus: A Question of Identity* (London: SPCK)

Isherwood, Christopher
1965: *Ramakrishna and His Disciples* (London: Methuen, and New York: Simon & Schuster)

James, William
1890: *The Principles of Psychology,* Vol. I (New York: Henry Holt, and London: Macmillan [1891])

1960: *Varieties of Religious Experience* [1902] (London: Collins Fontana)
Jeremias, Joachim
1966: *The Eucharistic Words of Jesus* (London: SCM Press, and New York: Scribner)

Kasper, Walter
1976: *Jesus the Christ* (London: Burns & Oates, and New York: Paulist Press)
Kee, A. and E.T. Long
1986: *Being and Truth: Essays in Honour of John Macquarrie* (London: SCM Press)
Kee, Howard
1990: *What Can We Know About Jesus?* (Cambridge University Press)
Kena Upanishad
1953: Trans. S. Radhakrishnan, *The Principal Upanishads* (London: Allen & Unwin, and New York: Harper)
Kierkegaard, Søren
1985: *Philosophical Fragments* [1844] (Princeton: Princeton University Press)
Klostermaier, Klaus
1969: *Hindu and Christian in Vrindaban* (London: SCM Press [reissued 1993]) and *In the Paradise of Krishna* (Philadelphia: Westminster Press)
Knox, John
1967: *The Humanity and Divinity of Jesus* (Cambridge University Press)
Kushdeva Singh
1974: *In Dedication,* 2nd edition (Patiala: Guru Nanak Mission)

Lakoff, George, and Mark Johnson, eds.
1980: *Metaphors We Live By* (University of Chicago Press)
Lampe, Geoffrey
1977: *God As Spirit* (Oxford University Press)
Lewis, C.S.
1955: *Mere Christianity* (London: Collins Fontana, and New York: Macmillan [1964])

Mackintosh, H.R.
1912: *The Doctrine of the Person of Christ* (Edinburgh: T. & T. Clark)
Macquarrie, John
1977: 'Christianity without Incarnation?' in Green, ed., *The Truth of God Incarnate*

1990: *Jesus Christ in Modern Thought* (London: SCM Press, and Philadelphia: Trinity Press International)
1995: *The Mediators* (London: SCM Press)
1998: *Christology Revisited* (London: SCM Press)
2002: *Stubborn Theological Questions* (London: SCM Press)
Mascall, Eric
1977: *Theology and the Gospel of Christ* (London: SPCK)
1985: *Jesus: Who He Is and How We Know Him* (London: Darton, Longman & Todd)
Maxwell, Meg, and Verena Tschuden
1990: *Seeing the Invisible: Modern Religious and Other Transcendent Experiences* (Harmondsworth: Penguin)
McDonald, Durston R.
1979: *The Myth/Truth of God Incarnate* (Wilson, Connecticut: Barlow)
McFague, Sallie
1982: *Metaphorical Theology* (Philadelphia: Fortress Press)
Meyendorff, John
1987: *Byzantine Theology* (Fordham University Press)
Meynell, Hugo
1986: *The Theology of Bernard Lonergan* (Atlanta, Georgia: Scholars Press)
Minsky, Marvin
1985: *The Society of Mind* (New York: Simon & Schuster, and London: Heinemann [1987])
Morris, James
1968: *Heaven's Command* (London: Faber & Faber, and New York: Harcourt, Brace, Jovanovich [1973])
Morris, Thomas V.
1986 a: *The Logic of God Incarnate* (Ithaca, N.Y. and London: Cornell University Press)
1986 b: 'Reduplication and Representational Christology', in *Modern Theology*, Vol. 2, No. 4
1989: 'The Metaphysics of God Incarnate', in Feenstra & Plantinga, eds.
Moulder, James
1986: 'Is a Chalcedonian Christology Coherent?', in *Modern Theology*, Vol. 2, No. 4
Moule, C.F.D.
1977: *The Origin of Christology* (Cambridge University Press)

Neusner, Jacob
1988: *The Incarnation of God* (Philadelphia: Fortress Press)
Newman, Paul W.
1987: *A Spirit Christology* (New York and London: University Press of America)

Nicholson, R.E., trans.
    1978: *Rumi: Poet and Mystic* (London and Boston: Unwin Mandala)
Nineham, Dennis
    1977: 'Epilogue' in Hick, ed., *The Myth of God Incarnate*

O'Collins, Gerald
    1983: *Interpreting Jesus* (London: Geoffrey Chapman, and Ramsey, N.J.: Paulist Press)
Ogden, Schubert
    1982: *The Point of Christology* (New York: Harper & Row, and London: SCM Press)
Ornstein, Robert
    1986: *Multimind* (Boston: Houghton Mifflin, and London: Macmillan)
Ortony, Andrew
    1979: *Metaphor and Thought* (Cambridge University Press)
Otto, Rudolf
    1932: *Mysticism East and West* (New York: Meridian Books)

Page, Ruth
    1991: *The Incarnation of Freedom and Love* (London: SCM Press, and New York: Pilgrim Press [1993])
Paine, Thomas
    1890: *The Theological Works of Thomas Paine (The Age of Reason)* (Chicago: Belford Clarke)
Pannenberg, Wolfhart
    1968: *Jesus: God and Man* (Philadelphia: Westminster Press, and London: SCM Press)
Peck, Anne Merriman
    1941: *The Pageant of South America* (New York: Longmans, Green)
Pelikan, Jaroslav
    1985: *Jesus Through the Centuries* (Yale University Press)
Percy, J.D.
    1961: *Facing the Unfinished Task* (Grand Rapids, Michigan: Eerdmans)
Prestige, G.L.
    1936: *God in Patristic Thought* (London and Toronto: Heinemann)
Puccetti, Roland
    1968: *Persons* (London: Macmillan)

Quesnell, Quentin
    1987: 'Aquinas on Avatars' in *Dialogue and Alliance,* Vol. l, No. 2
Qur'an
    1988: Ahmed Ali, trans. (Princeton University Press)

Race, Alan
    1983: *Christians and Religious Pluralism* (London: SCM Press, and Maryknoll, N.Y.: Orbis)

Radhakrishnan, S.
1953: *The Principal Upanishads* (London: Allen & Unwin, and New York: Harper)
Rahner, Karl
1965: *Theological Investigations,* Vol. I, 2nd ed. (London: Darton, Longman & Todd)
Ramsey, Michael
1980: *Jesus and the Living Past* (Oxford University Press)
Ratzinger, J.
1987: *Journey Toward Easter* (Slough, England: St Paul Publications)
Ricocur, Paul
1978: *The Rule of Metaphor* (University of Toronto Press)
Robinson, John A.T.
1963: *Honest to God* (London: SCM Press, and Philadelphia: Westminster Press)
Ruether, Rosemary
1974: *The Theological Roots of Anti-Semitism* (New York: Seabury Press)
1983: *Sexism and God-Talk* (Boston: Beacon Press, and London: SCM Press)
1989: *To Change the World* (London: SCM Press, New York: Crossroad)

Sabatier, Auguste
1904: *The Doctrine of the Atonement* (London: Williams & Norgate)
Sacks, Sheldon, ed.
1979: *On Metaphor* (University of Chicago Press)
Sanders, E.P.
1985: *Jesus and Judaism* (London: SCM Press, and Philadelphia: Fortress Press)
Schillebeeckx, Edward
1979: *Jesus: An Experiment in Christology* (London: Collins, and New York: Seabury Press)
Schmaus, M.
1972: *The Church: Its Origin and Structure,* Vol. 4 of *Dogmatic Theology* (London: Sheed & Ward)
Schleiermacher, Friedrich
1956: *The Christian Faith,* trans. H.R. Mackintosh and J.S. Stewart (Edinburgh: T. & T. Clark)
Schweizer, E.
1971: *Jesus* (London: SCM Press, and Richmond, Virginia: John Knox Press)
Smart, Ninian
1960: *A Dialogue of Religions* (London: SCM Press)

Smith, H. Maynard
1926: *Frank, Bishop of Zanzibar* (London: SPCK, and New York: Macmillan)
Smith, Wilfred Cantwell
1991: *The Meaning and End of Religion* (1962) (Minneapolis: Fortress Press and London: SPCK [1978])
Sonn, Tamara
1989: Wei-hsun, Charles, and Gerhard E. Spiegler, eds. *Religious Issues and Interreligious Dialogue* (New York and London: Greenwood Press)
Soskice, Janet
1985: *Metaphor and Religious Language* (Oxford: Clarendon Press)
Stump, Eleanor
1988: 'Atonement According to Aquinas', in Thomas Morris, ed., *Philosophy and the Christian Faith* (University of Notre Dame Press)
1989: 'Atonement and Justification'. in Ronald Feenstra and Cornelius Plantinga, eds., *Trinity, Incarnation and Atonement* (University of Notre Dame Press)
Sturch, Richard
1991: *The Word and the Christ: An Essay in Analytic Christology* (Oxford: Clarendon Press)
Swinburne, Richard
1989 a: 'Could God Become Man?' in Godfrey Vesey, ed., *The Philosophy in Christianity* (Cambridge University Press)
1989 b: *Responsibility and Atonement* (Oxford: Clarendon Press).
1992: *Revelation* (Oxford: Clarendon Press)
Sykes, Stephen
1986: 'The Strange Persistence of Kenotic Christology' in A. Kee and E.T. Long, eds., *Being and Truth: Essays in Honour of John Macquarrie* (London: SCM Press)

Thatcher, Adrian
1990: *Truly a Person, Truly God* (London: SPCK)
Turbayne, Colin
1962: *The Myth of Metaphor* (Yale University Press)

Vermes, Geza
1983: *Jesus and the World of Judaism* (London: SCM Press, and Philadelphia: Fortress Press)
1991: 'Jesus the Jew', in James H. Charlesworth, ed., *Jesus' Jewishness* (New York: Crossroad)

Ward, Keith
1991: *A Vision to Pursue: Beyond the Crisis in Christianity* (London: SCM Press)

Ware, Timothy
1963: *The Orthodox Church* (Harmondsworth: Penguin)
Welch, Claude
1965: *God and Incarnation in Mid-Nineteenth Century German Theology* (New York: Oxford University Press)
Weston, Frank
1914: *The One Christ: An Enquiry into the Manner of the Incarnation*, 2nd edition (London: Longmans, Green)
Wheelwright, Philip
1962: *Metaphor and Reality* (Indiana University Press)
White, Vernon
1991: *Atonement and Incarnation* (Cambridge University Press)
Whitehead, A.N.
1929: *Process and Reality* (Cambridge University Press)
Wiles, Maurice
1963: 'The Christology of D.M. Baillie', in *Church Quarterly Review*
1974: *The Remaking of Christian Doctrine* (London: SCM Press, and Philadelphia: Westminster Press [1978])
Winckworth, Susanna, trans.
1937: *Theologia Germanica* (London: Macmillan)

Young, Frances
1977: 'A Cloud of Witnesses', in Hick, ed., *The Myth of God Incarnate*
1983: *From Nicaea to Chalcedon* (London: SCM Press, and Minneapolis: Fortress Press)
1991: *The Making of the Creeds* (London: SCM Press, and Philadelphia: Trinity Press International)

Index